IMAGES
of America

NORTH OGDEN

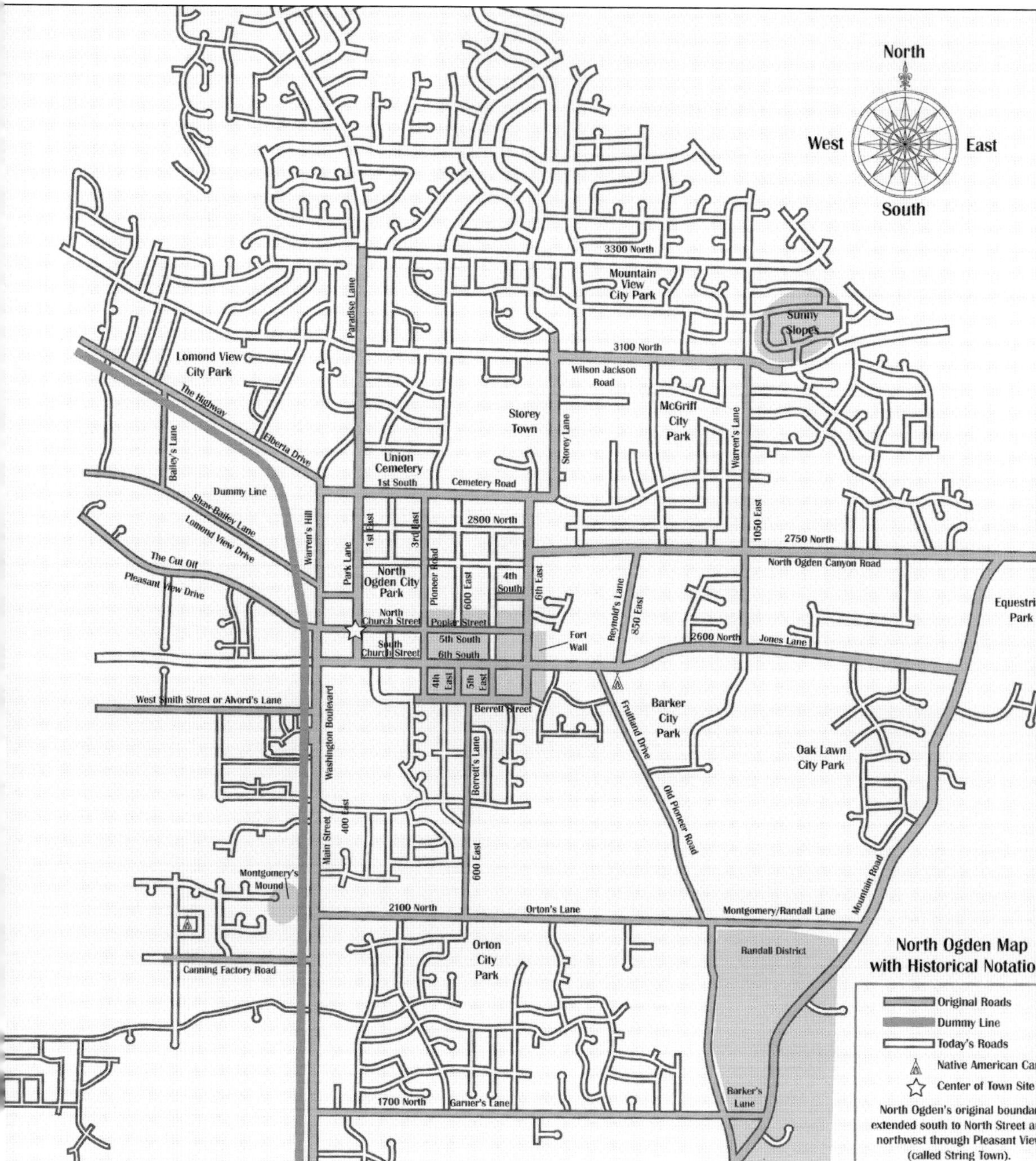

North Ogden's original boundary extended south to North Street and northwest through Pleasant View (called String Town). (Graphics by Amber Hansen, courtesy of Leslie Liechty and Bruce Spackman.)

On the Cover: Audrey Ann Montgomery and Eleanor Randall enjoy the view across North Ogden and toward Ben Lomond Peak. They are standing in Lewis Randall's orchard among the cherry tree blossoms. The photograph was taken around 1950 from Fruitland Drive, displaying a much less developed city at that time. (Courtesy of North Ogden Historical Museum.)

IMAGES
of America

NORTH OGDEN

North Ogden Historical Museum

ARCADIA
PUBLISHING

ISBN 978-0-7385-8460-6

Published by Arcadia Publishing
Charleston, South Carolina

Printed in the United States of America

Library of Congress Control Number: 2009940066

For all general information, please contact Arcadia Publishing:
Telephone 843-853-2070
Fax 843-853-0044
E-mail sales@arcadiapublishing.com
For customer service and orders:
Toll-Free 1-888-313-2665

Visit us on the Internet at www.arcadiapublishing.com

To history lovers everywhere and to those who have gone before, we appreciate the great city of today.

Contents

Acknowledgments

Since the founding of the North Ogden Historical Museum in 2006, gathering and preserving historical photographs and histories has been a major priority. We are grateful for the opportunity to transfer many of these treasured photographs into book form for all to enjoy. Images of America: *North Ogden* has been written and compiled by Holly W. Fuller and Lana B. Tolman. This book would not have been possible without the museum volunteers and members who have contributed many hours toward preserving the history of North Ogden. We greatly appreciate their dedication and determination. We are honored to have the support and encouragement of the community. Thanks to the generous donors of photographs and histories, including the Weber State University Library Special Collections Department.

Thanks to Arcadia Publishing for their guidance through the publishing process. It has been a very rewarding experience.

We would like to express our gratitude to North Ogden's former mayor Gary A. Harrop for writing the foreword included in the book, and also for being instrumental in the creation of our historical organization. Our appreciation goes to North Ogden City for allowing us to utilize one of their facilities to house our archives and artifacts, and for supporting the museum in all aspects.

The museum members are indebted to our city's prior historians and journal keepers, as well as the authors of the first North Ogden history books, *A History of North Ogden, Beginnings to 1985* and *Our North Ogden Pioneers: 1851–1900.*

A special thank-you is extended to the family of Lettice Rich for lending her beautiful poetry.

All images appear courtesy of the North Ogden Historical Museum unless otherwise noted.

The Board of Directors for the North Ogden Historical Museum includes:

Aloma Blaylock
Richard Blaylock
Penny Clendenin
LaVern Cottrell
Curtis Fuller
Holly Fuller
Amber Hansen
Dean Holbrook
Susan Holbrook
Debbie Jones
Rosemary Jones
Leslie Liechty
Todd Perkins
Bruce Spackman
Lana Tolman
Alice Wyatt

Foreword

I have always been fascinated by history—its facts and many related aspects. Often I have picked up one of my favorite historical novels and drifted away to another time and place as the author paints a picture in my mind using only words. Perhaps it's the morning sun as it ascends the face of Ben Lomond, or maybe it's the same sun as it sinks behind the purple mountains beyond the Great Salt Lake. History creates interesting and awe-inspiring pictures, much like novels, if we avail ourselves of the time to read.

Here in the elbow of the Wasatch Mountains, we are blessed because of the adventuresome men and women who wanted to learn what might lie beyond the next mountain peak or valley. Early trappers, including Jim Bridger and Peter Skeen Ogden, charted this area. Later Mormon pioneers, under the direction of Brigham Young, entered the area and began to settle. Our own local pioneers envisioned the community we now call North Ogden. Our historical brown and white street signs represent the city and people of the past as they guide us through our community today. These early settlers must have witnessed the sun rising to shine on the face of Ben Lomond and watched it disappear behind the western mountain range. As those early settlers surveyed the beauties of this area, I'd like to think they experienced, as we do today, peace and euphoria.

There are so many fascinating and interesting historical facts to be learned and enjoyed concerning the wonderful city in which we live. History is both a barometer and a yardstick for our generation to measure up to and live by. We should build on the past, while not repeating those mistakes of long ago, as we look to the future. May God bless America and its people—the past, present, and future generations. Enjoy this book as a presentation of the history of our own North Ogden.

—Gary A. Harrop

Introduction

The history of North Ogden is a combination of the people, the land and landmarks, the climate, and the resources. Throughout the years, there have been many changes; however, there are also many constants. The sweeping vistas and beautiful mountain ranges, as well as the breathtaking sunsets, remain much the same as they must have appeared to the early settlers. Ben Lomond Peak has always risen like an invitation into the skyline, luring many hikers, past and present, to conquer its vistas. The early settlers encountered challenges beyond imagination while striving to achieve better lives for their families. This same pioneer spirit lives on in the citizens of today, as they continue to strive for excellence in themselves and to prepare for future generations.

The members of the North Ogden Historical Museum would like to take readers on a journey through the past to the era of the early settlers and the first 100 years of North Ogden's history. Our book is not a complete history, but contains a treasure trove of photographs, offering a glimpse into the past. The many accounts of courage, strength, and determination will have an impact on every reader. Several of these stories illustrate how much easier our lives are today. The dugout houses where families were raised, the premature deaths of loved ones, and the laborious tasks required for survival were not a deterrent to the valiant pioneers. The happy celebrations, social activities, and education continued in spite of the many challenges, and the economy thrived with bartering, business, and ingenuity. The North Ogden Historical Museum invites you to delve into a page from our town's history to learn about and appreciate the great city of today.

—Holly W. Fuller

Silent Sentinel

by Lettice O. Rich

To Ben Lomond, beloved mountain of our home town:
You stand in silent majesty, unchanged by age or wind-lashed storms,
Guardian of a home-filled valley cradled in your mighty arms.
Sculptured by a Master Hand, of earth and tree and craggy stone,
Each season paints an overlay and claims your splendor all its own.
Your snow-capped peak, cloud-mantled, reaches up to azure blue,
Where silver beams pierce fluffy clouds to let the moonlight through.
In the solemn stillness of a winter's listening night,
Your beauty seems transplanted from some celestial sight.
Oh Symbol of Strength, I wonder—if words were yours to speak,
Would history be unfolded beneath your towering peak?
Did you see the roaming red man wing arrows at deer or moose?
Or a patient dark-skinned mother croon to her small papoose?
Did you feel their apprehension when the white intruders came?
Encroaching on their homeland, killing their fish and game?
Did you smell the fragrant upturned earth, see sagebrush cleared for schools,
Marvel at channeled mountain streams, with bare hands and faith for tools?
Did you feel their pangs of hunger, slow numbing of winter's cold,
The sorrow of parting with loved ones, too weak for life to hold?
Remember a Scottish mother—homesick, discouraged, and alone,
Who named you "Old Ben Lomond," because you brought memories of home?
Did you hear their fervent prayers for peace when menacing clouds of war
Tore men from home and family for freedom's fight afar?
Was your heart a little fearful when machines gouged the valley wide,
Replacing farms with highways, planting houses side by side?
Did you miss the fragrant cherry trees, white-blossomed in early spring,
The laughing cherry-pickers and the songs they used to sing?
You've seen so much of living as you've stood here through the years—
Prosperity, wars, peacetime—laughter, heartache, tears.
I wonder what you think of us and the way we live each day,
If you could speak, Ben Lomond—I wonder what you'd say!

One

Surroundings and Early Times

Mountain Magnetism

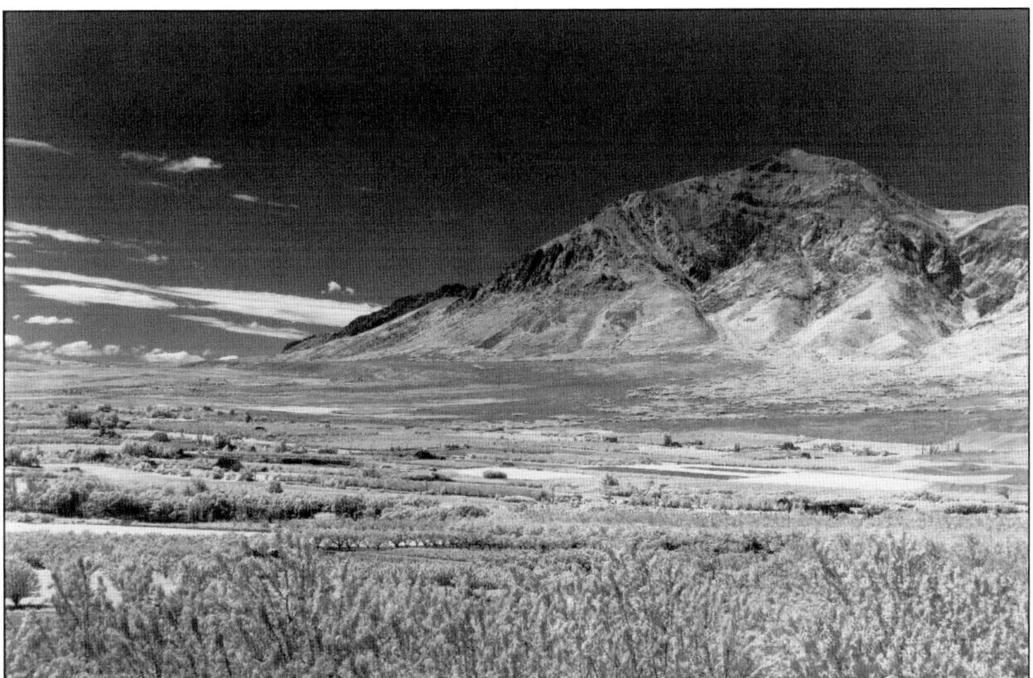

North Ogden was settled at the base of majestic Ben Lomond Peak in 1851 by early pioneers. The floor of North Ogden's valley is a remnant of Lake Bonneville, an ancient, great inland sea, which left rich, fertile soil for farming. Evidence of the lake's shoreline is still visible on Ben Lomond and surrounding mountain ranges, even though the lake's waters receded over 10,000 years ago. The city was incorporated August 6, 1950.

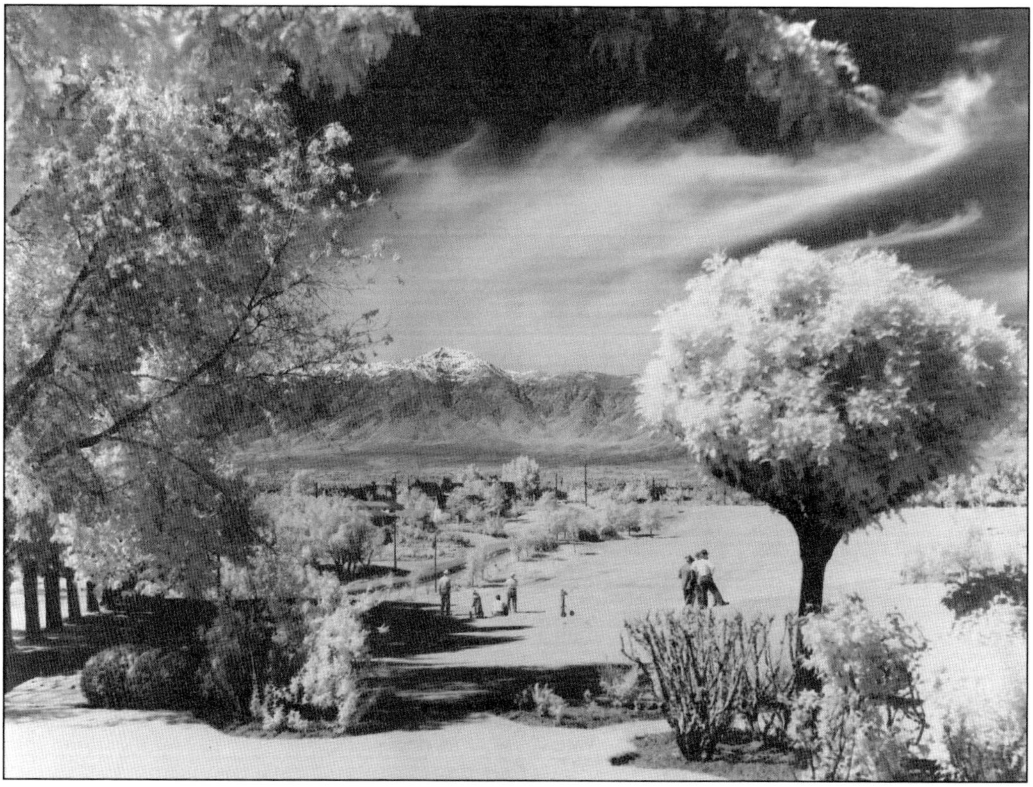

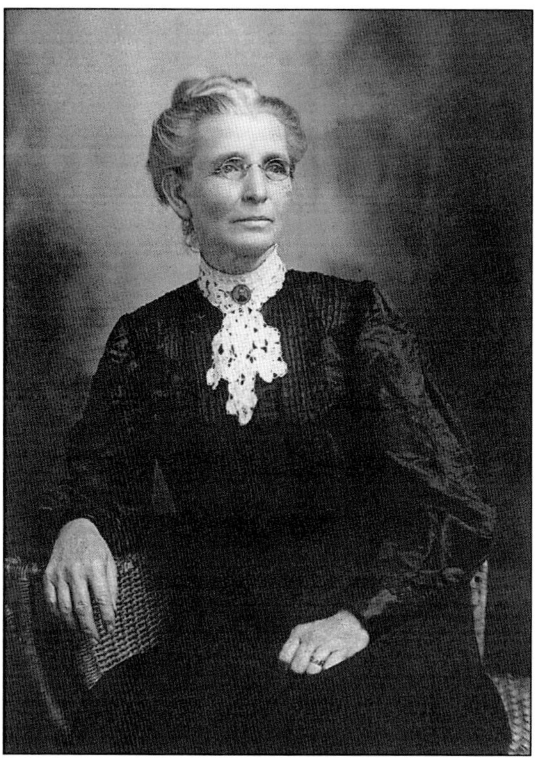

The exceptional photograph above of snow-capped Ben Lomond Peak was taken in the 1940s from the Ogden Golf and Country Club. The peak's annual snowfall is 150–200 inches. North Ogden was settled in the pristine foothills of the prominent pyramid-shaped mountain in 1851. The peak was named by early pioneer Mary (Wilson) Montgomery (seen in the image at left) because it resembled Ben Lomond Peak, which sits at the edge of Loch (Lake) Lomond near her beloved hometown in Scotland. Ben Lomond (*Beinn Laomainn* in Scottish Gaelic) translates to "Beacon Mountain."

Jonathan Campbell Jr. and his nephew Samuel Campbell were among the first settlers in North Ogden. They entered the valley in 1850, set up tents, and dreamed of building a settlement. They were driven out by Native Americans, but returned the following spring to remain as permanent residents. Pictured are Jonathan Jr., son Nephi, and wife Phoebe Campbell.

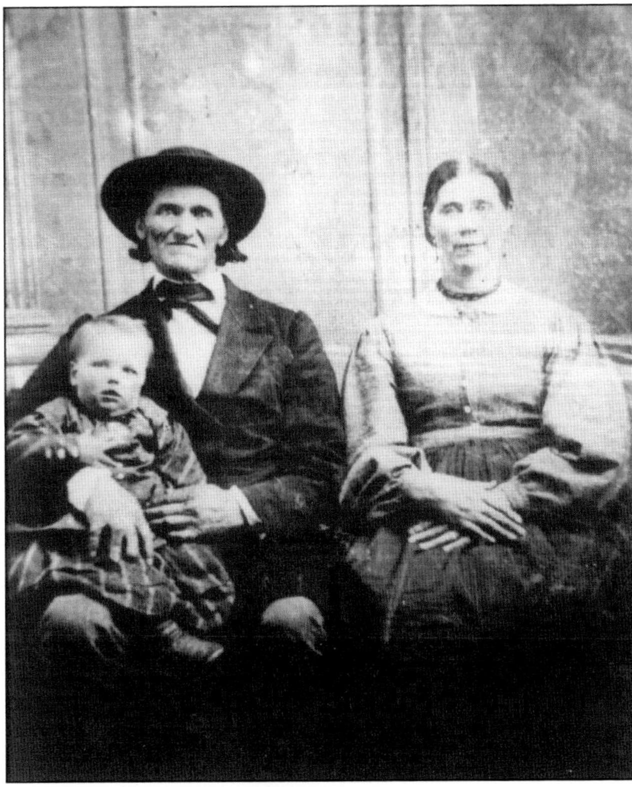

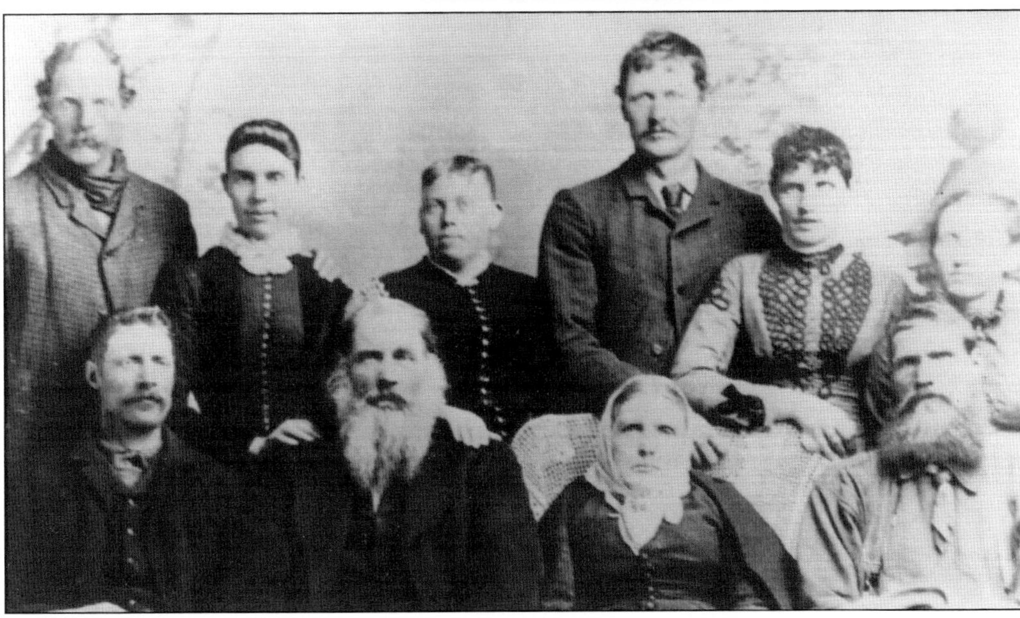

The Campbells were the first pioneers to arrive and settle in North Ogden. Pictured from left to right are (first row) Ben Campbell, Samuel and wife C. R. Frances (Hall) Campbell, and J. Heber Campbell; (second row) Samuel Joseph Jr. and wife Clarissa (Reynolds) Campbell, Anna (Darling) Campbell (wife of Ben), Jake and wife Polly (Chapman) Campbell, and Sarah Alois (Henry) Campbell (wife of Heber).

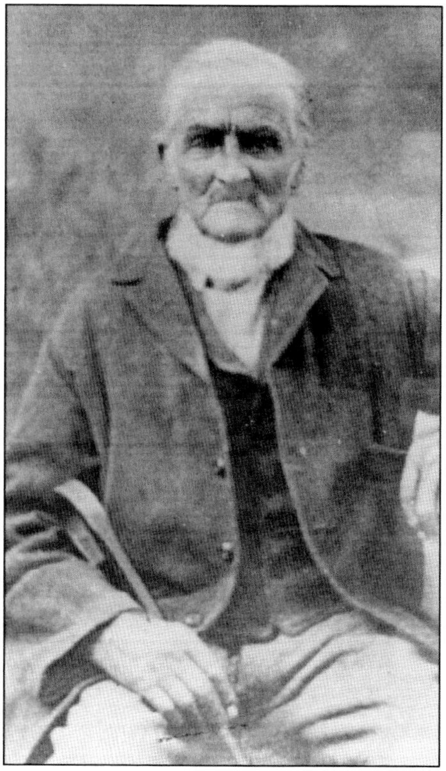

John Riddle (left) and his son Isaac moved north from Ogden with 200 head of cattle in 1850. The men wintered them in North Ogden and lived in a dugout through the winter. They retreated to Lorin Farr Fort in Ogden when tension escalated with Native Americans. The region's Shoshone were reluctantly forced to share the land with the incoming pioneers. They called the area "Opecarry," which meant "stick in the head." In the spring of 1851, John and Isaac returned to the dugout location to establish a farm and plant crops. The Campbells and Riddles, the first pioneers in the area, were followed by about 18 additional families by October of the same year. The 1920s photograph below was taken of Ben Lomond, providing a glimpse of the area in early times.

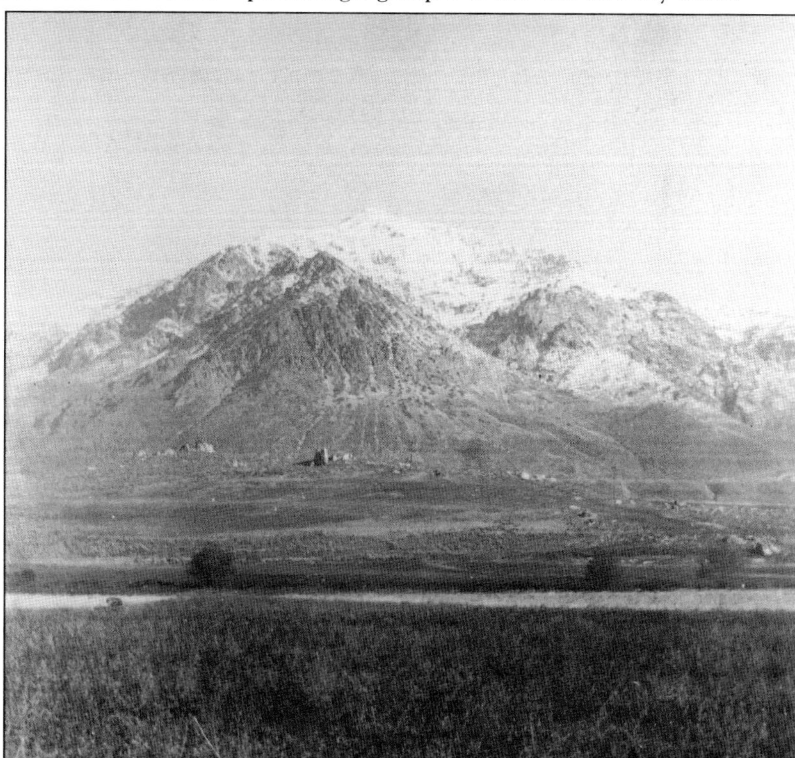

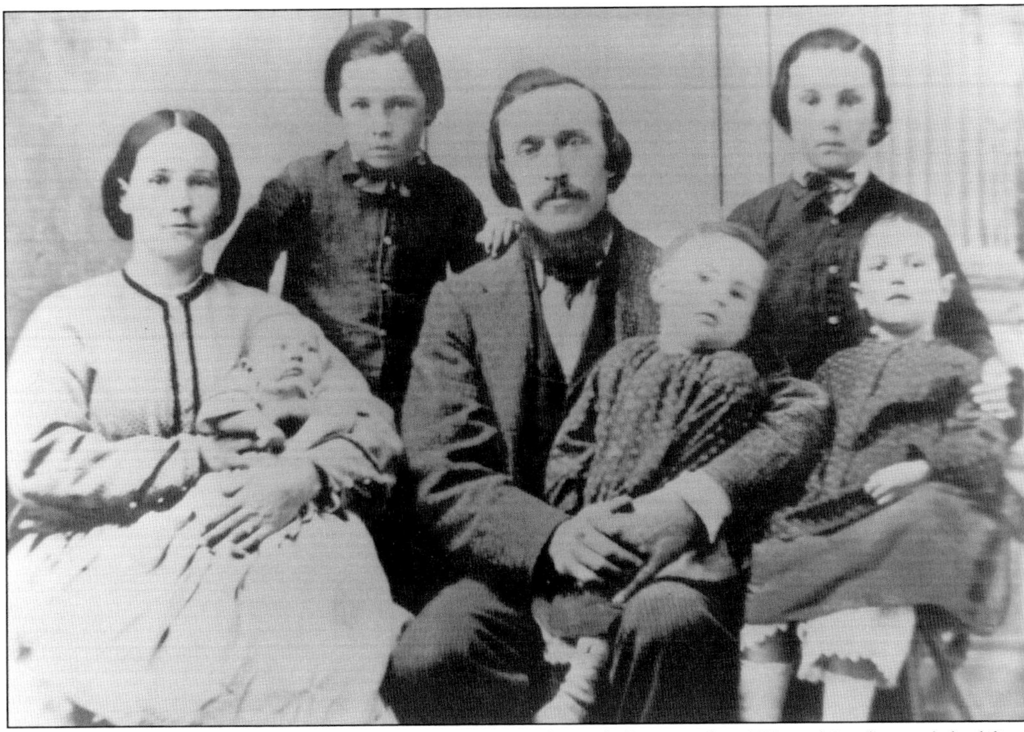

The members of the Henry Holmes family are, from left to right, Ellen (Anderson) holding Mary Ellen, William Robert, Henry holding Heber Chase, Henry John, and Elizabeth Ann. The early pioneer couple lived on Mud Creek Farm on the north side of 1700 North with their eight children. Henry was well known as a schoolteacher, brick maker, builder, farmer, bishop, and North Ogden's first postmaster.

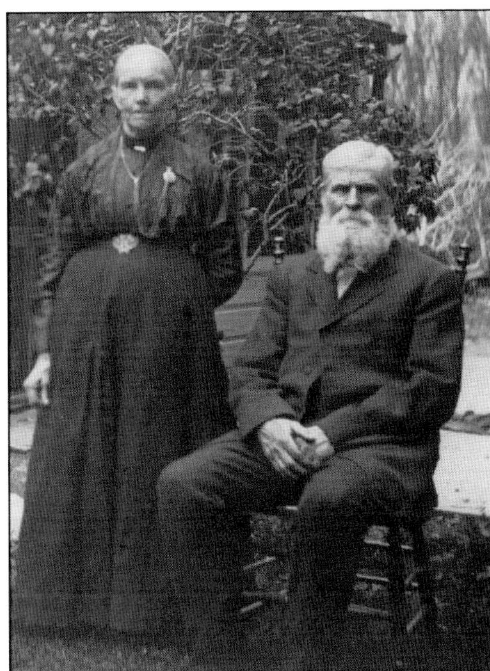

Sarah (Garrard) and Greenleaf Blodgett Sr. were from early pioneer families. Greenleaf was born in 1850, while his family was crossing Wyoming on their way to Utah. It was said that he was the first white child to be born in Wyoming. Sarah was lovingly called "Aunt Kit," her nickname for carrying a black medical kit. She received medical training in England and compassionately tended to many in North Ogden.

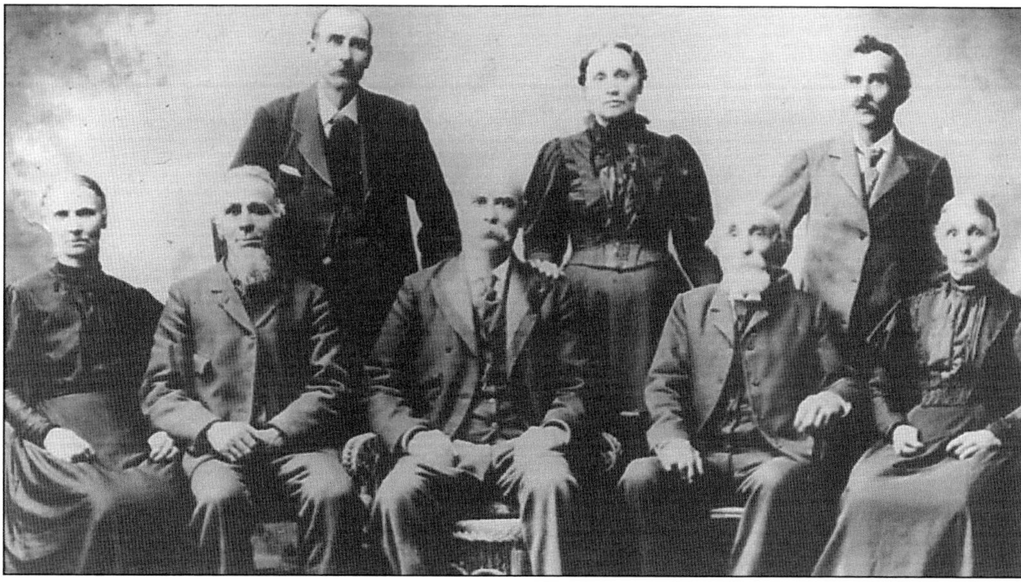

The family of Robert and Mary (Wilson) Montgomery is pictured in the early 1900s. From left to right are (first row) Isabel (Cazier), Robert Jr., Nathaniel, James, and Margaret (Gardner); (second row) William, Mary Elizabeth (Bailey), and Alma. In 1853, early pioneers began constructing fort walls surrounding the area at the center of town to protect families and livestock in case of Native American conflicts. After tensions subsided, construction of the fort was abandoned.

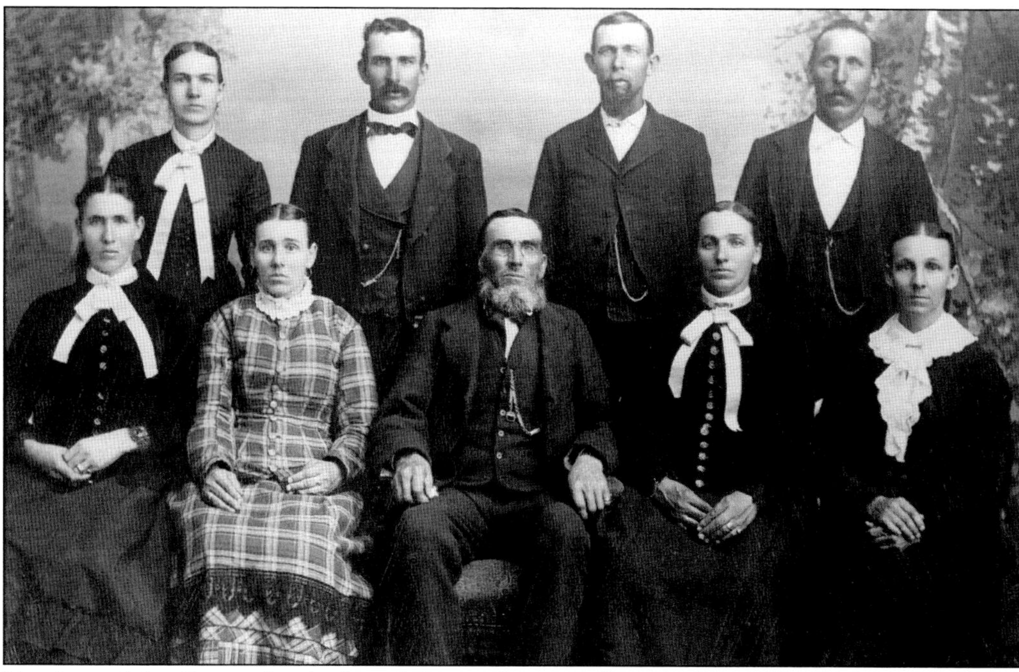

Members of the Garner family, from left to right, were (first row) Amelia Jane, Fannie Marilla, David (father), Louisa Ann, and Mary Marinda; (second row) Lydia, Charles, William Franklin, and David Edmond. The first five children born in the family made the 1,300-mile journey across the plains mostly barefoot. Their bleeding feet were bound with rags to avoid leaving blood-stained tracks for wild animals to follow.

James and Polly Emeline (Blodgett) Barker built their first home in North Ogden in early 1853. The one-room log cabin with a rock fireplace at one end sheltered 11 children. James was an excellent farmer, and Polly became known as a doctor among early settlers and Native Americans. She had a special talent with herbal medicines, helping deliver babies, and setting broken bones—often using a tree branch splint.

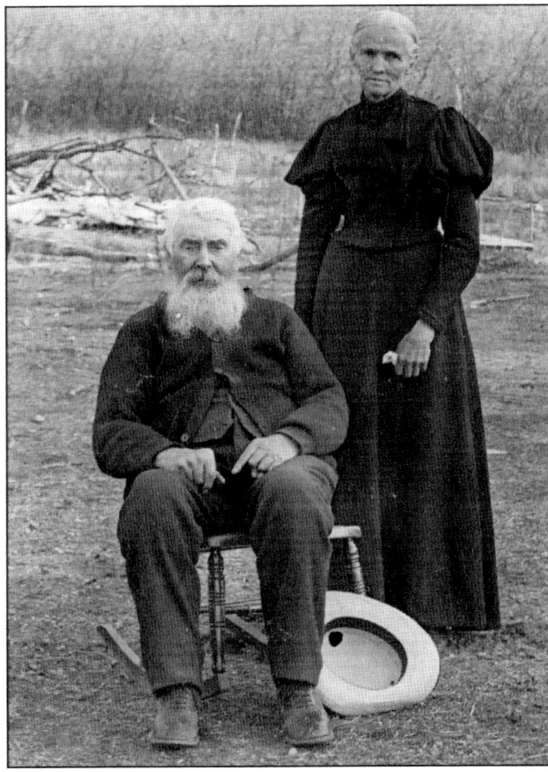

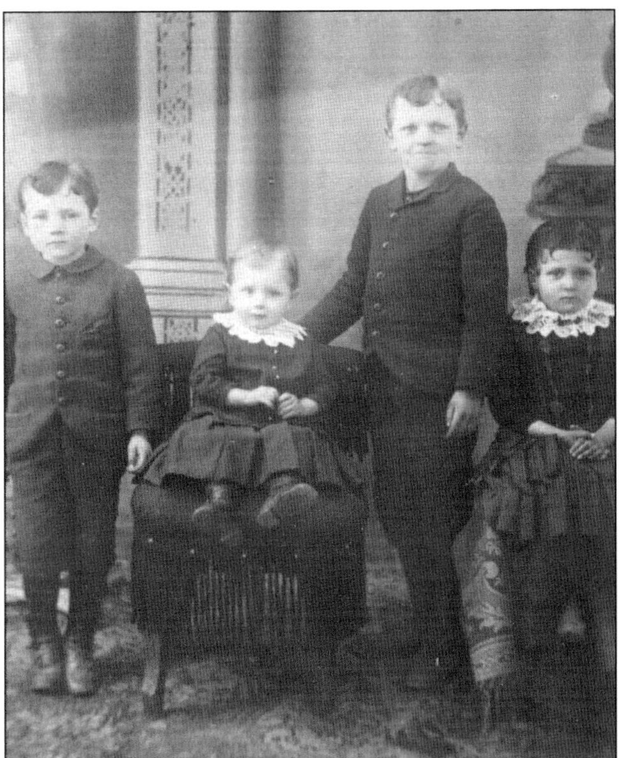

Early North Ogden settlers Gideon and Sarah Ann (Shupe) Alvord had 11 children. The four pictured here are, from left to right, Edmund Riley, William Mathias, Ira John, and Stella. Gideon was a hard worker and was well known for his farming and stock-raising practices. The couple tragically lost three children to diphtheria in one week's time. Eight Alvord children reached adulthood.

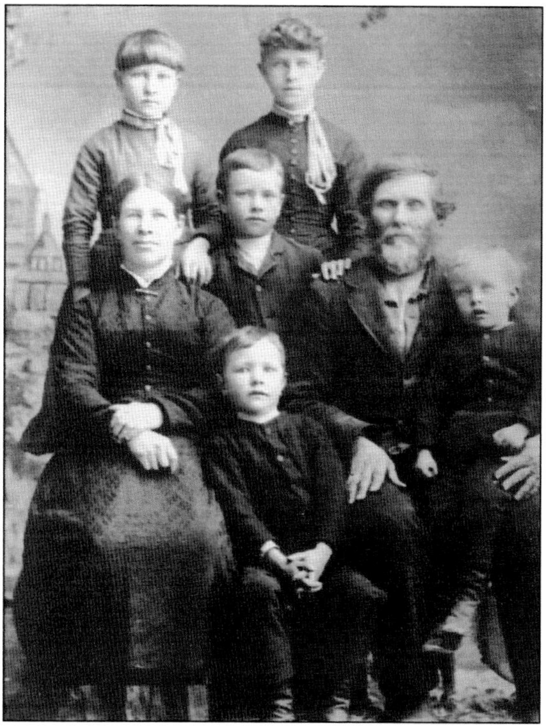

These early settlers arrived in 1857 and found a village of Native Americans living nearby. When the family began farming and fencing the property, the Native Americans left, but secretly returned to steal produce and horses. Pictured is the William Hill family, from left to right, (first row) Joseph and Hyrum; (second row) Elizabeth (Humphries,) George, and William John; (third row) Harriet Ann (Jones) and Rachel (Ellis).

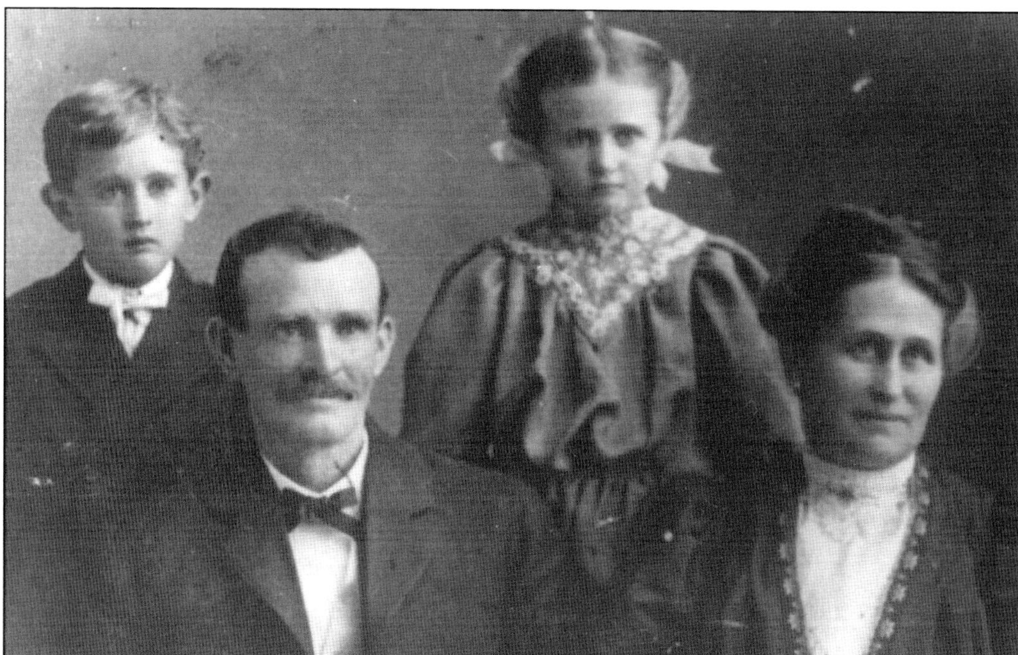

Thomas B. and Olive (Chadwick) Storey were the parents of four children. Olive died after her last child was born. Thomas later married Mary Ann (Stimpson), and two more children joined the family. Pictured from left to right in 1910 are Karl S., Thomas B., Maurine, and Mary Ann. Living in Storey Town, Mary Ann was a schoolteacher, and Thomas worked for Amalgamated Sugar Company.

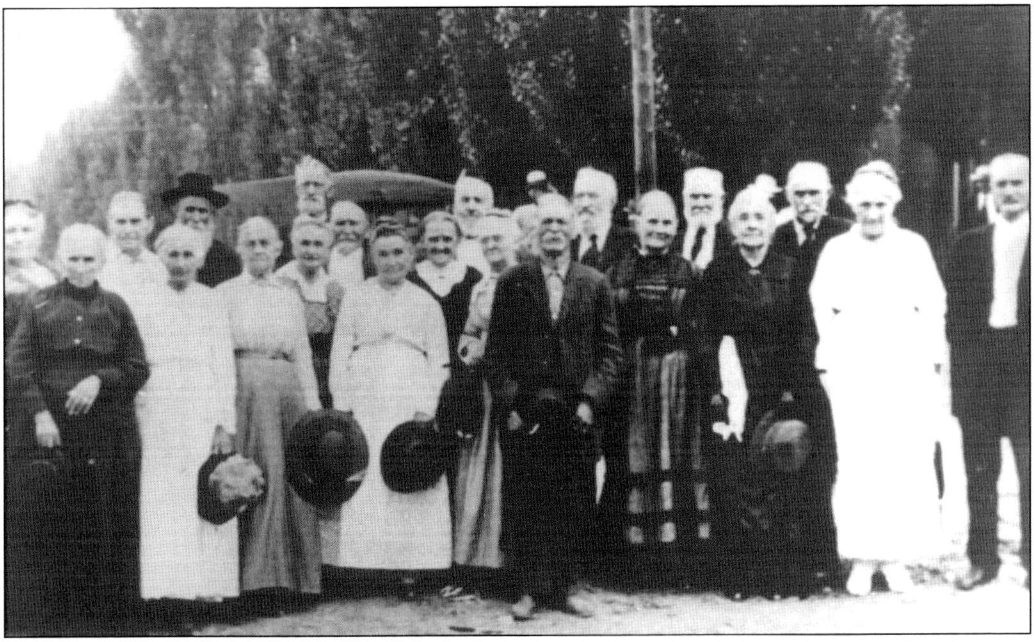

In 1921, the pioneers who crossed the plains before 1869 gathered for a photograph. The men are Greenleaf Blodgett, George Brown, Thomas Norris, John Woodfield, James Deamer, James Ward, William Hill, Ezekiel Blodgett, and Charles Jones. The women are Catherine Mariah (Kate) Jones, Elizabeth Montgomery, Elizabeth Williams, Mary Warren, Emma Dean, Jennie Norris, Annie Deamer, Elizabeth Marshall, Sarah Garner, Eliza Brown, Electa Montgomery, and Barbara Brown.

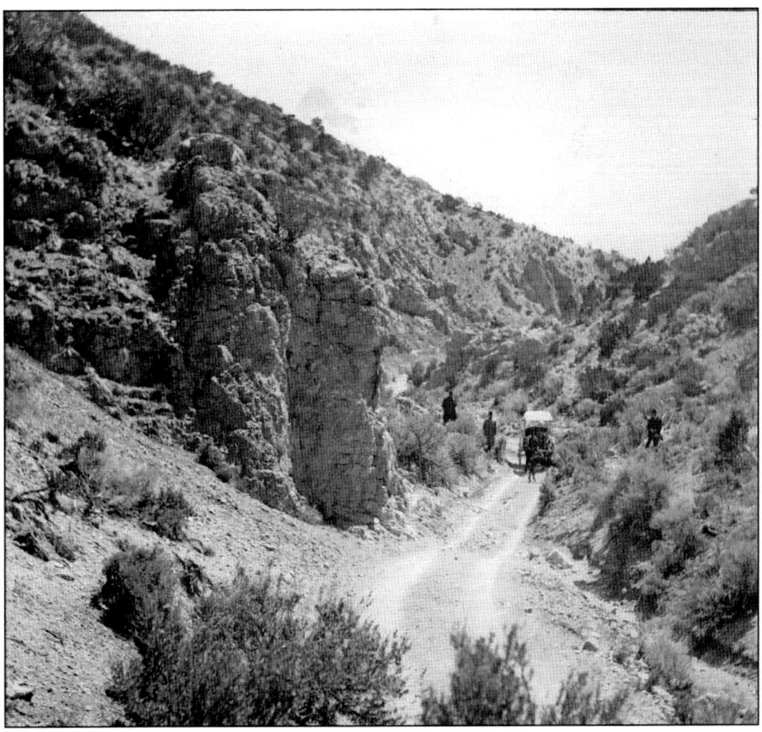

In early times, North Ogden Canyon was the only access to Ogden Valley, and the trail was frequented by Native Americans and trappers long before the pioneers arrived. Shown is the original route through the bottom of the canyon, known as the Lodge Pole Trail. In 1934, a road costing $73,500 was constructed higher up the mountainside as an economic relief project. The project utilized 315 workers and 300 pounds of blasting powder.

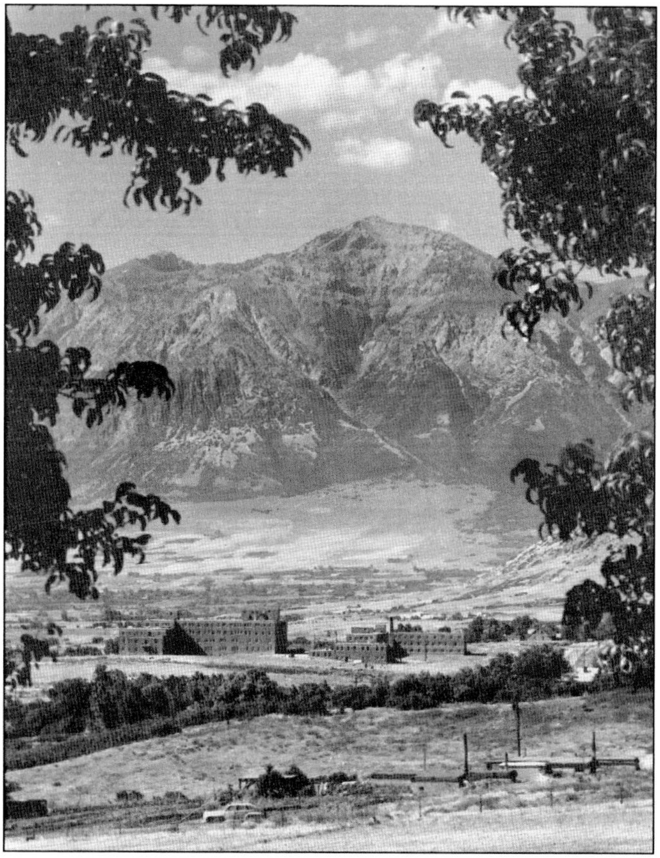

A distant view of Ben Lomond Peak is seen from Ogden's east bench in the 1940s. The main canyons across the mountain are, from left to right, Maguire, Pine, Ridge, and Berrett Canyons. On the left is Willard Peak (elevation 9,763 feet), about 2 miles to the northwest. That peak stands 51 feet above Ben Lomond's elevation of 9,712 feet. Snow often lingers on the peaks until the beginning of July.

In 1913, Charles Jones organized an expedition to erect a flagpole at the top of Ben Lomond Peak. The flag could be seen for many years from the heart of North Ogden. Included in the expedition were Charles Jones, William Hall, and Henry C. Hall. The Cutler trail is a steep 5-mile hike to the peak. The Ben Lomond trail is longer (7.6 miles) but easier to navigate.

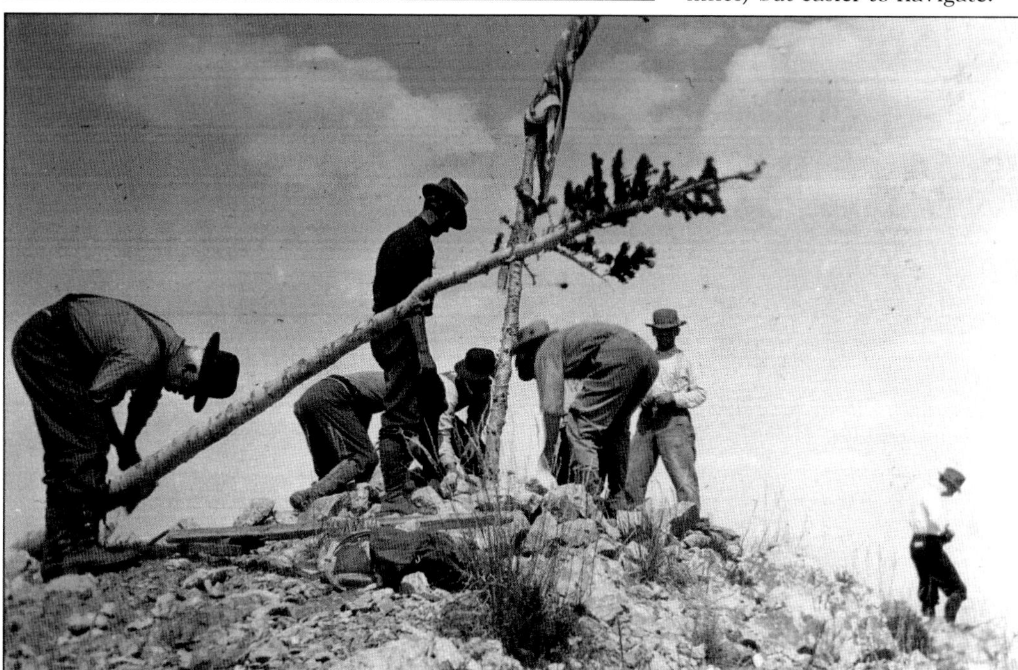

Many photographs have been taken through the years capturing the splendor of Ben Lomond Peak. This photograph taken in the early 1900s provides the ultimate view of North Ogden below from the viewpoint of one of the many who have hiked the Ben Lomond Peak trail. Legend says Ben Lomond Peak was the inspiration for the original version of Paramount Pictures' famous logo.

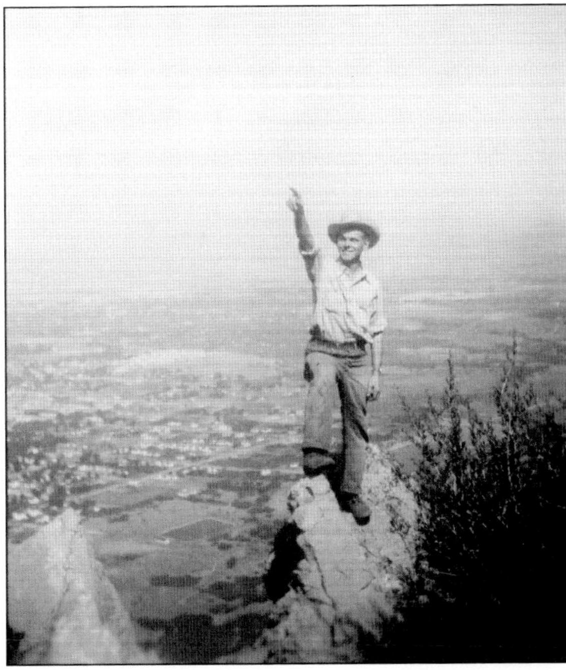

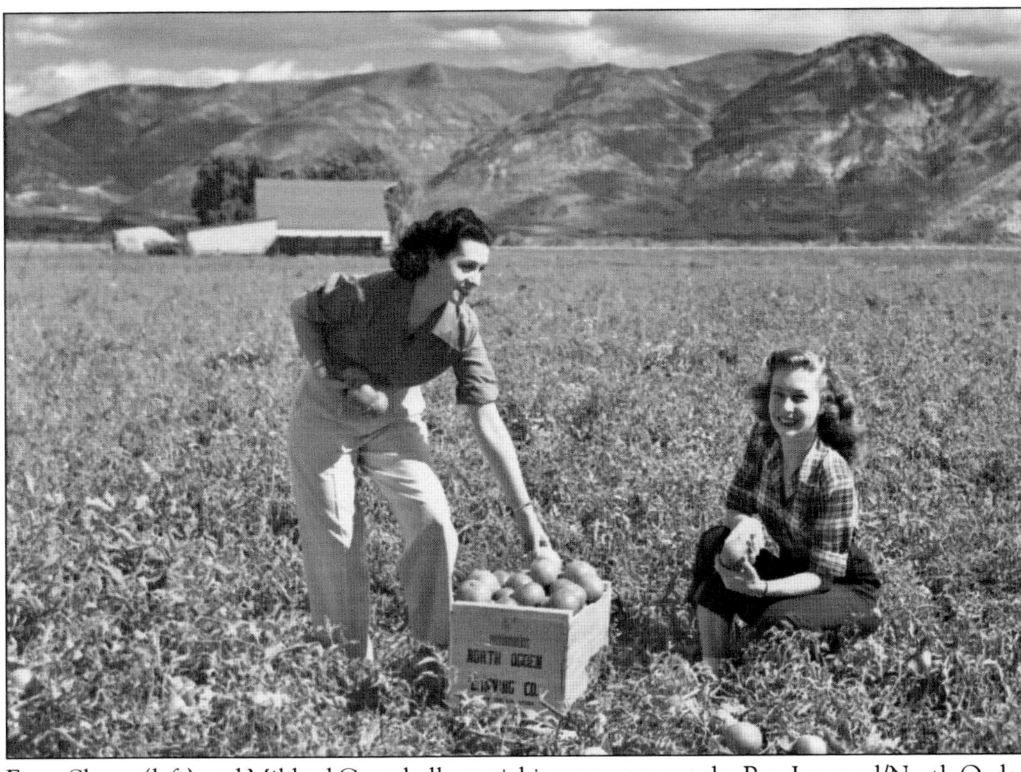

Erma Shupe (left) and Mildred Campbell are picking tomatoes at the Ben Lomond/North Ogden Stake Farm in 1940. North Ogden's eastern mountain range looms in the background, showing from left to right, North Ogden Canyon, Cold Water Canyon, and One Horse Canyon, with Lewis Peak at the right. The elevation of Lewis Peak is 8,031 feet.

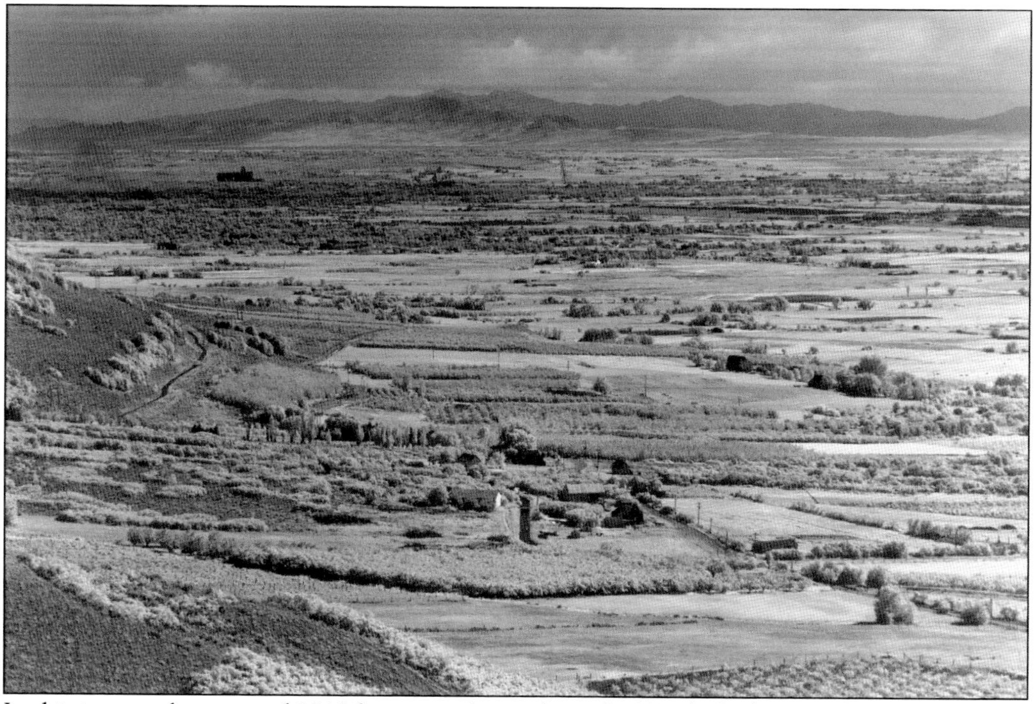

In this image taken around 1946 facing southwest from the North Ogden Divide road, the area's farmland and orchards are visible, along with the distant Stansbury mountain range. On a clear day, Antelope Island, the Stansbury Mountains, and the Oquirrh Mountains can be seen in the distance. Antelope Island is the largest of the 11 islands located in the Great Salt Lake.

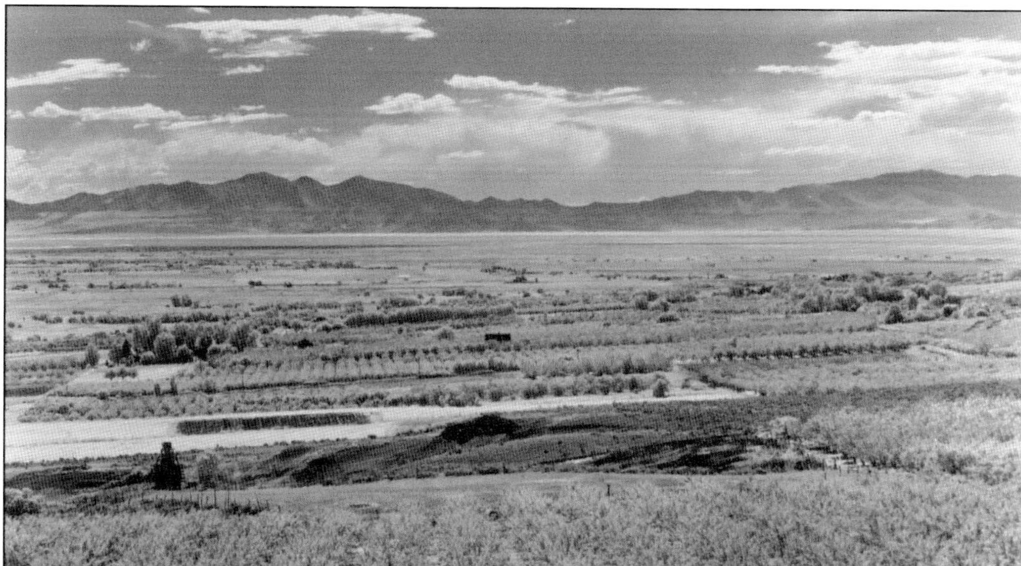

A 1946 overview of North Ogden's orchards and farmland extends to the west. In the distance, the Promontory mountain range can be seen, with a glimmer of the Great Salt Lake at the base. The lake circles around the mountain range, and the furthermost tip to the south is known as Promontory Point. Promontory Summit is where the "Golden Spike" was driven May 10, 1869, completing the first transcontinental railroad.

Two

Settlers
Humble Homes and Homesteaders

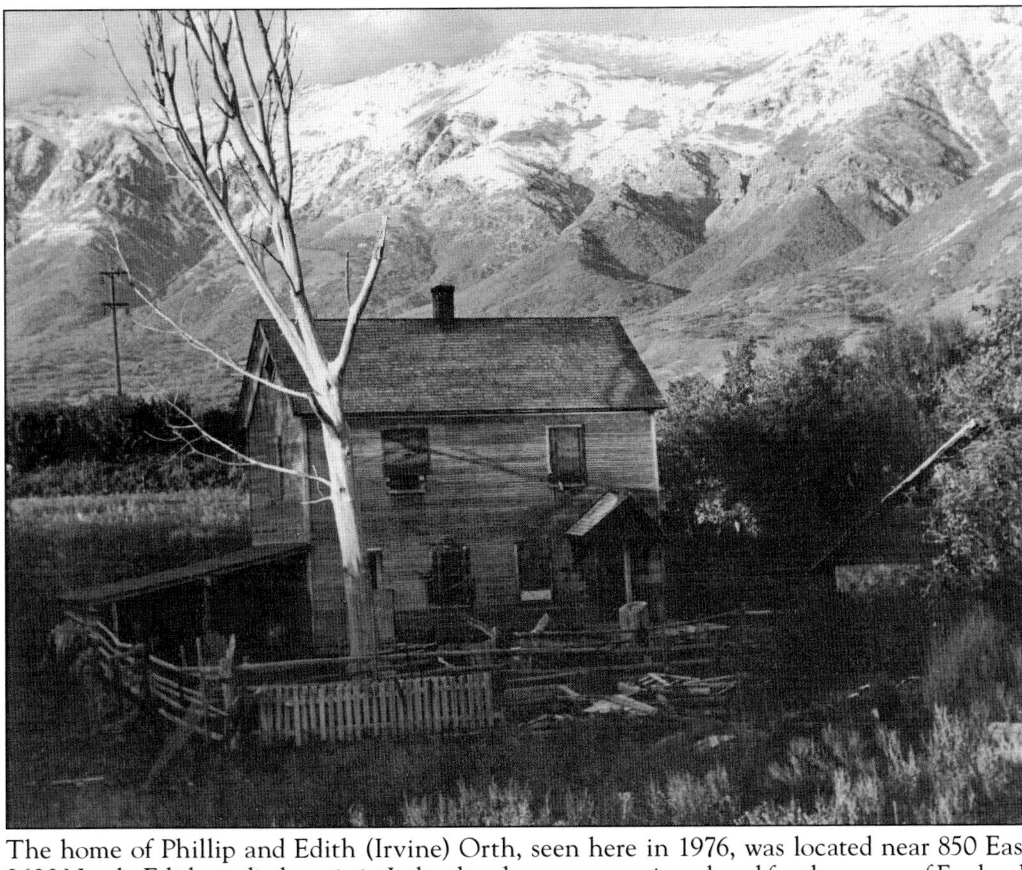

The home of Phillip and Edith (Irvine) Orth, seen here in 1976, was located near 850 East 2600 North. Edith studied music in Ireland and on one occasion played for the queen of England. She came to Utah alone in 1915. Many children came to her home for piano lessons, and Edith exhibited unusual patience with each one. She was also the church organist at the North Ogden Ward for 35 years. For many years, children thought the house was haunted. (Courtesy of Marijane Johnson.)

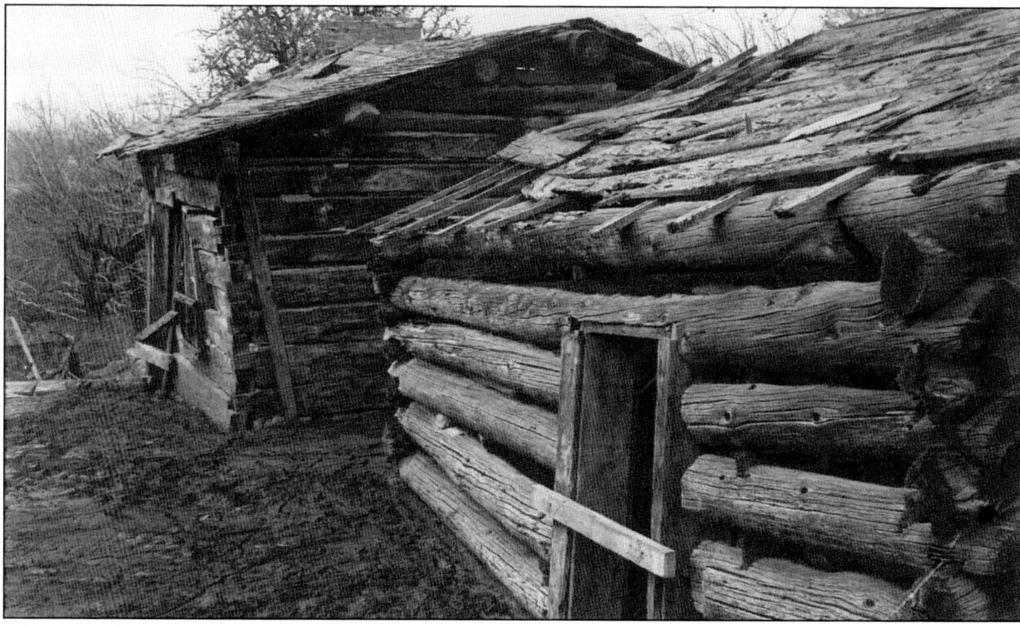

The log cabin homestead at 2351 Fruitland Drive was built in 1853 by James and Polly (Blodgett) Barker. The first pioneers in North Ogden lived in dugouts, with rocks to stabilize the walls. Sapling trees formed the roofs, which were then covered with grass and topped with three feet of earth. A stone fireplace provided heat, light, and a cooking area. Animal hides covered the doorway and windows.

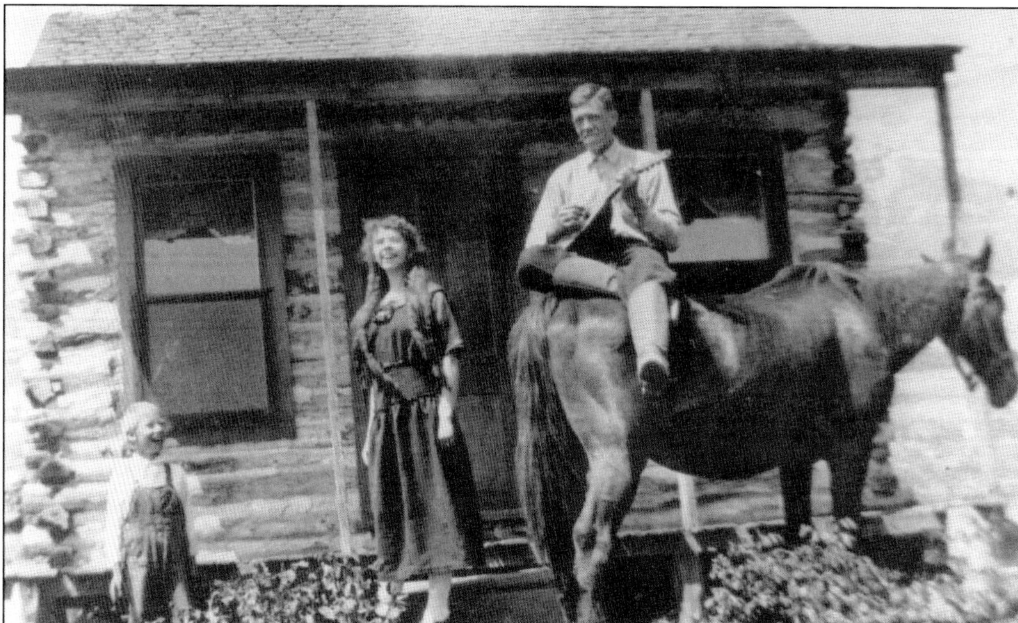

The William Blaylock cabin was constructed in 1914 near 450 East 3300 North. Pictured are Golda (Clifford) Blaylock with her son Angus (left). Golda's brother, Archie Clifford, is sitting on the horse. Golda and her husband, William Levi Blaylock, lived with their two children in the cabin during the summer. Their winter home was located in North Ogden at 223 East Elberta Drive.

Alfred Berrett, standing at right, arrived in North Ogden in 1853. He later constructed this two-story home for his family near 581 East 2600 North. This began four generations of Berretts, who have milked cows in the area for over 127 years. Alfred's son Marlon stands on the wagon. Of Alfred's 14 children, only six reached maturity.

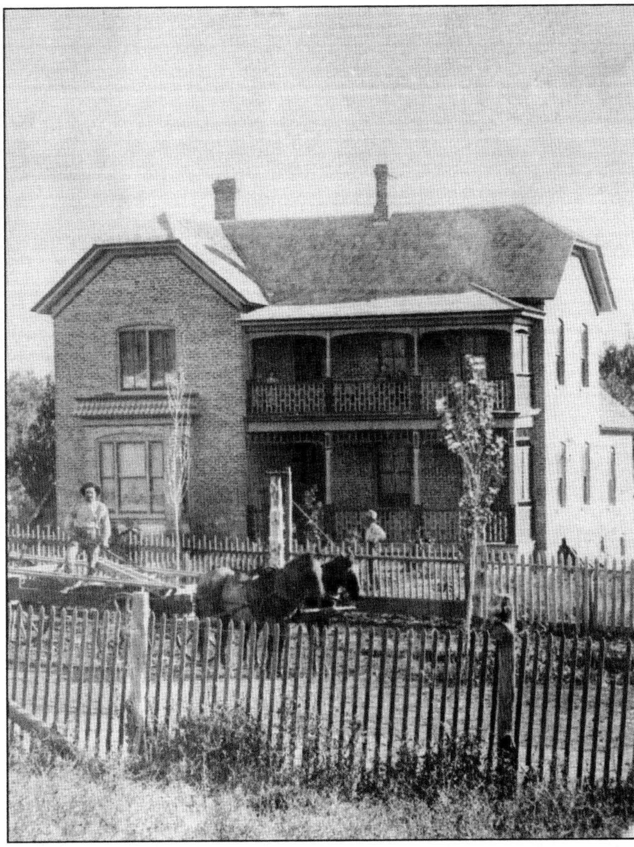

Thomas Dunn traveled from New York to Illinois in 1839 and helped build the Church of Jesus Christ of Latter-day Saints' (LDS) Nauvoo Temple. He later immigrated to Utah and became the first bishop of the church's North Ogden Ward. His home was located on the corner of 650 East 2600 North, and was used as the North Ogden city office building from 1952 to 1956.

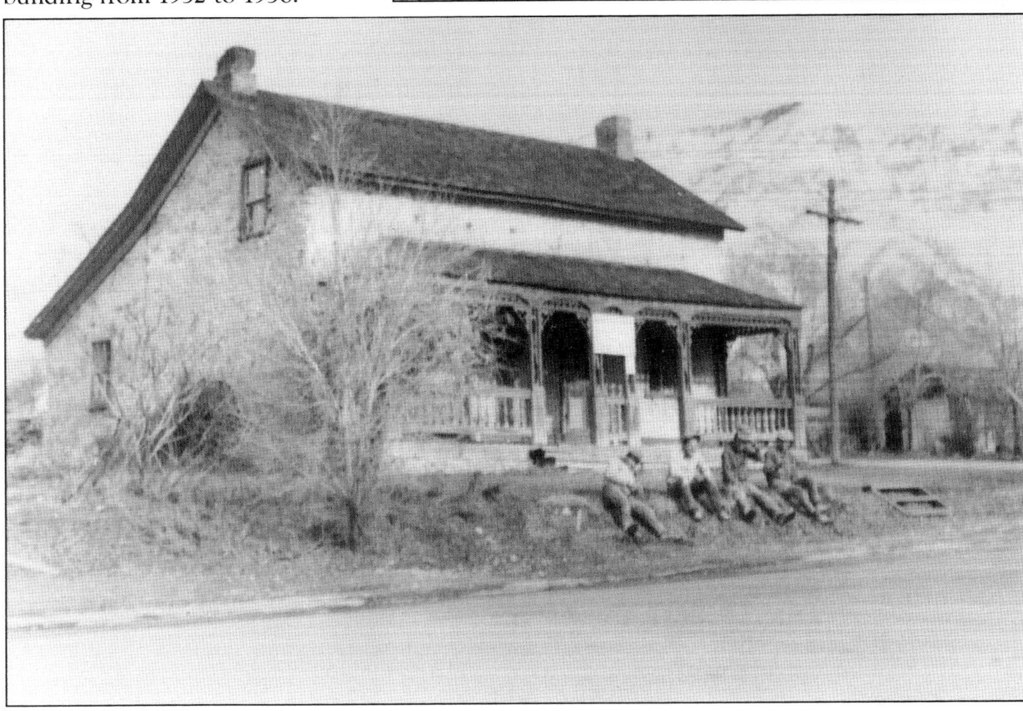

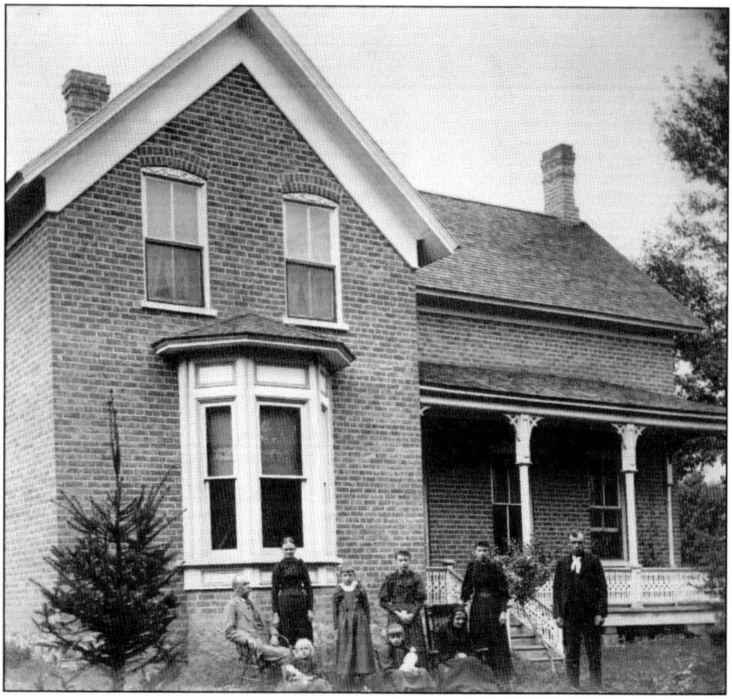

Nathaniel Montgomery helped settle North Ogden, where he farmed and planted a large orchard. He and Nancy Maria (Clark) raised six children (two others died in infancy) at their home, built in 1891, at 192 East Elberta Drive. Pictured at the home are, from left to right, (first row) Grace (Harris), Florence (Snooks), and grandmother Lillias Barbour Clark; (second row) father Nathaniel, mother Nancy (Clark), Kate (Barker), Margaret (Taggart), Lillias (Randall), and Nathaniel Robert.

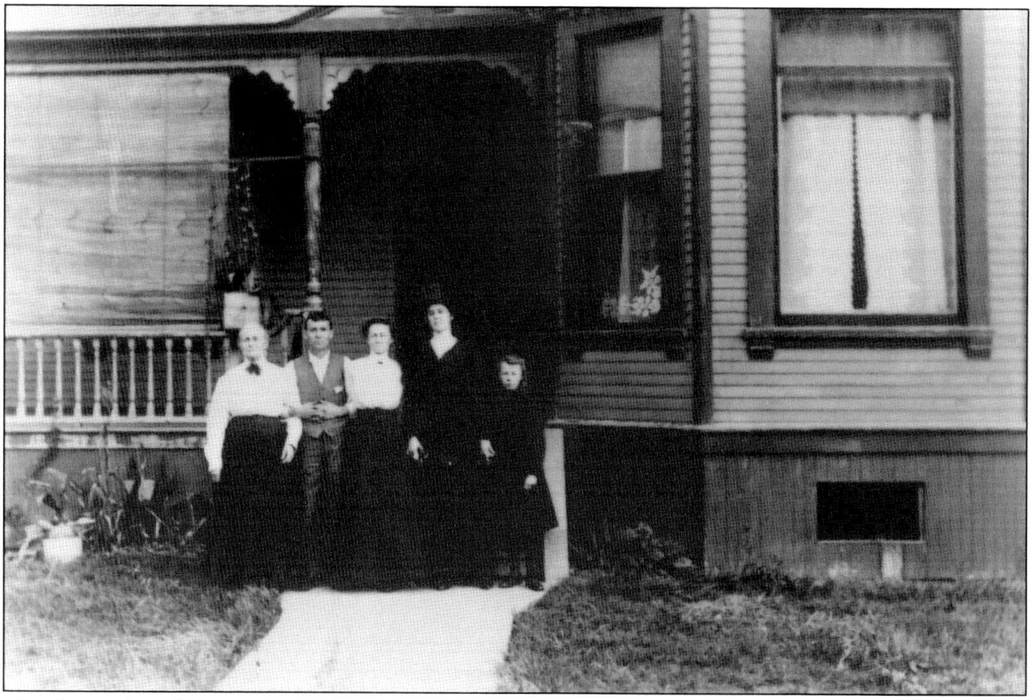

The Samuel and Emma Dean home is pictured above. From left to right are Emma (Norville) Dean, George and Martha Worton, unidentified, and Emma (Worton) Leavitt. In 1863, Samuel Dean opened the first known store in North Ogden near 450 East 2650 North. Emma was only 13 years old when she married. She was widowed in her 40s and raised 10 children alone. The family survived by selling homemade cheese, butter, soap, and candles.

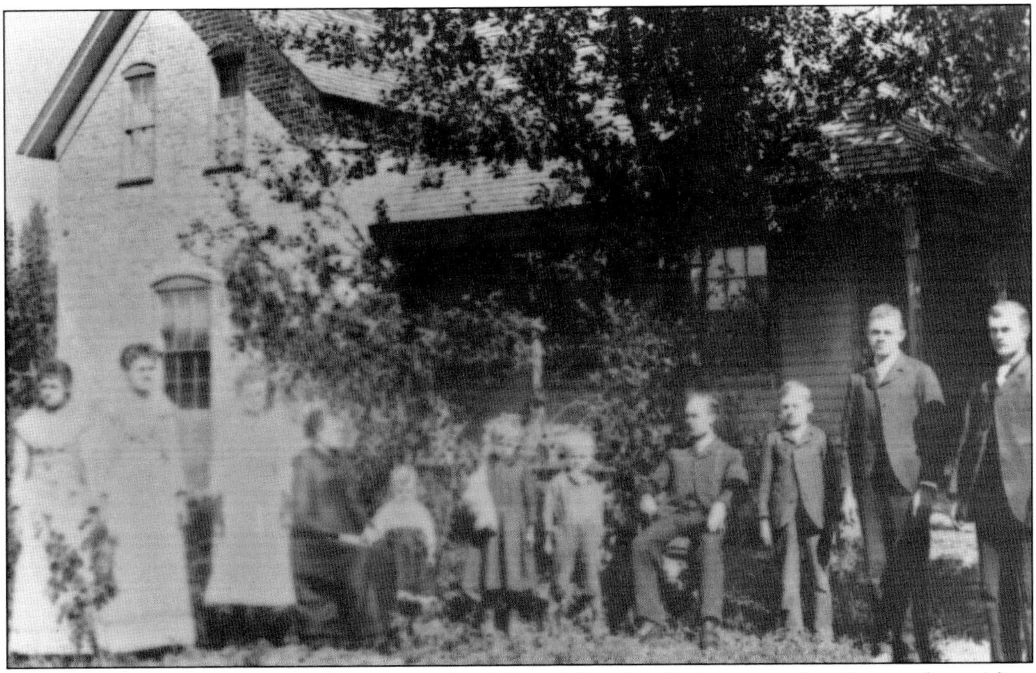

Pictured from left to right at the Frederick William Ellis family home are family members Alice (Storey), Susan (Field), Cora (Miller), Susan Keziah (Davis), Claude, Sarah Esther (Andrew), Parley, Frederick W., Joseph, Charles, and Frederick G. Susan (Davis), Frederick's first wife, raised 10 children in their home near 450 East 2700 North. Frederick's second wife was Sarah Jane (Barker), who raised their six children in Pleasant View.

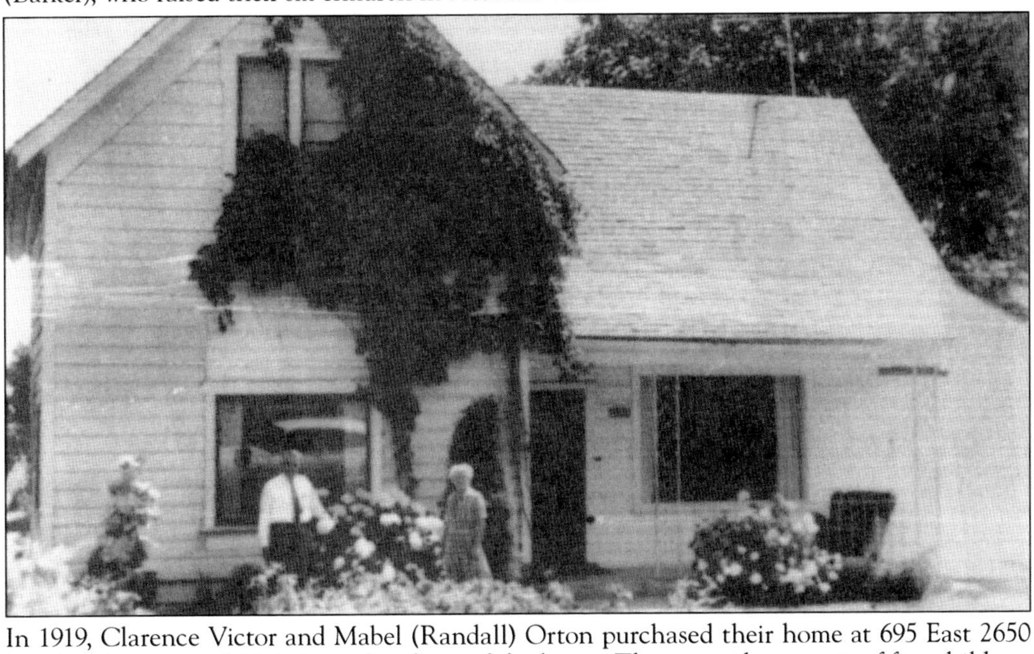

In 1919, Clarence Victor and Mabel (Randall) Orton purchased their home at 695 East 2650 North. Clarence and Mabel stand in front of the home. They were the parents of five children: Allene (Atkinson), Lettice (Rich), Eldon, Clarence, and Nona Jean (Searle). The family initially purchased a farm in Huntsville and then moved back to North Ogden after six years.

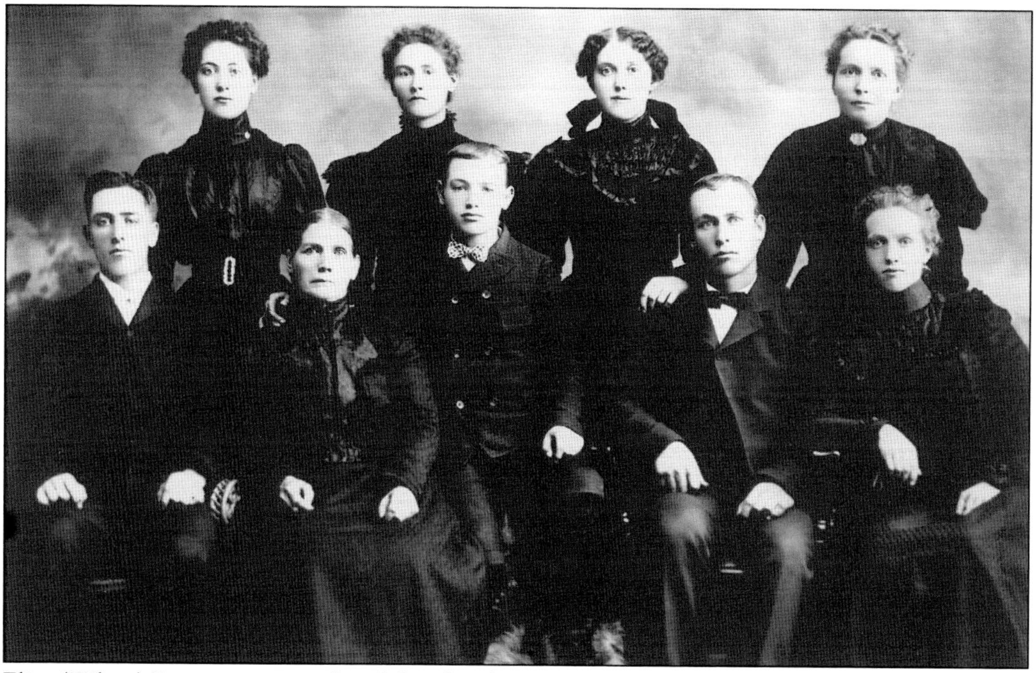

Eliza (White) Brown is pictured with her family. From left to right are (first row) George E., Eliza (mother), Nephi J., John, and Ellen Berrett; (second row) Emily Folkman, Annie Montgomery, Harriet Berrett, and Mary Campbell. After the death of her first husband, John White, Eliza became a plural wife of Thomas B. Brown. Thomas' first wife, Jane, died at an early age, leaving Eliza to raise 18 children.

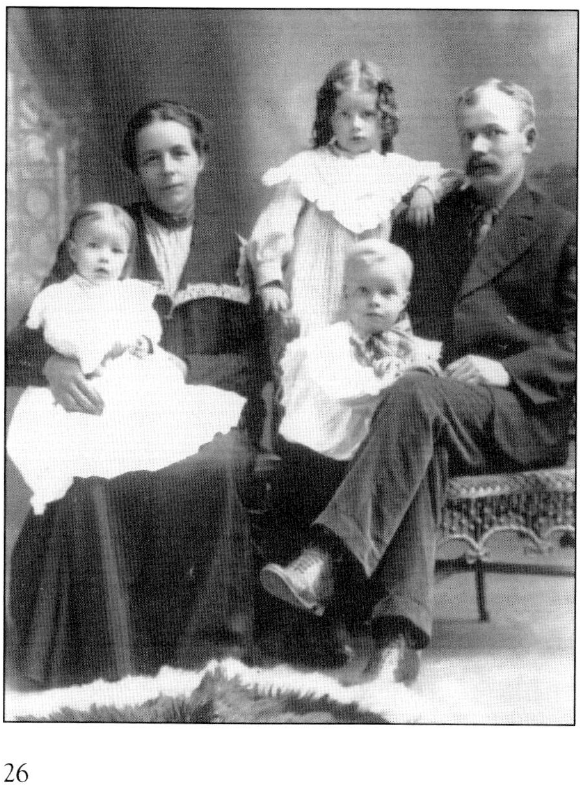

Thomas C. and Sarah (Campbell) Shupe are pictured around 1900 with their children Lottie (left), Wright, and Ellen (standing). Thomas died at age 31, leaving Sarah with four small children. Sarah took in laundry and sold milk from the family cow to support the children. She later remarried and lived happily in Ogden, with enough property for flowers, a garden, and an orchard.

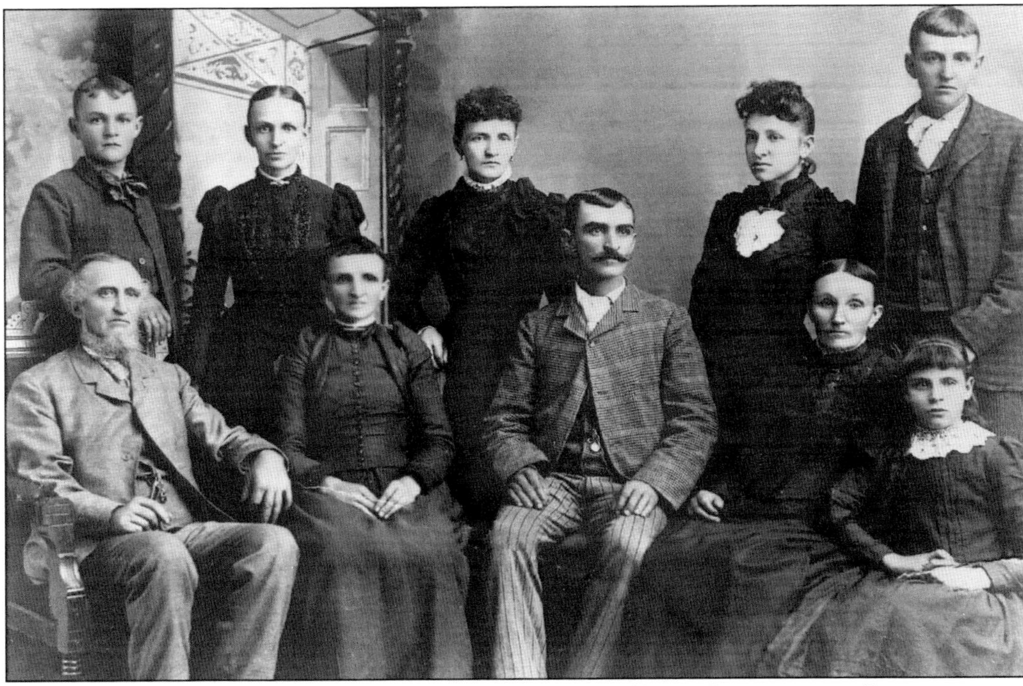

Francis Dudman was an early pioneer businessman. He and his wife, Mary, initially ran a notions store in one room of their home on 2750 North, as seen below, and later built a general merchandise store. They sold homemade ice cream, root beer, and lemonade at every celebration in the area. They took their grandson Earl along and put him in an apple box under the counter to nap. Pictured above are, from left to right, (first row) Francis (father), Sarah Jane (Waldram), James Alfred, Mary Bult (mother), Ida Maud (Stahr) Brown; (second row) John Thomas Bult, Susan Ann (Brown), Ellen (Waldram), Martha Elizabeth (Holmes), and Francis William.

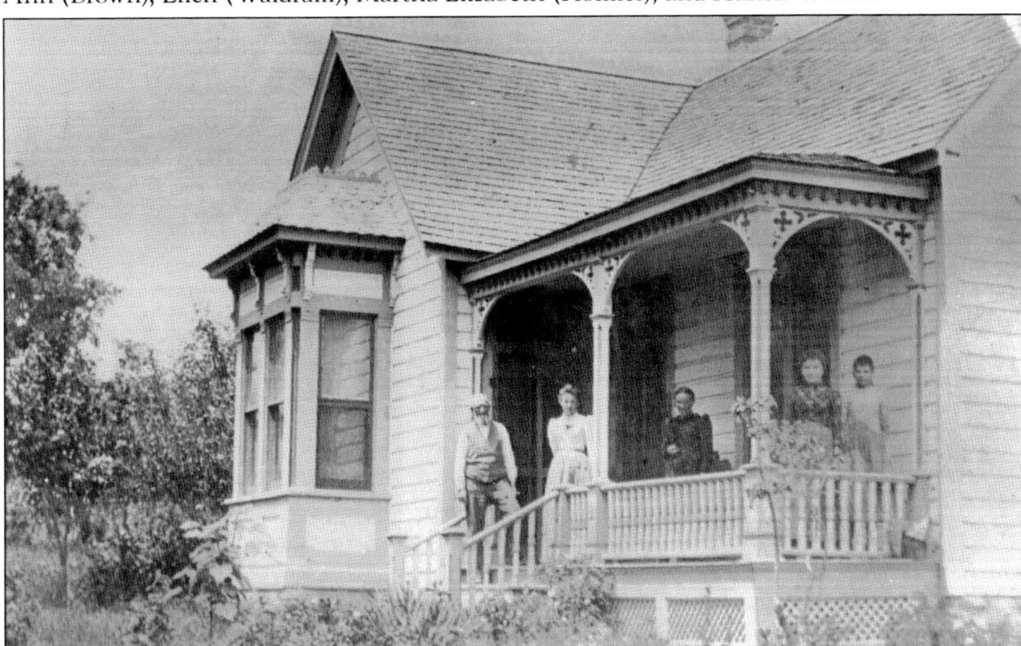

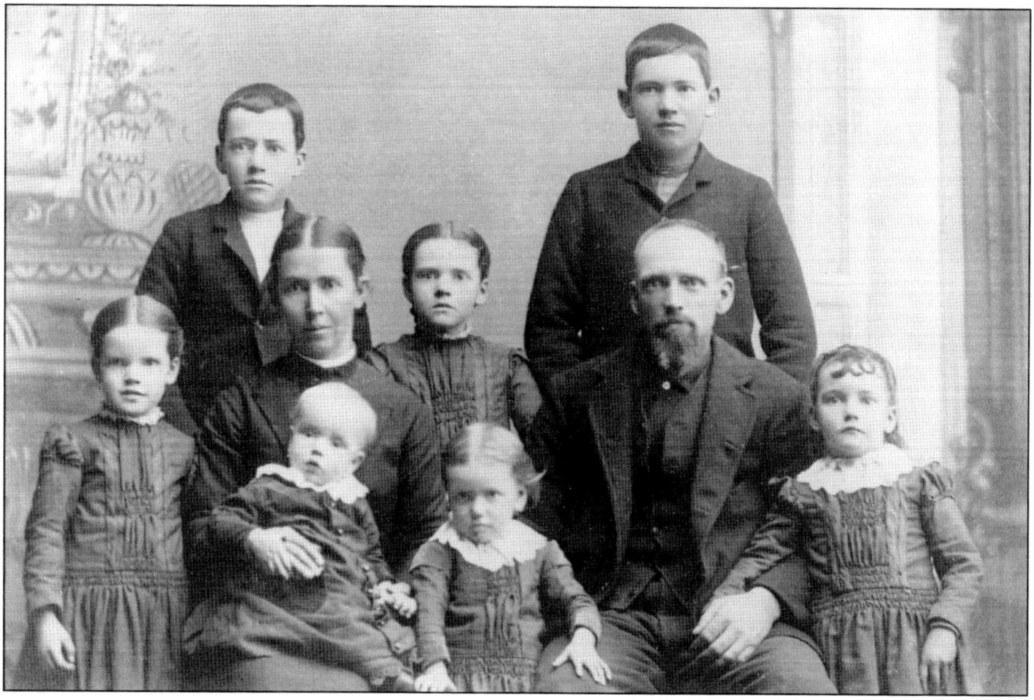

This 1890 photograph shows the members of the John Jones family. They are, from left to right, (first row) Mary Elizabeth, Robert, Charlotte Emily, and Jennie May; (second row) mother Rhoda (Berrett), Rhoda Pearl, and father John; (third row) Charles William and John Arthur. John, being gifted in singing and dancing, built The Jones Hall, which had a stage, benches, kerosene lamps, and a pot-bellied stove. Many citizens were entertained with dances, roller-skating, and theater productions. The building was also used for meetings, reunions, and sometimes for school. John and Rhoda had to be creative and ambitious to provide for their large family. John was a blacksmith, a cobbler, a miner, and a farmer. They persevered through scarlet fever (losing one child, Robert) and their home burning in 1892. The Jones home, seen below, was located at 656 East 2650 North.

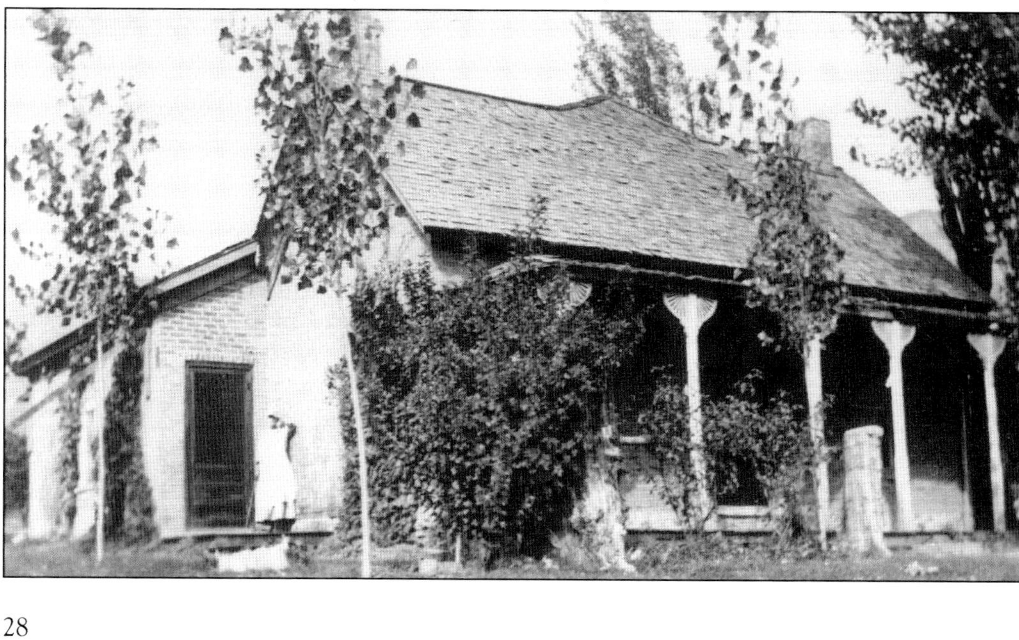

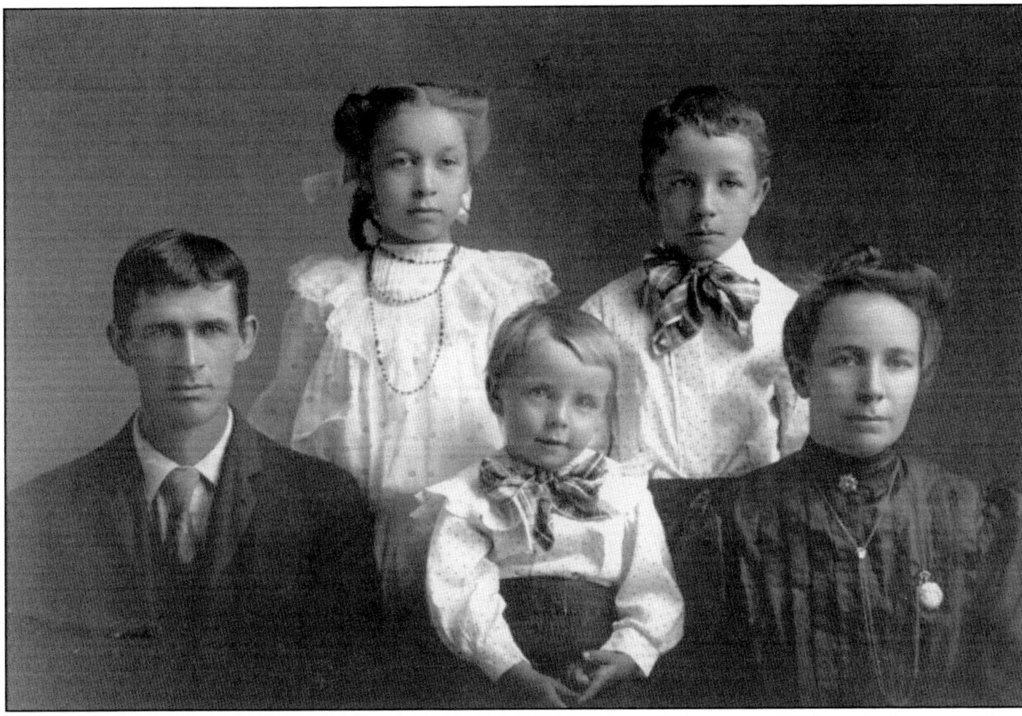

Greenleaf Jr. and Alice Eliza (Wheeler) Blodgett are pictured above in 1905 with their children Carl Joseph (center), Nancy Alice (Taylor), and Greenleaf Ray. Greenleaf Jr. recalled stories about his early years at the Red Brick School. He played a prank on the teacher by climbing up to cover the chimney. The school filled with smoke, creating the need for an extra recess. Pictured below, the family home at 2299 North Fruitland Drive originally had two rooms, with four more added as their family grew. Greenleaf Jr. owned one of the first dairy herds in the area. He herded his cows to meadows in the Hot Springs area to graze in the winter months, as there was less snow at that location.

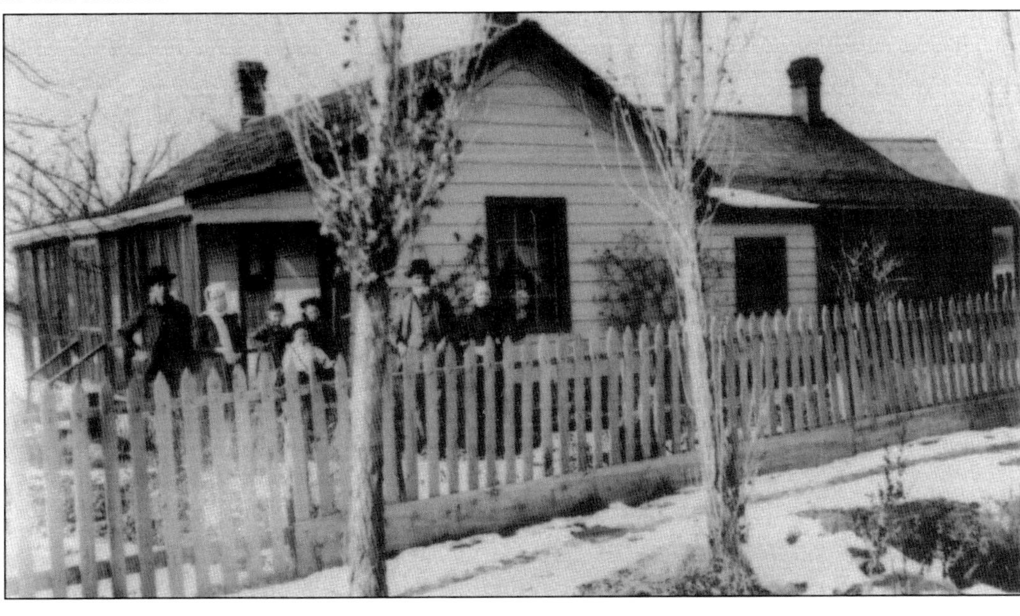

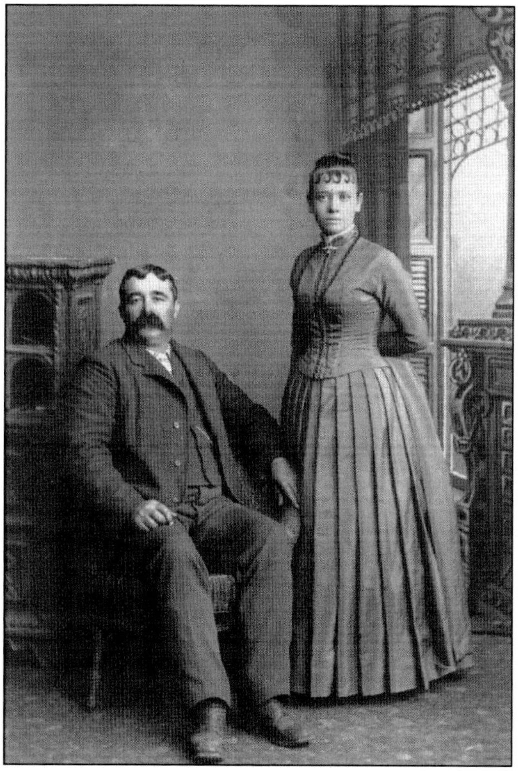

Pictured below is "The Castle," an elegant home built in 1892 by Abiathar Richard Cydney (Dick) Smith at 161 East 2550 North. The home was elaborately constructed and completely furnished for Dick's fiancée, Martha Jane Alvord, shown at left with Dick. A smokehouse, icehouse, granary, and two large barns were constructed on the 65-acre farm. He also owned 14,000 acres of grazing land around the area. Known as the "Sheep King," Dick was one of the most prominent financial entrepreneurs in North Ogden. Tragically Jane died of diphtheria on their wedding day. He later married Rebecca Nichols, and they became the parents of two children. The home was later sold to Lorenzo and Mary (Barker) Ward. It was destroyed by fire following a remodeling project in 1971, displacing the family of Steven and Sheryl Ward.

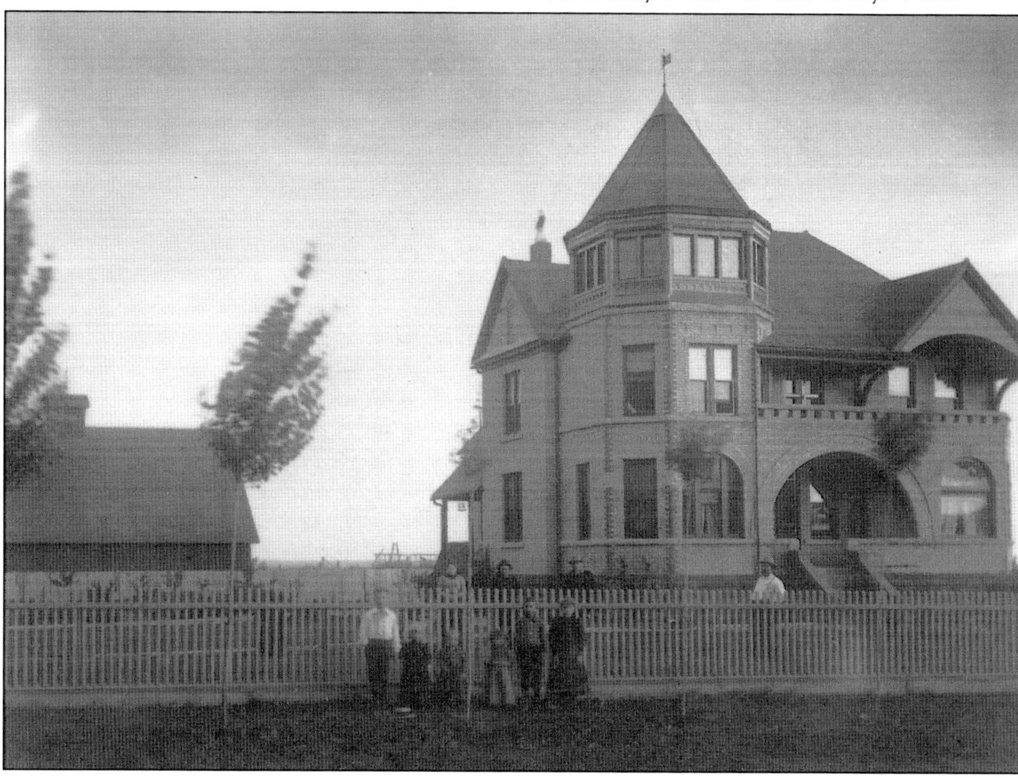

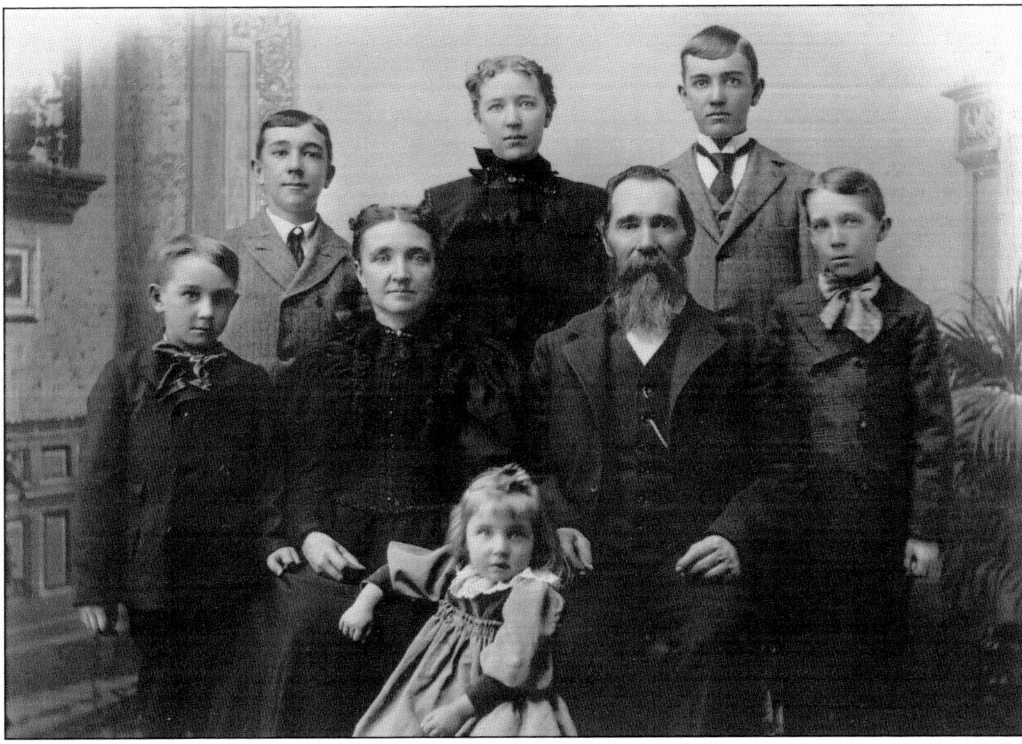

Pictured above is the Richard Thomas Berrett family around 1900. They are, from left to right, (first row) Edna Caroline (Lyon); (second row) Earl Ray, Annie Elizabeth (Toone), Richard Thomas, and Orson Toone; (third row) Walter Herbert, Emily Louise (Blaylock), and Thomas Francis. This was Richard's second family, as his first wife died shortly after having their eighth baby. The Berrett home, seen in the photograph below, was constructed in 1883 and was located on the southwest corner of 2600 North 650 East. Edna, Richard, and Annie are standing behind the fence. Richard hauled supplies to mining towns in Idaho and Montana by using teams of mules and large freight wagons. In the mid- to late 1850s, gold rush fever helped freighting become a lucrative business. Flour, bacon, molasses, dried fruit, and potatoes were some of the food supplies hauled to the miners and traded for gold.

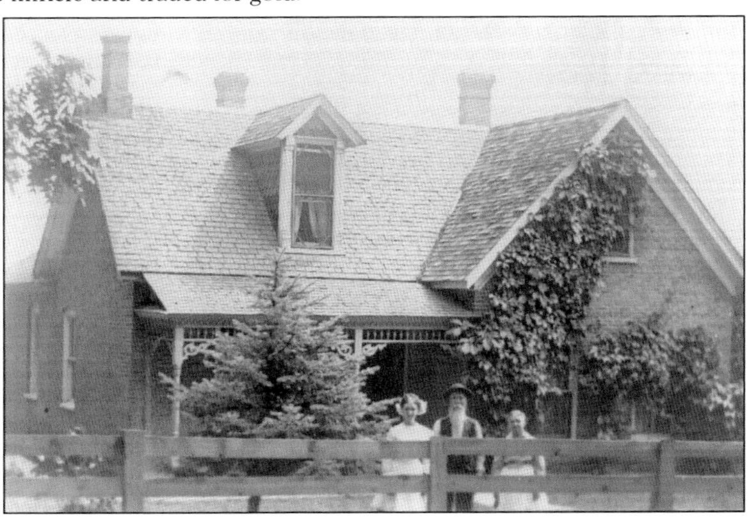

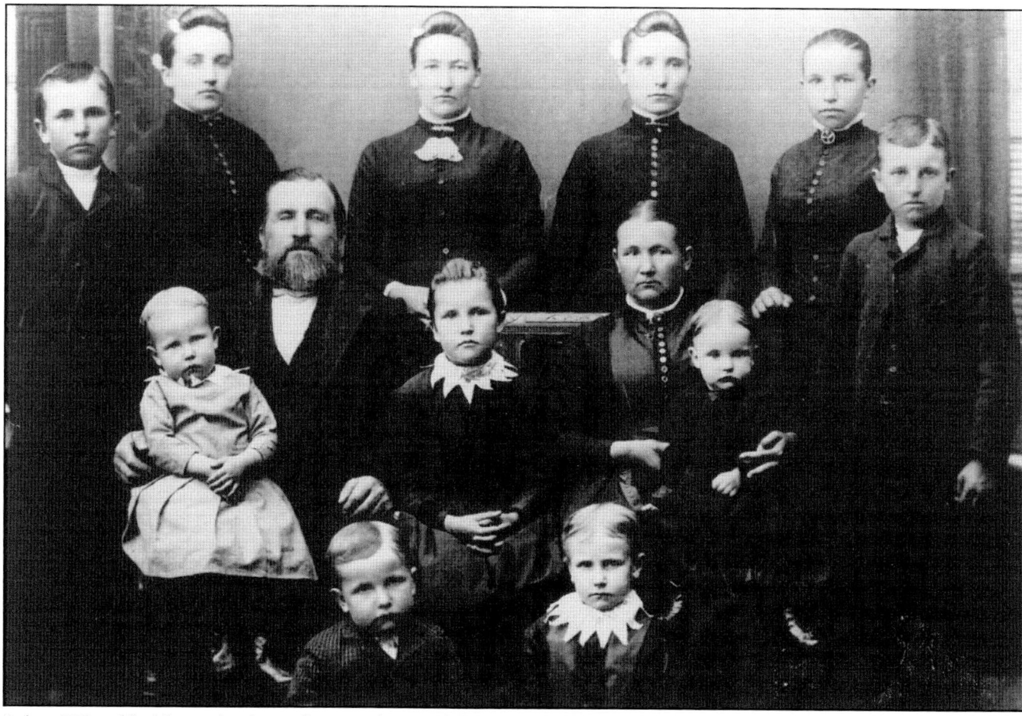

John Woodfield worked in the gardens of Queen Victoria at age six, following the death of his father. His payment was one shilling per week, which helped support his mother and 10 siblings. He came from England to North Ogden in 1862, carrying all his possessions in a handkerchief tied to a stick. John built a one-room log home, which was later replaced with a brick home. He married Rachel Roylance in 1865, and they were the parents of 12 children. Pictured above are, from left to right, (first row) William George and Emily Jeanette; (second row) Rosene Maria, John (father), Isabel, Rachel (mother), and Harriet Ellen; (third row) John Aaron, Jane, Mary Ann, Charlotte, Elizabeth, and Thomas Alma. Pictured below in 1887 is the Woodfield's two-story brick home at 1808 North 400 East.

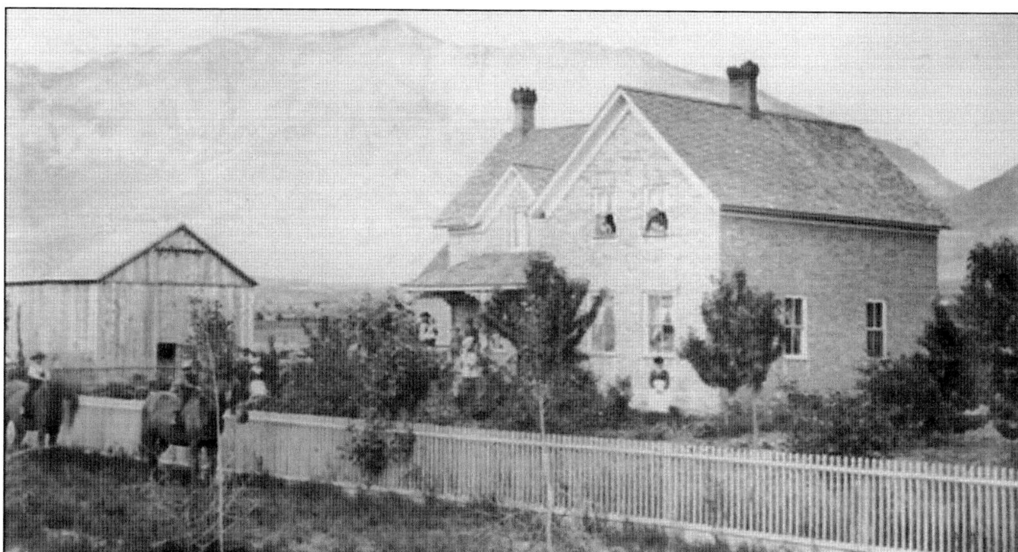

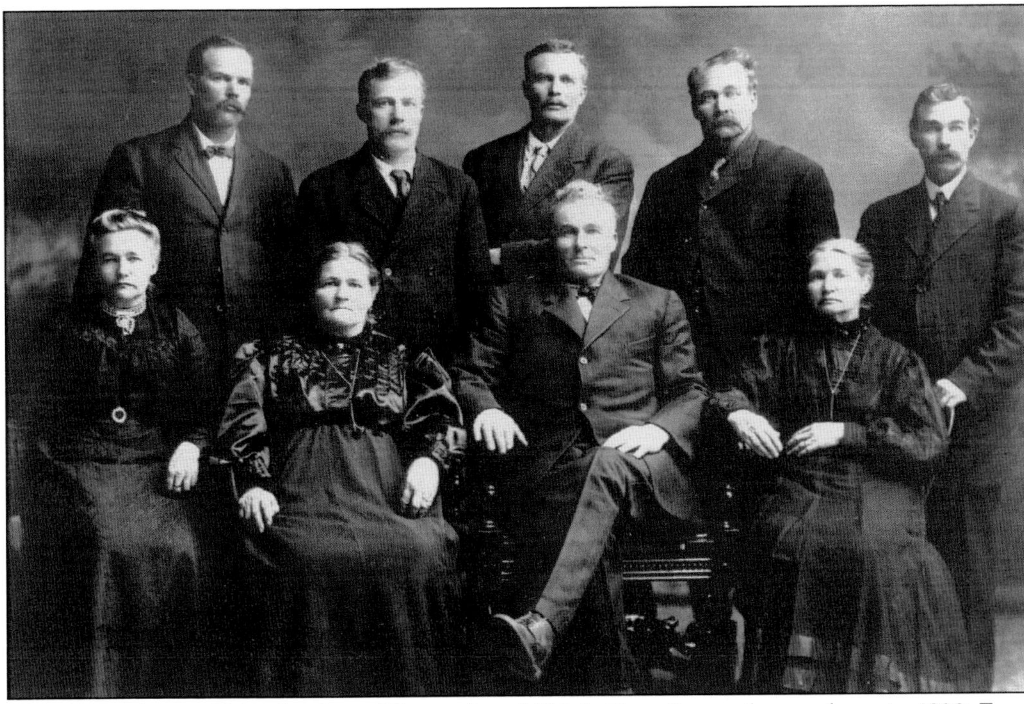

The descendents of Martha Ann (Thomas) and Elijah Shaw Jr. are shown above in 1890. From left to right are (first row) Amelia, Laura, William Orson, and Martha Ellen; (second row) George, John, Elijah III, Edmund Riley, and Samuel. Upon their arrival in North Ogden in 1858, the Shaws purchased land and built a two-room log cabin. They raised 11 children in the cabin, eventually constructing a two-story brick home in 1878, pictured below. The home was located at 344 West Pleasant View Drive and included a large ballroom on the top floor, which made the home a social center for many years. The generous Shaw family often helped others in need, including Native Americans.

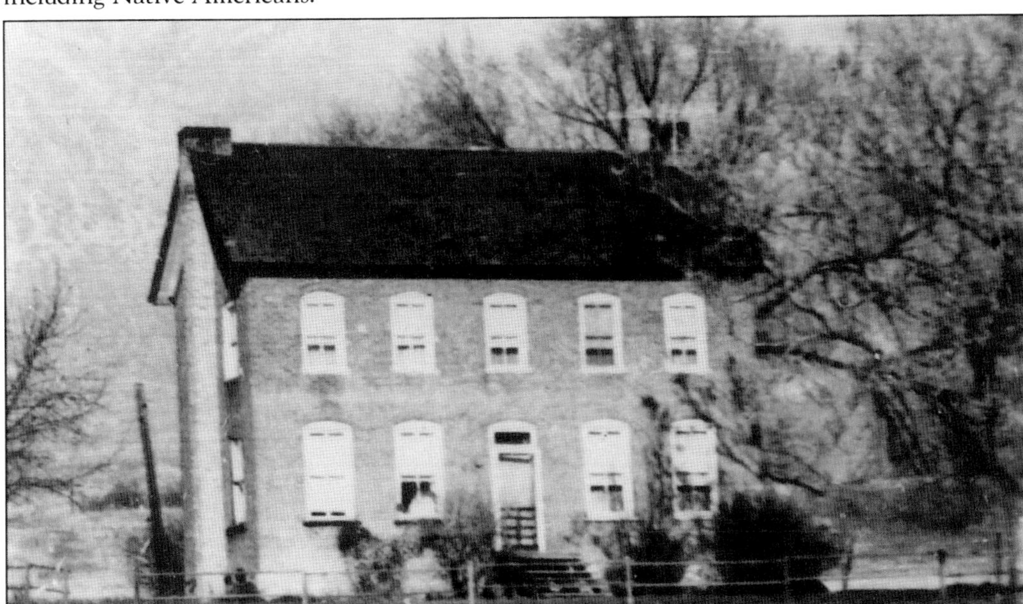

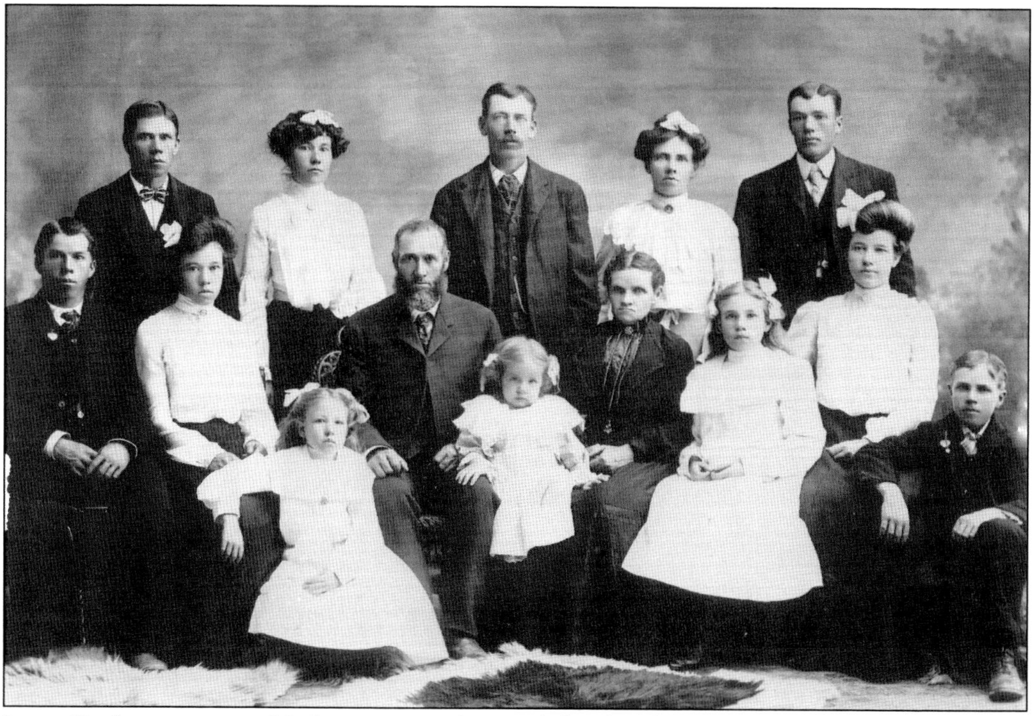

James Roylance came to Utah as a young boy with his family in 1853. James was a farmer and a well driller. He married Georgina Barnett in 1871, and after the birth of their sixth child, Georgina nearly died from blood poisoning. James amputated her foot himself to try to save her, as the doctor had given up hope. She finally recovered and went on to give birth to seven more children, 13 in all. The family members above are, from left to right, (first row) Edna, Myrtle, Serena, and Heber; (second row) John, Rachel, James (father), Georgina (mother), and Virtue; (third row) Alma, Maria, James H., Mary Ann, and George. Seen below, the Roylance home, located at the corner of 1700 North and 400 East, was a two-story structure constructed with bricks that Georgina's father made.

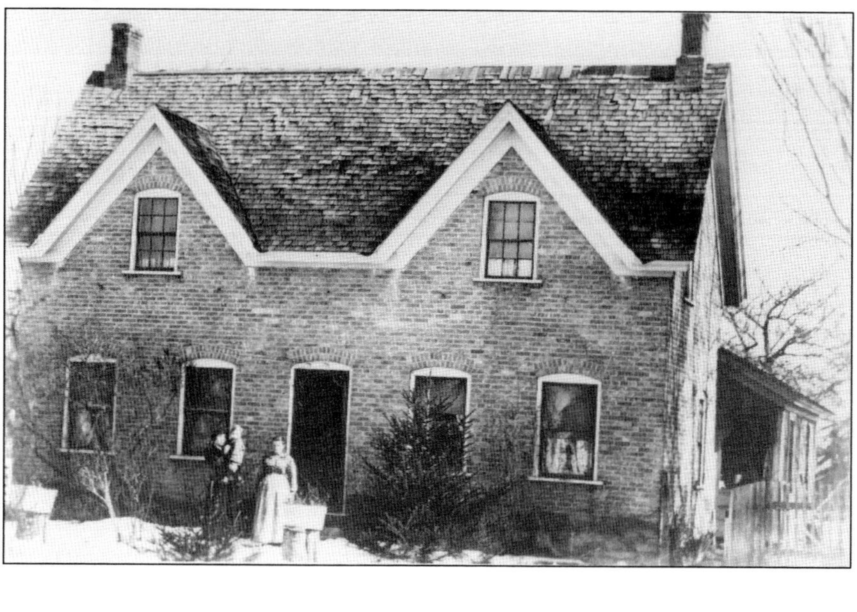

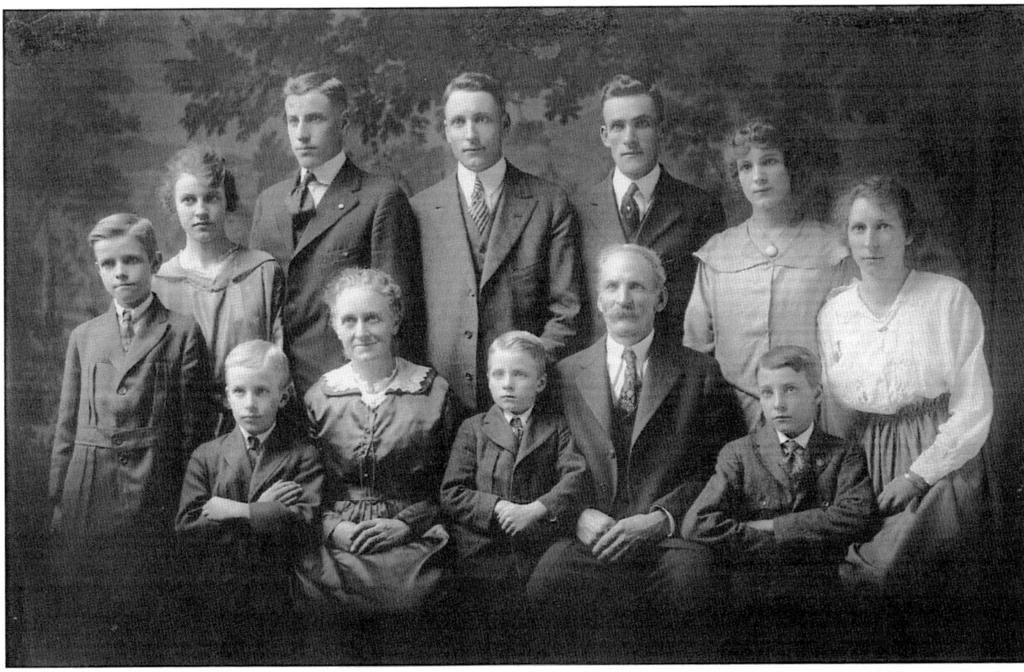

James Enoch Randall was born in 1864 and grew up on a farm in the eastern area of North Ogden. In addition to farming, he worked for the railroad, and enjoyed baseball, hunting, and fishing. He married Isabella Chadwick in 1889 and built a five-room frame house near the Randall property. They later constructed a two-story red brick home at 2060 North 1200 East, as seen below. The impressive 15-room home was spacious enough for their growing family of 10 children. Isabella always had flower gardens outside and beautiful plants and ferns inside, along with several pet canaries that she enjoyed. The Randall family members are pictured above, from left to right, (first row) Clarence Edward, Leroy David, Isabella (Chadwick), Leslie Elwood, J. Enoch, Charles Horace, and Mary Luetta; (second row) Sarah Ethel, Earl Abraham, James Walter, Lewis Alfred, and Lottie Elizabeth.

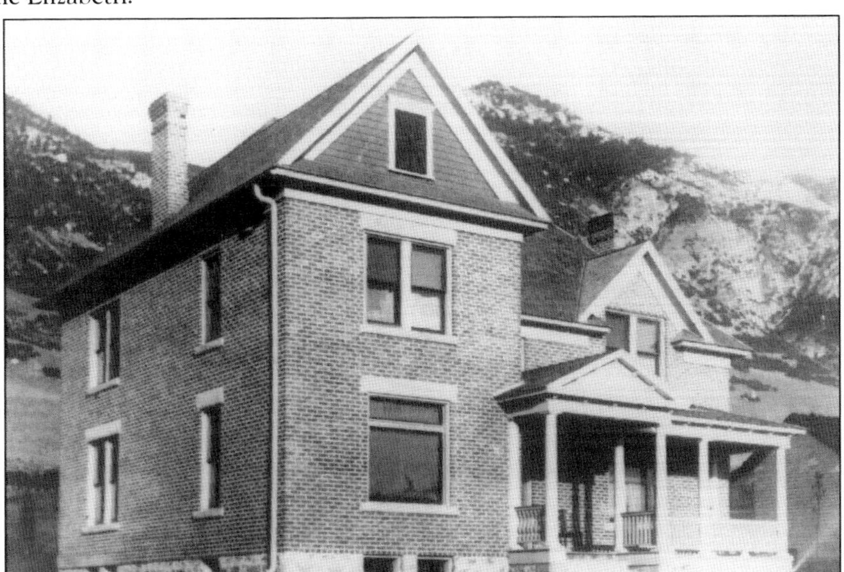

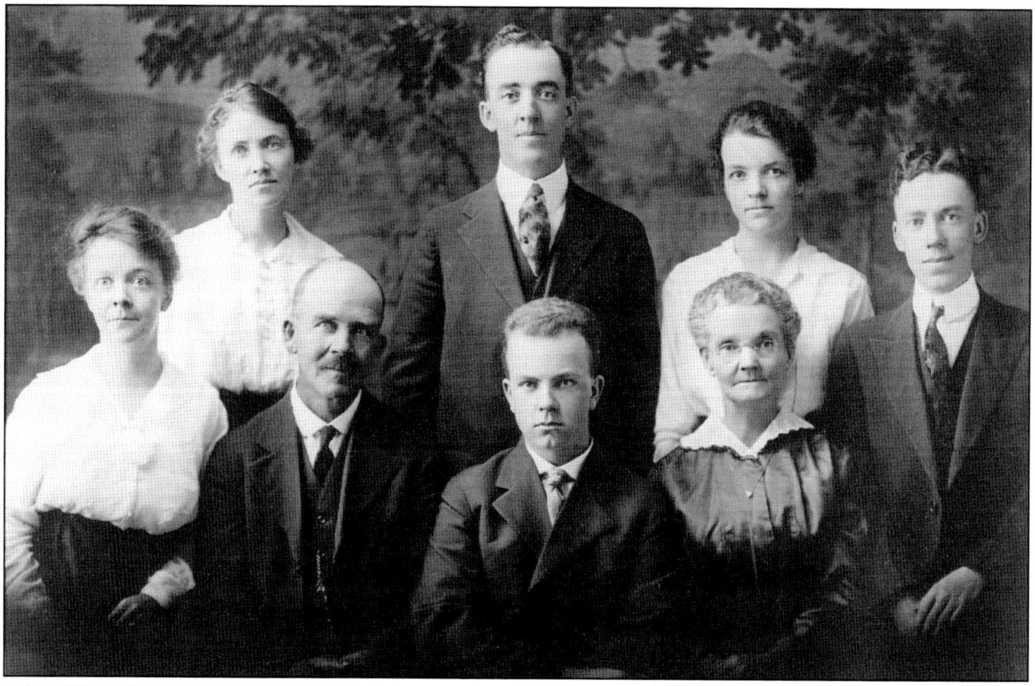

John W. Gibson was a prominent historian and educator. The journals he kept have been an important source of data containing many historical records of North Ogden's past. He was a prominent schoolteacher and had hundreds of books neatly stacked in his home, which he loaned out to North Ogden residents. He was elected Weber county assessor in 1898. John and Charlotte were the parents of six children and provided them with a pleasant home atmosphere. The family members in this photograph taken around 1916 are, from left to right, (first row) Charlotte Jeanette "Nettie" (Berrett), John William Sr., Leland Wallace, and Charlotte (Berrett); (second row) Sarah Lillias (Ferrin), John William Jr., Margaret Eleanor (Taylor), and Robert Berrett. The John W. Gibson home at 474 East 2650 North is pictured below in 1910.

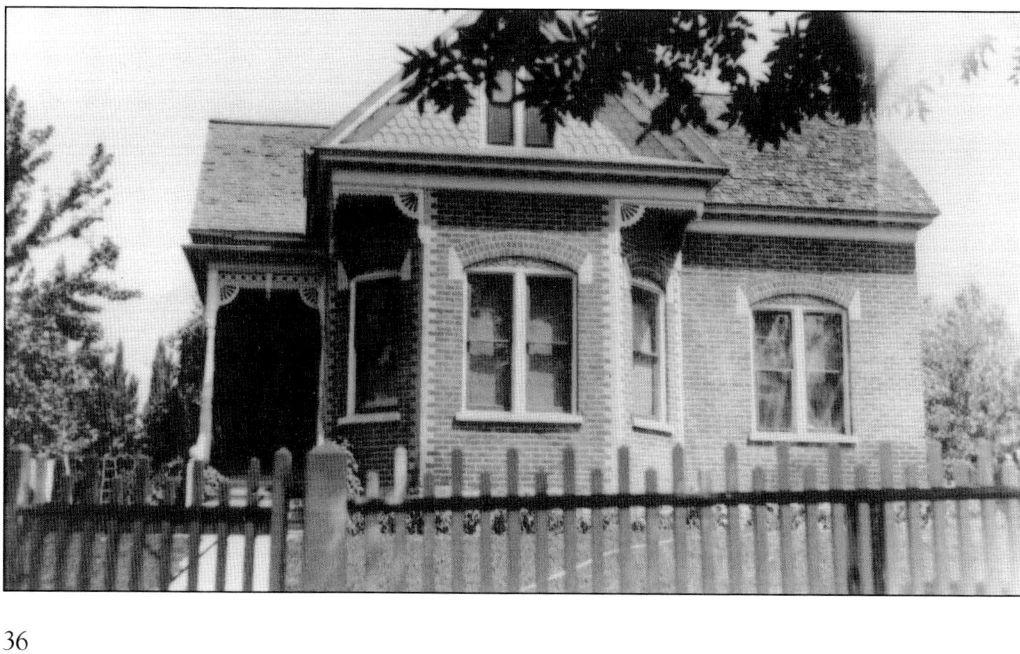

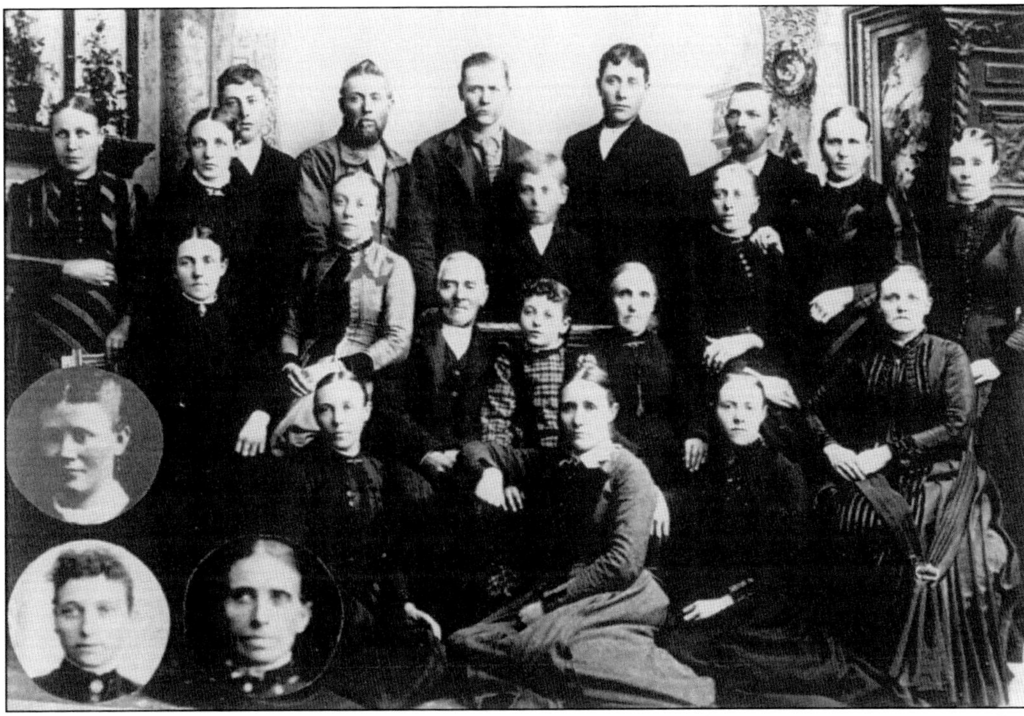

Abraham Chadwick was an early pioneer who engaged in plural marriage, marrying a total of five wives, four of whom were named Mary. Abraham was arrested for polygamy and received a six-month jail sentence. The Abraham Chadwick family members in this 1890 photograph above are, from left to right, (first row) Ellen Adelia (Bailey), Mary Louise (Shaw), and Francis Alice (Barker); (second row) Elizabeth (Montgomery), Eliza Ann (Randall), Abraham (father), Margaret May (Woodfield), Mary (Wheeler, third wife), Isabella (Randall), and Esther Caroline (Barker); (third row) Ann (Montgomery), Clarissa (Storey), Thomas Henry, Alonzo, Abraham Jr., John Charles, George, John Samuel, Mary Jane (Rose), and Olive Alberta (Storey); (inset, first row) Elizabeth Ann (Linford), and Mary Ann (Newby, fourth wife); (inset, second row) Eva Elizabeth (Clark). Below is the home of Abraham and Mary Ann (Newby) Chadwick near 1380 North 400 East around 1925. According to records, Abraham fathered a total of 27 children.

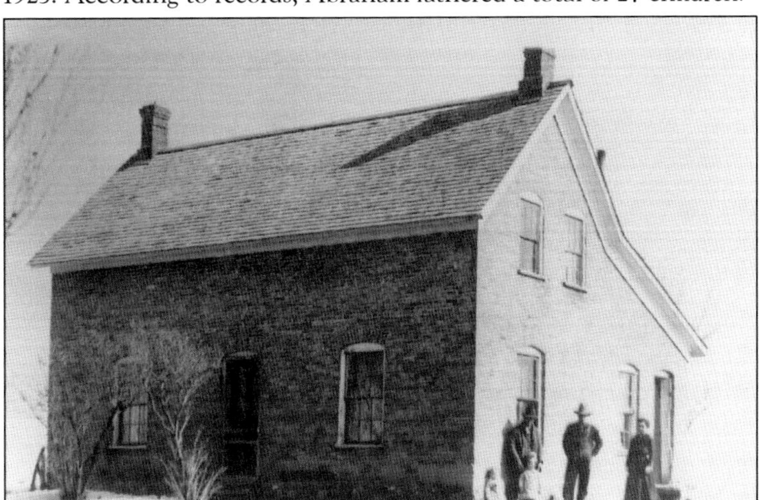

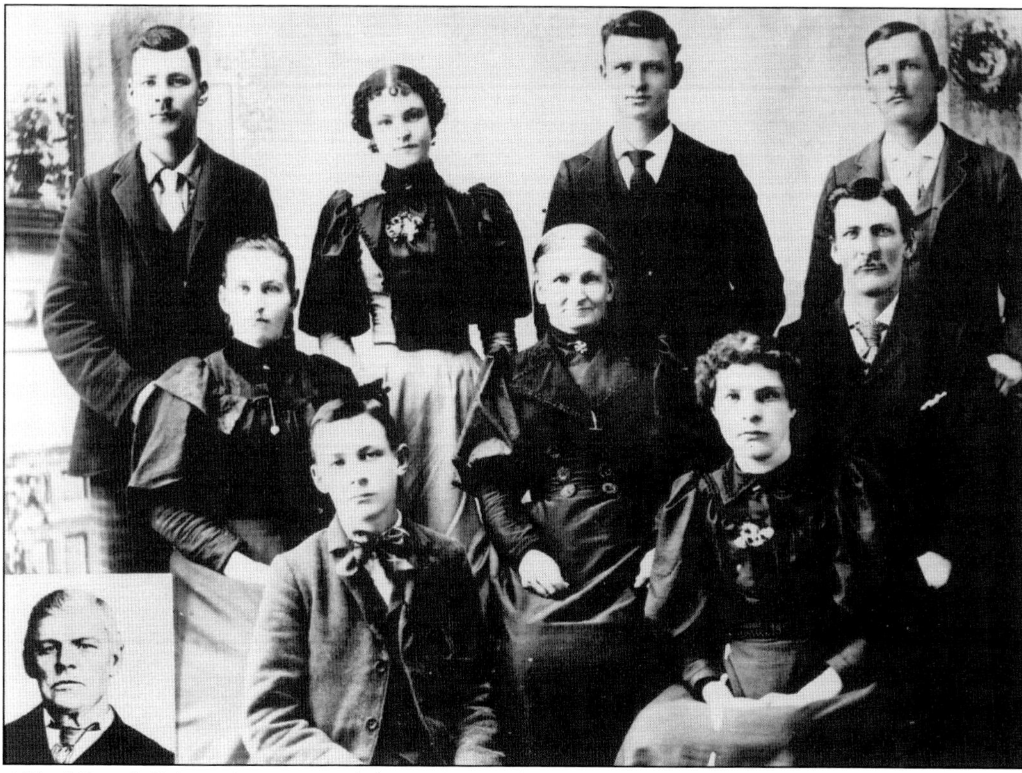

Alfred Randall (inset) was one of the early North Ogden settlers to practice polygamy. Pictured above are his fourth wife, Hannah (Severn), and eight of their children. When Congress passed anti-polygamy legislation in 1862, the offenders were usually sentenced to a one-year prison term and a $300 fine. Prominent and influential men of the community practiced polygamy, causing a devastating loss to the families during incarceration. Pictured below is Alfred Randall with his five wives. From left to right, they are (first row) Margaret (Harley) and Emerette (Davis); (second row) Mildred (Johnson), Hannah (Severn), and Elsie (Anderson). Hannah (his North Ogden wife) and Alfred were the parents of nine children. Alfred was a wheelwright and carpenter by trade, building and operating Ogden Woolen Mills near Twelfth Street and Harrison Boulevard in Ogden from 1867 to 1876. Alfred fathered a total of 33 children.

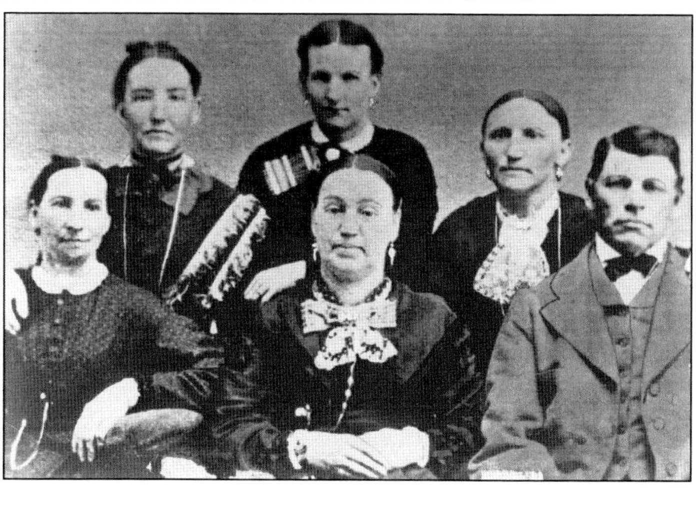

Three

Agriculture and Survival

Cherries, Chickens, and Churning

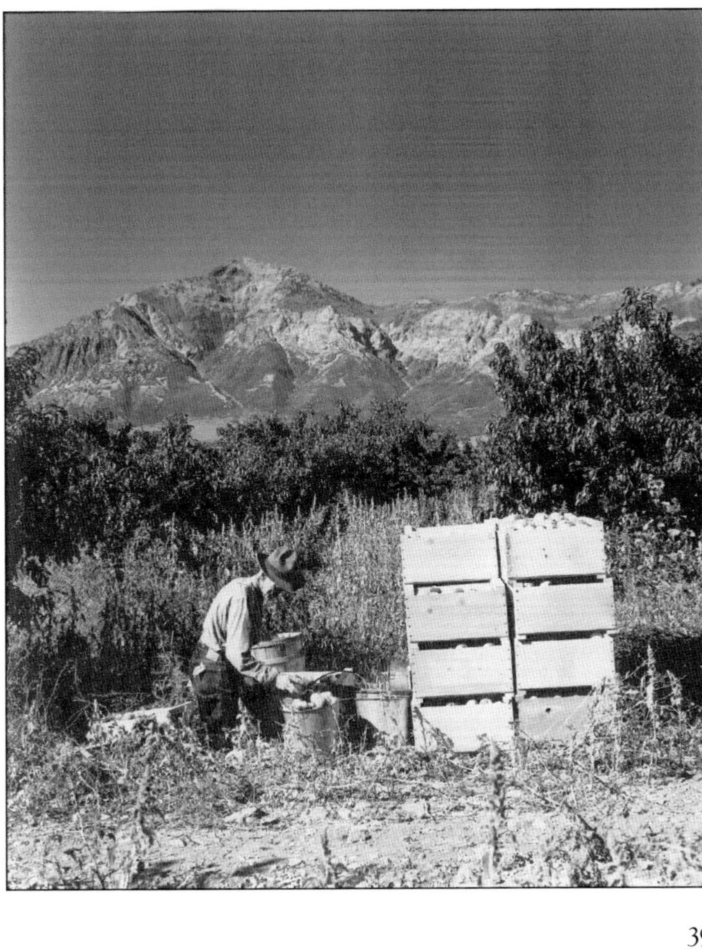

The peach harvesting season is shown with Ben Lomond Peak in the background. When the settlers first arrived in the area, they found wild fruit growing abundantly on hillsides and in marshes. They picked wild plums, chokecherries, thimbleberries, and currants, as well as strawberries and raspberries. The pioneers planted apples, peaches, cherries, pears, and apricots that had been transported across the plains. Large orchards developed, providing fruit to surrounding areas.

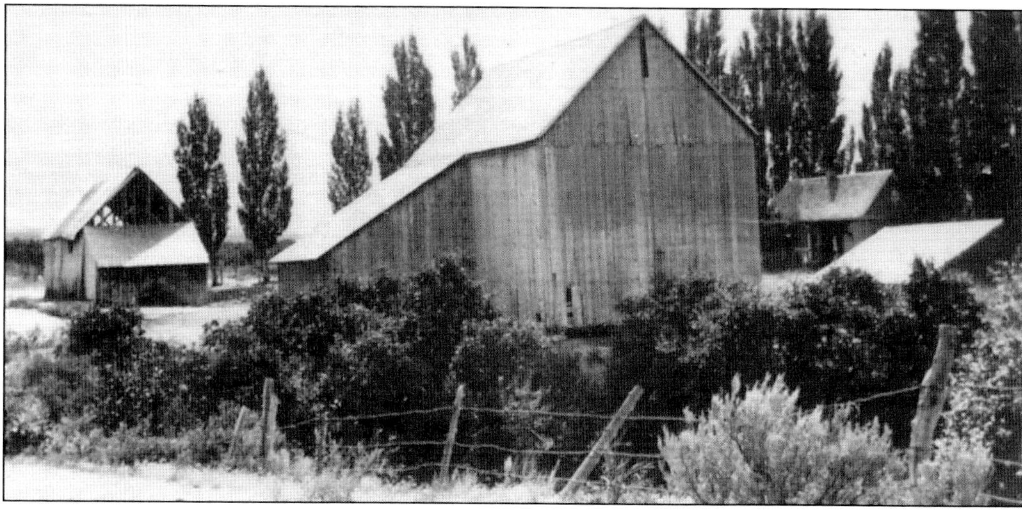

The barn above, located near 2750 North 1050 East, belonged to Emil and Florence Chatelain. Born in 1889, Emil was active in community affairs and tended to a large productive orchard and farm with the help of his wife and family. The original Chatelain home still stands, but the barn has been demolished. Many of the early barns were constructed with wooden pegs when metal nails were unavailable. Dairy barns were equipped with a Jackson Fork, which aided the farmers with winter hay storage. In 1932, William Nathan Barker constructed the barn seen below near 2400 North Fruitland Drive. Two barns previously built on the same site were destroyed by fire, once by boys playing with matches. W. Nathan was a well-respected North Ogden farmer with a very successful egg business. The barn is a prominent North Ogden landmark.

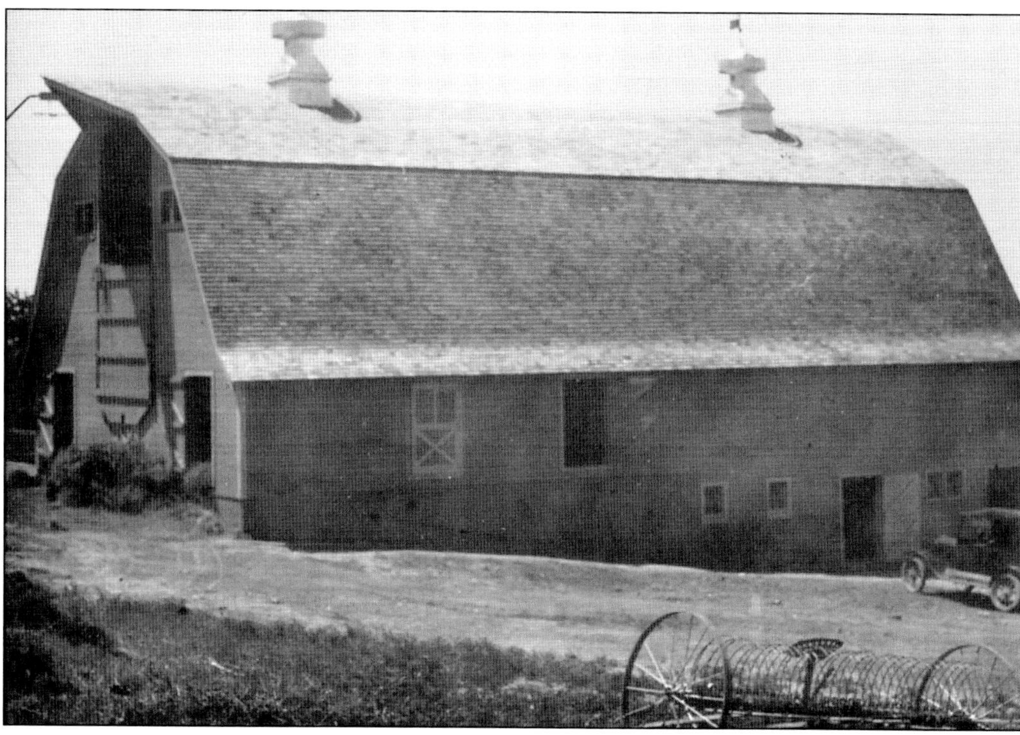

Nathaniel Montgomery constructed this barn in 1875. His son-in-law LeRoy Snooks called each of his cows by name at milking time, and they complied by coming in the order called. LeRoy's grandchildren Barbara and Roy Wyatt are pictured at right. Located near 200 East Elberta Drive, the barn was demolished in 1970. Earlier a nearby granary was burned, and a long-forgotten stash of dynamite exploded, creating quite a commotion in the neighborhood.

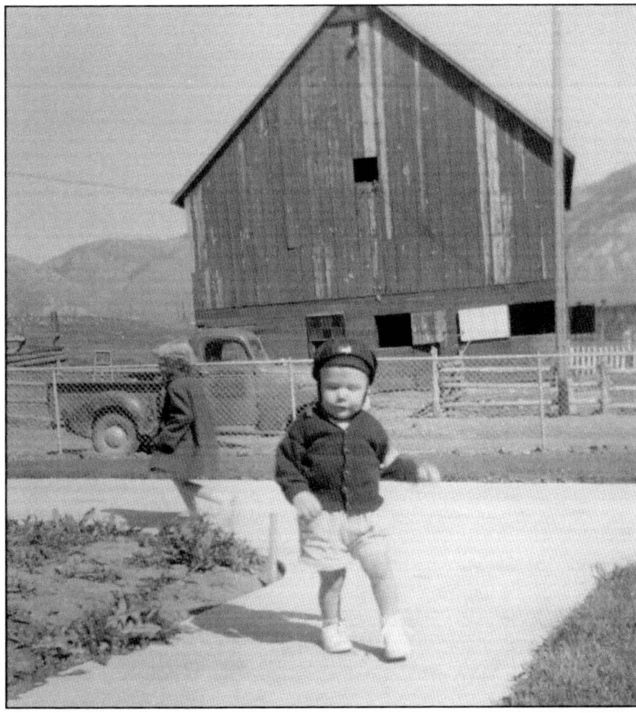

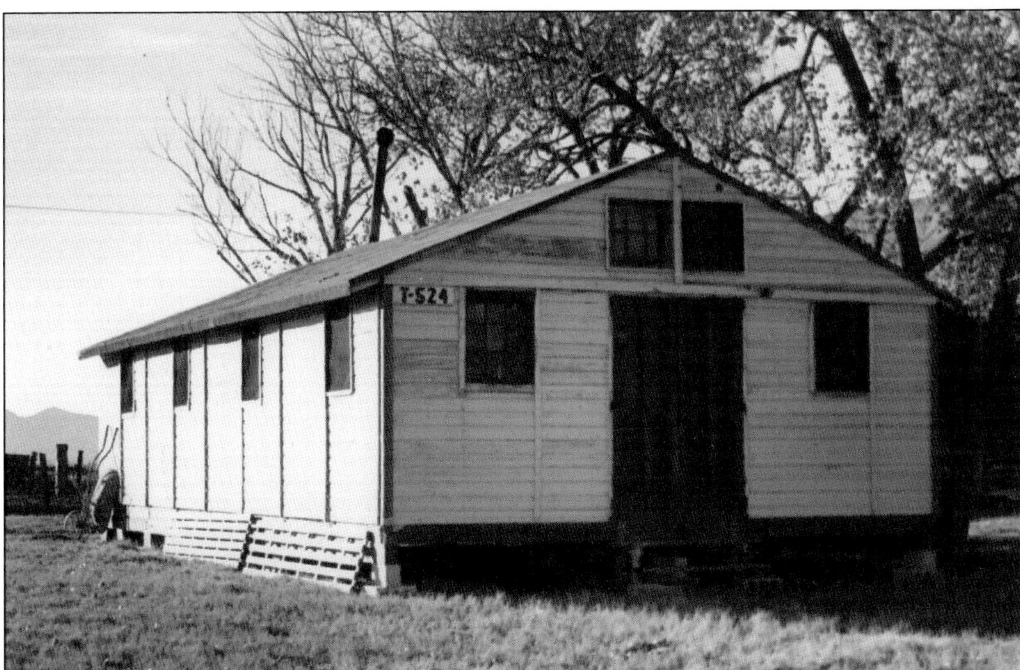

Farm labor was always needed, and many farmers provided migrant workers with housing, such as the building seen above. Mexican nationals, as well as German and Italian prisoners of war, worked on local farms around 1943. Prisoners were paid by fruit companies, and their meals were provided by the army. Native Americans were also hired as farm laborers, in addition to approximately 150 young locals, who sometimes helped after working their regular jobs.

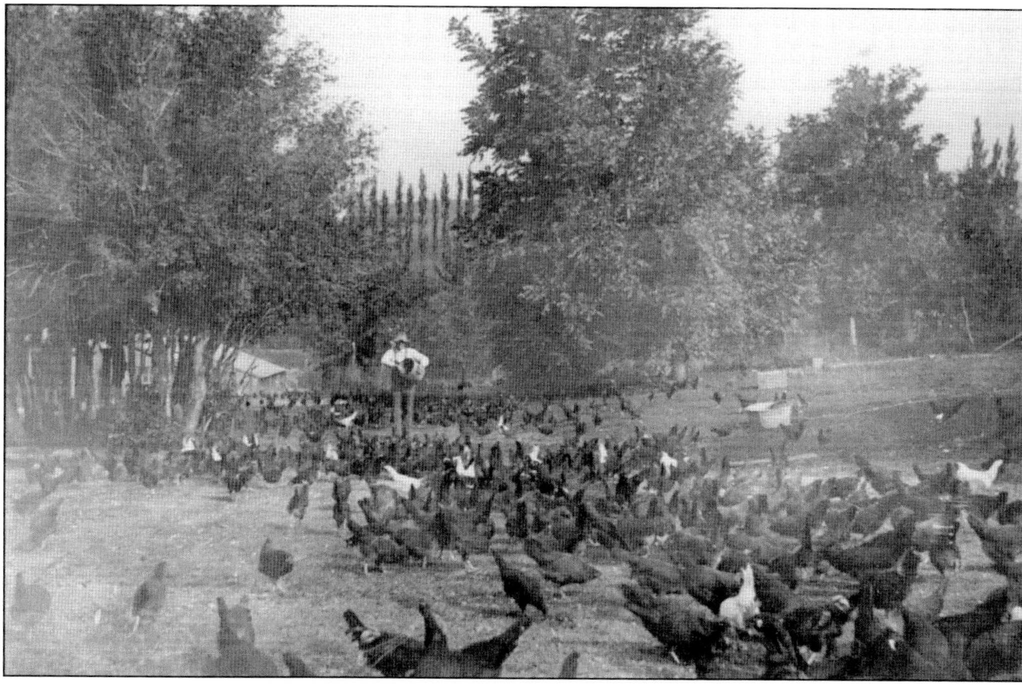

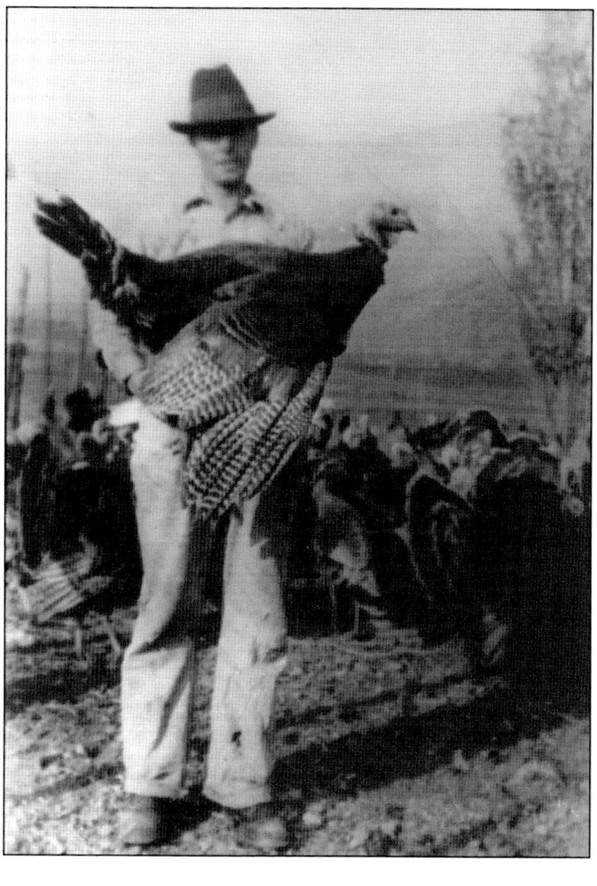

Almost every covered wagon entering the North Ogden valley carried a crate of chickens, which most early farmers raised. Joseph D. Barker, pictured here in 1910, is scattering feed for his chicken flock. Joseph was one of the first farmers in the area who raised chickens commercially, and he won many prizes at the state fair. Eggs were one of the first items used for bartering.

The dry, warm climate and an abundance of grasshoppers helped the turkey industry thrive. The turkey farmers received a double benefit when the birds ate the grasshoppers that threatened their crops and orchards. Byron W. Warren, pictured at left, and his cousin Will raised turkeys on the Sunny Slope Poultry Farm, "where the sun always shines" according to a popular slogan, near the mouth of North Ogden Canyon around the 1920s. The coops were heated with pipes circulating hot water.

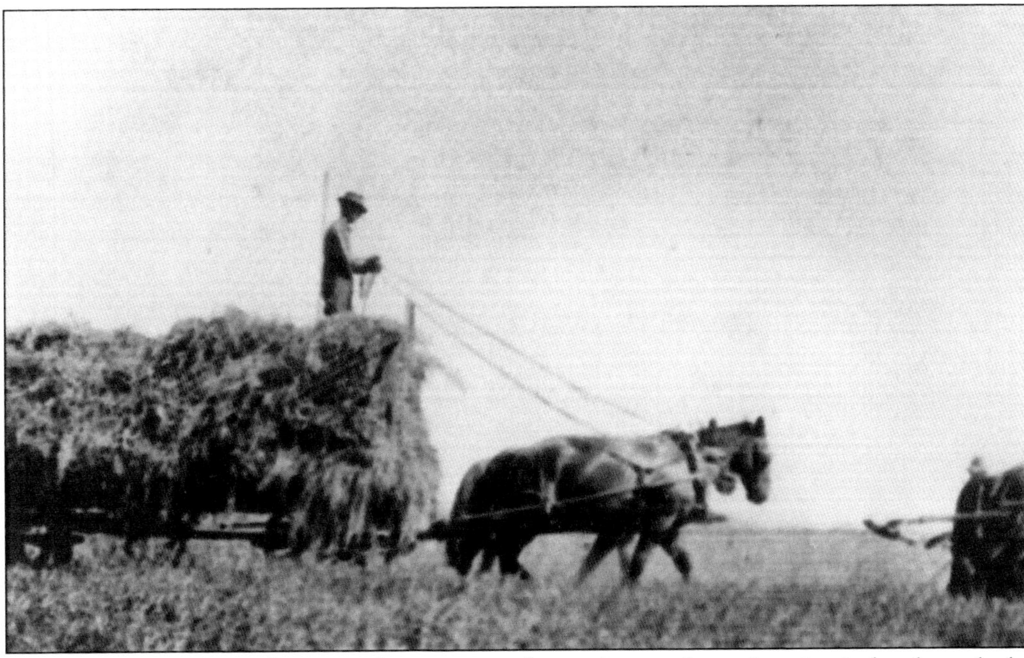

The horse-drawn hayrack was used to transport hay to barns, above, keeping it dry through the harsh winters. A derrick was used to load the hay onto the wagons. The grain threshing machine (pictured below) revolutionized the harvesting process, which was once laboriously done by hand. The first threshing machine was powered by horses. In 1856, John White and Alfred Berrett Sr. bought a steam-powered thresher. Sagebrush was burned to produce the steam. In 1897, William Hill and Milton Holmes purchased a Roaring Lion thresher and were hired to thresh much of the grain for miles around. Trained drivers knew by the roar of the machine whether the team of horses pulling the thresher should be hurried or slowed. Both photographs were taken around 1920.

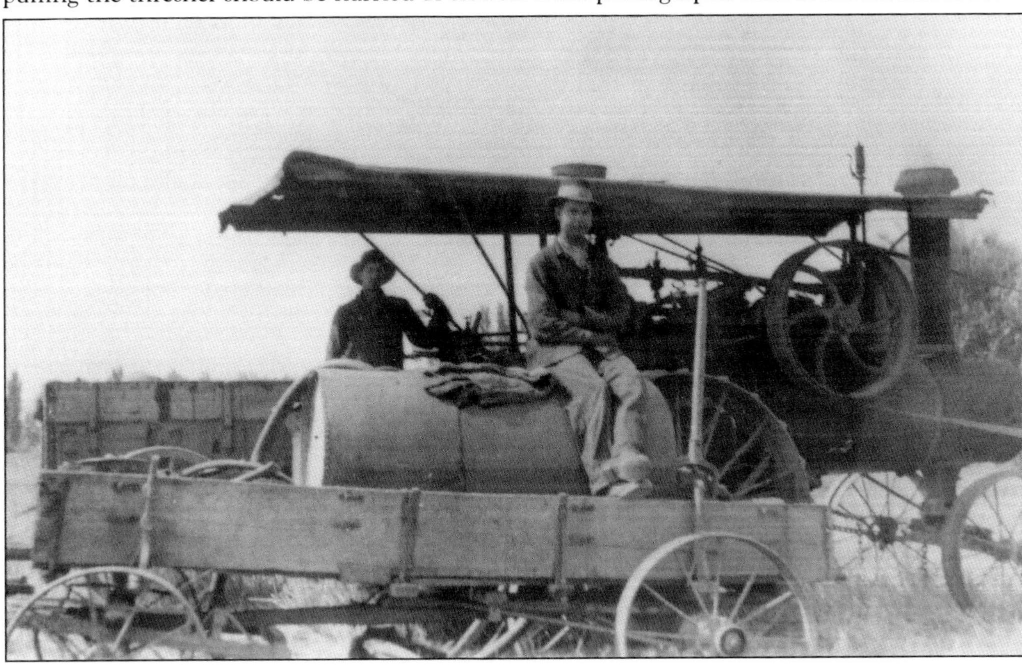

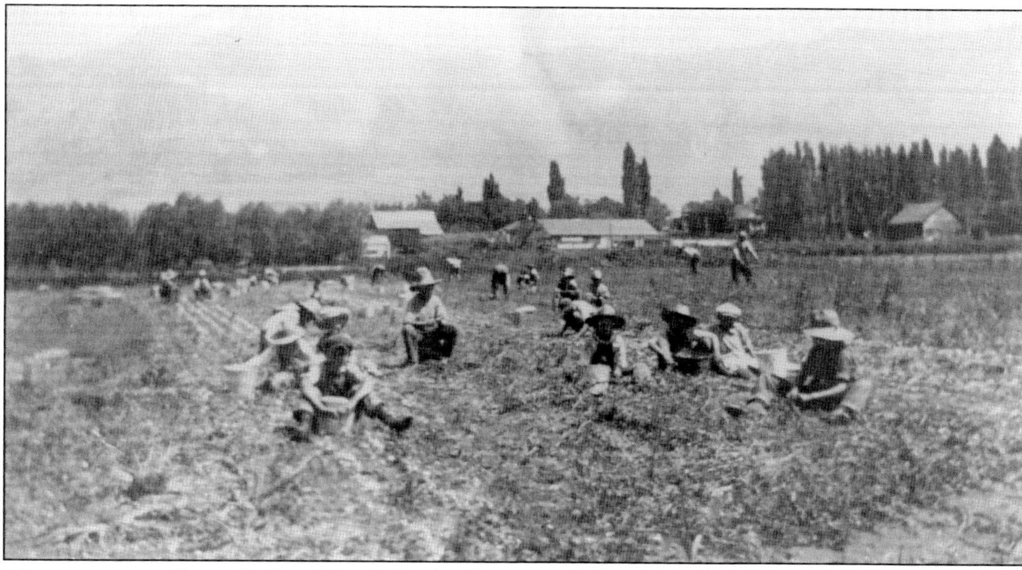

Many row crops flourished on North Ogden farms, including onions, green beans, cabbage, corn, tomatoes, beets, celery, potatoes, sugar beets, and pumpkins, as seen below. Some of the crops were sold fresh, while others were taken to the North Ogden Canning Factory for processing. Onion harvesting time around 1920 is pictured above at the Clarence M. Barker farm near 2559 North 400 East. The children of the family are shown helping with the harvest. The families helped with the planting, weeding, and harvesting, and also with preserving fruits and vegetables needed for winter. Some fruit was dried and some bottled. To preserve the fruit, early settlers heated the desired mixture and poured it into bottles. Egg white was painted on the rim of the bottle, and heavy paper was attached to this glue to form a seal.

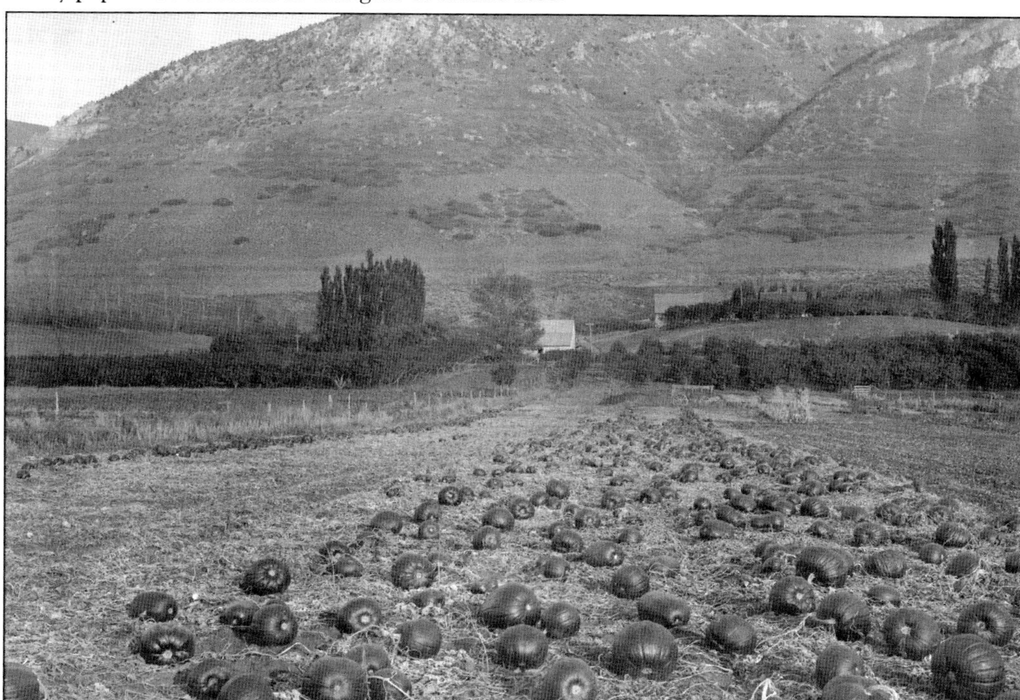

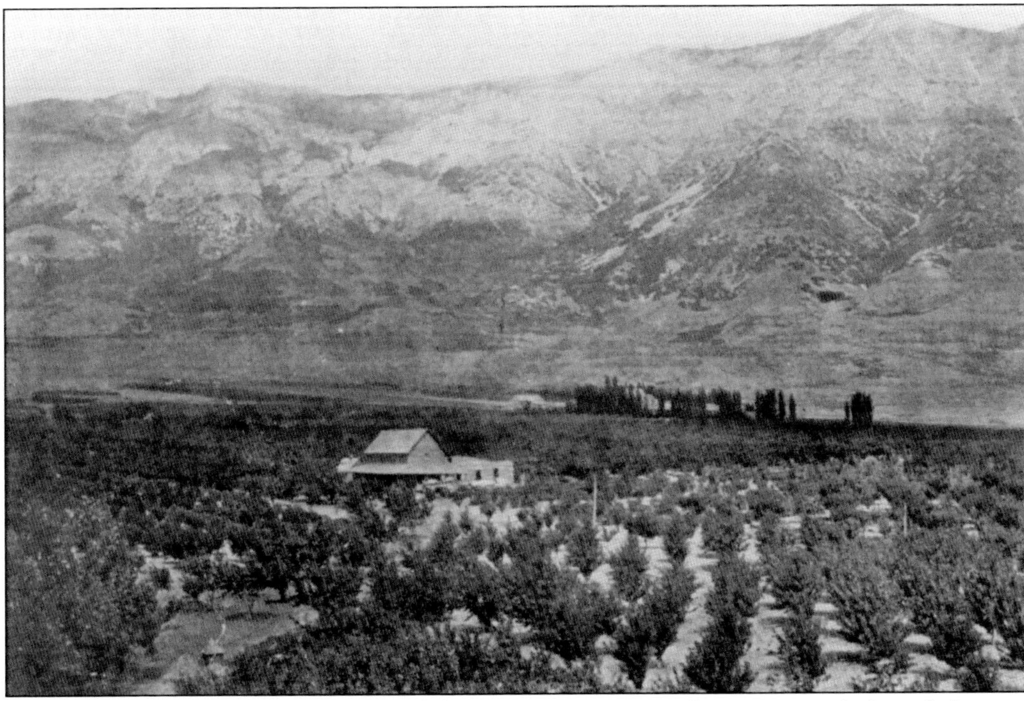

Almost every pioneer family planted fruit trees as soon as they were settled, and the area proved ideal for fruit growing. Shown above around 1910 is the Edwin G. McGriff orchard at approximately 900 East 2800 North. McGriff, a horticulturist from New York, transformed 80 acres of sagebrush-covered land into orchards with 7,000 peach, apricot, plum, and cherry trees, and 2,500 grapevines. The first year, his orchard was completely destroyed by grasshoppers. The orchard was replanted, and the grasshoppers were successfully poisoned. Seen below, the Ben Lomond Orchard home was occupied first by the McGriff family and later by the company's orchard managers. The impressive home was built by John T. Hall, and his family lived there from 1912 to 1945. The 14-room home included a dance floor on the upper level and a rock wine cellar.

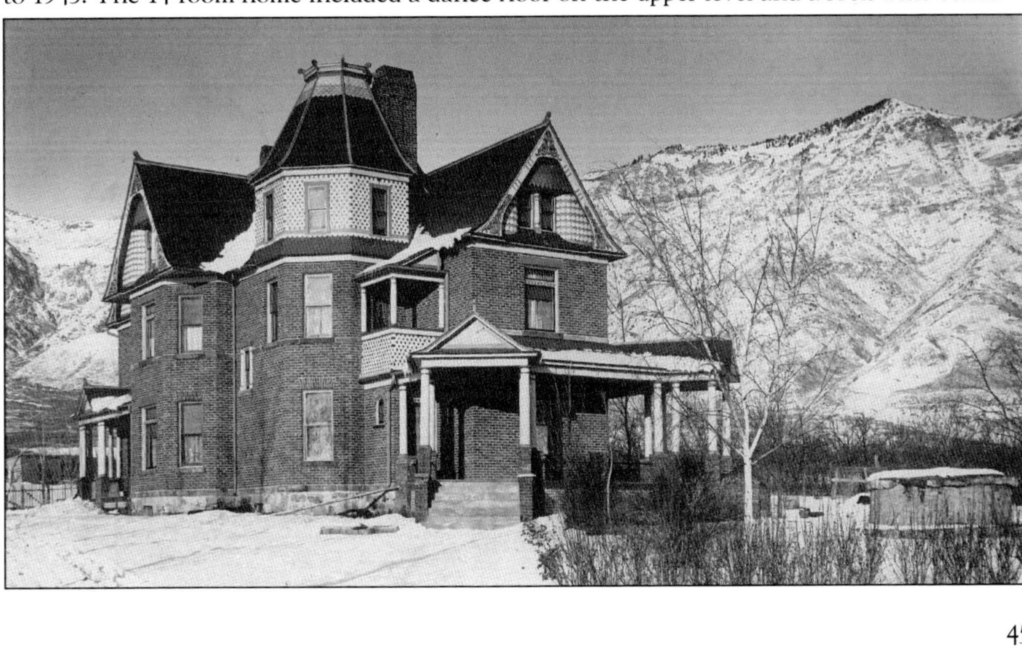

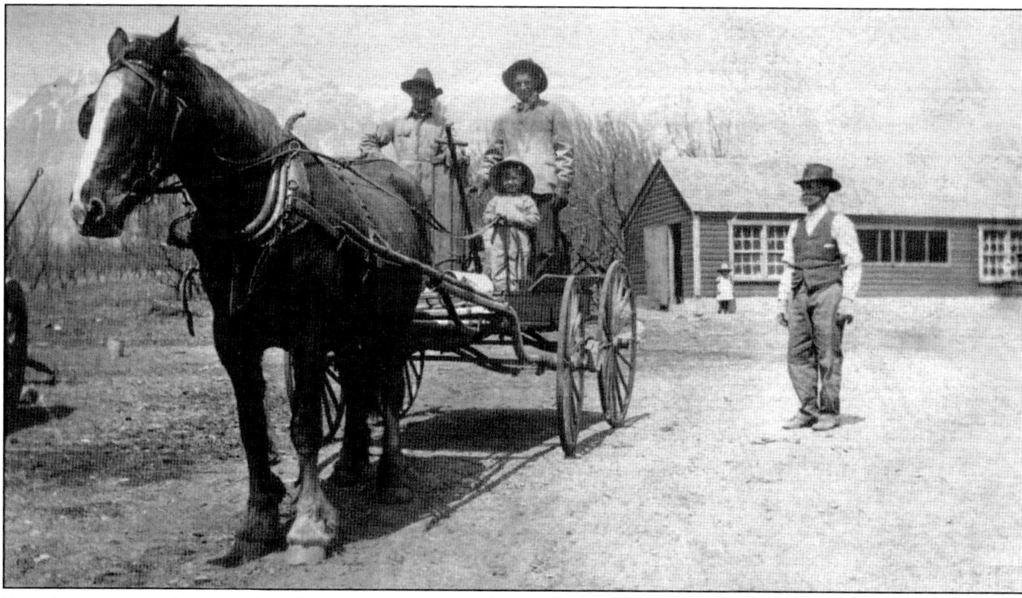

Ready to spray their orchards are the sons and grandson of Scott W. Campbell, who is shown to the right. On the wagon are Clyde, his young son Jay, and an unidentified man. Scott developed a successful fruit business, delivering to several Ogden stores. He built a house, purchased more land, and later formed a corporation with E. G. McGriff and James Storey. They built a fruit packinghouse and shipped to markets in the east.

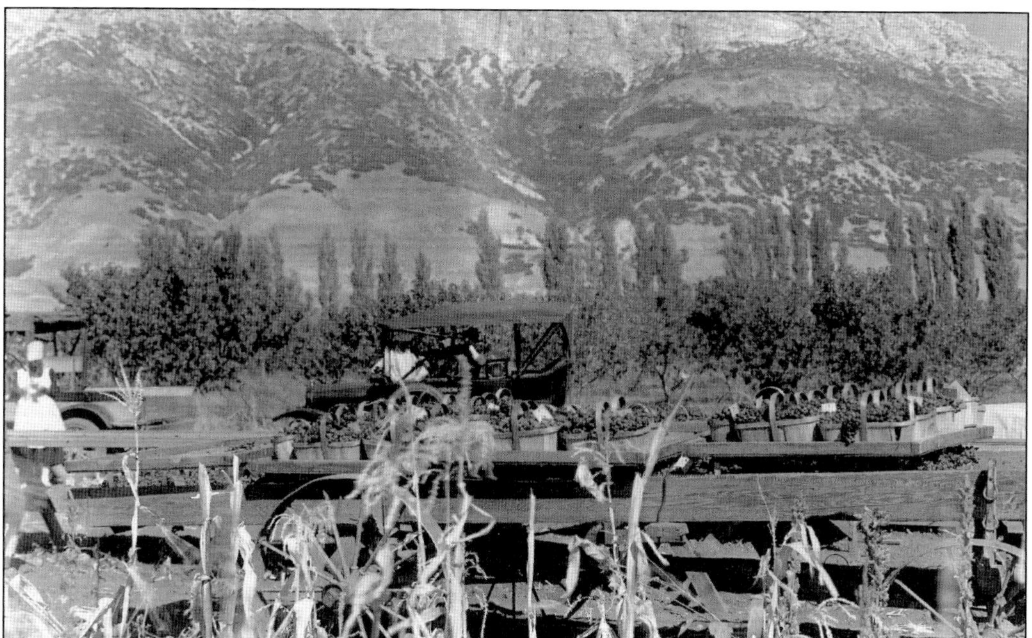

The grapes are being harvested and readied for shipment in the early 1920s. In 1900, E. G. McGriff bottled 3,000 gallons of excellent wine by using the leavings from grapes that were sold fresh. Bottled grape juice was also produced. Frank and Henry Stevens, Henry and Will Warren, Lige Shaw, John Hall, Frederick Barker, Will Norris, Emil Chatelain, and John Jones owned vineyards. Charles Pettigrew produced delicious seedless grapes through grafting.

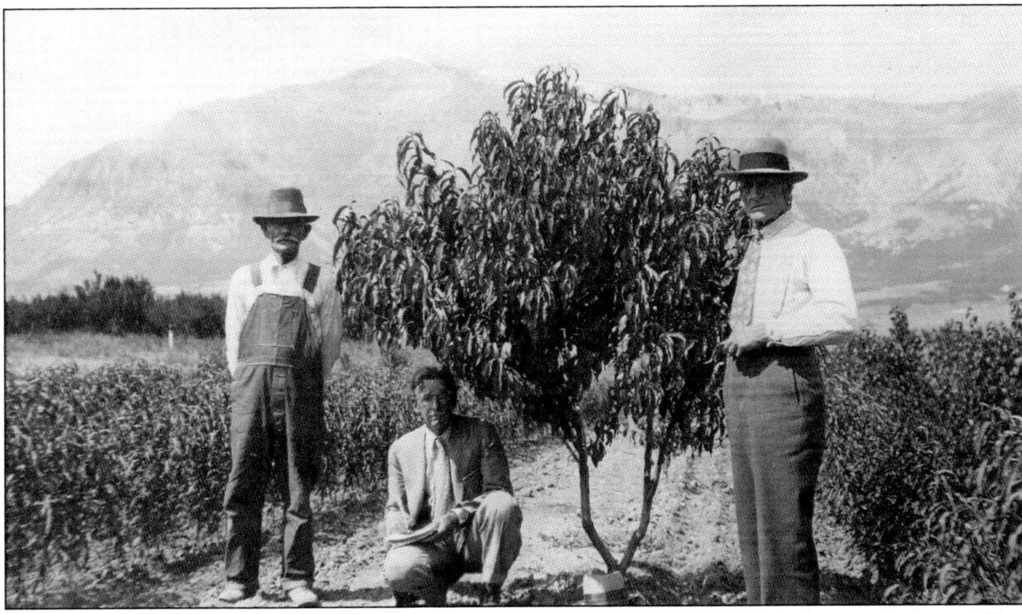

Elihu Nathan Warren is shown on the left, demonstrating his tree-grafting talent to fellow horticulturists around the 1920s. He created multiple varieties of fruit on one tree by grafting limbs onto a hardy rootstock. He also excelled in growing large fields of petunias in the spring, which were sold to people from miles around to beautify their homes and gardens.

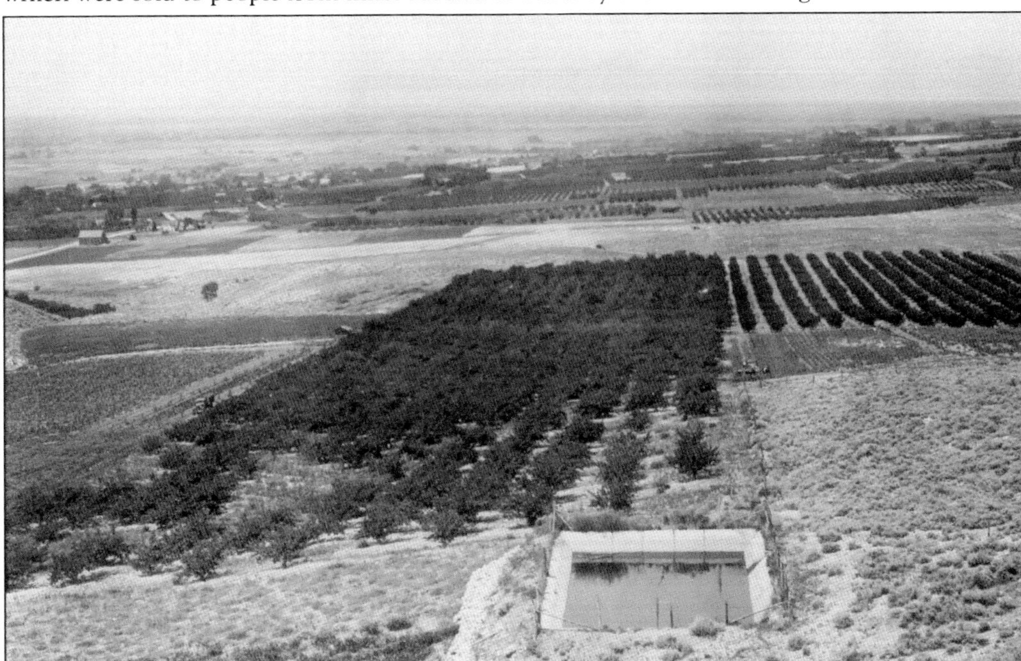

An early photograph shows the bench areas close to Ben Lomond that were dotted with orchards. Canals and reservoirs were constructed to divert water where needed. Fresh fruit was shipped around the United States from these orchards. Busy packinghouses and canning factories were once common in North Ogden, but the industry faded after many years. Home construction encroached on the area, and a mysterious disease destroyed many of the cherry trees.

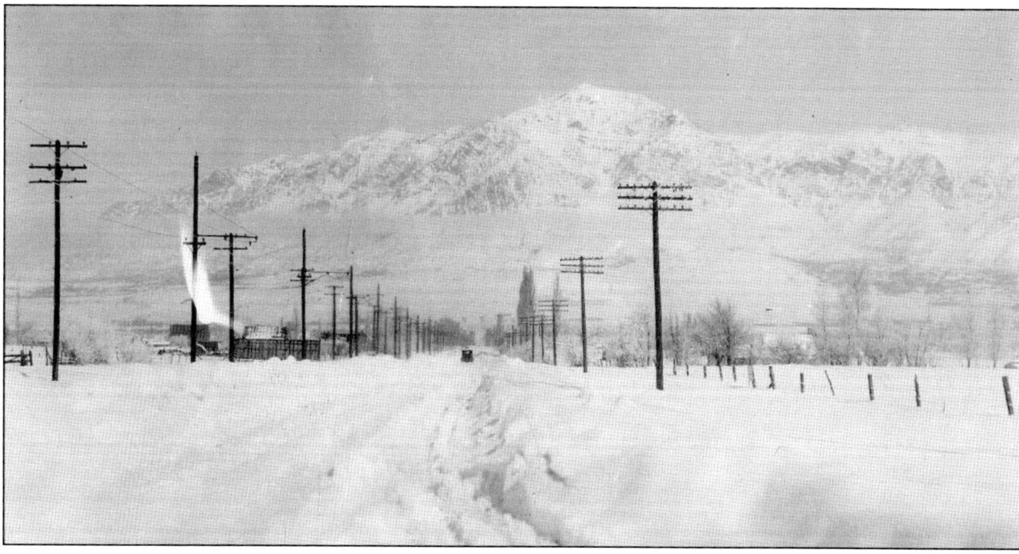

After heavy winter storms, as shown above, travel in North Ogden was nearly impossible. Pioneers used heavy timbers to build V-shaped snowplows that were pulled by three teams of horses. The photograph below, taken around 1920, shows an early plow working to clear the snow. Marlon H. Berrett was the road supervisor at the time. The plows measured up to 18 feet at the widest point, making it necessary to turn around at narrow bridges or roadways. In 1854, one of the hardest winters was recorded in Joseph Godfrey's diary. Lingering deep snow and below-freezing temperatures caused people and animals to run out of food. Animals were fed the straw from pioneers' beds, as well as tree branches, but hundreds did not survive. People resorted to gathering thistles and sego lily bulbs for survival.

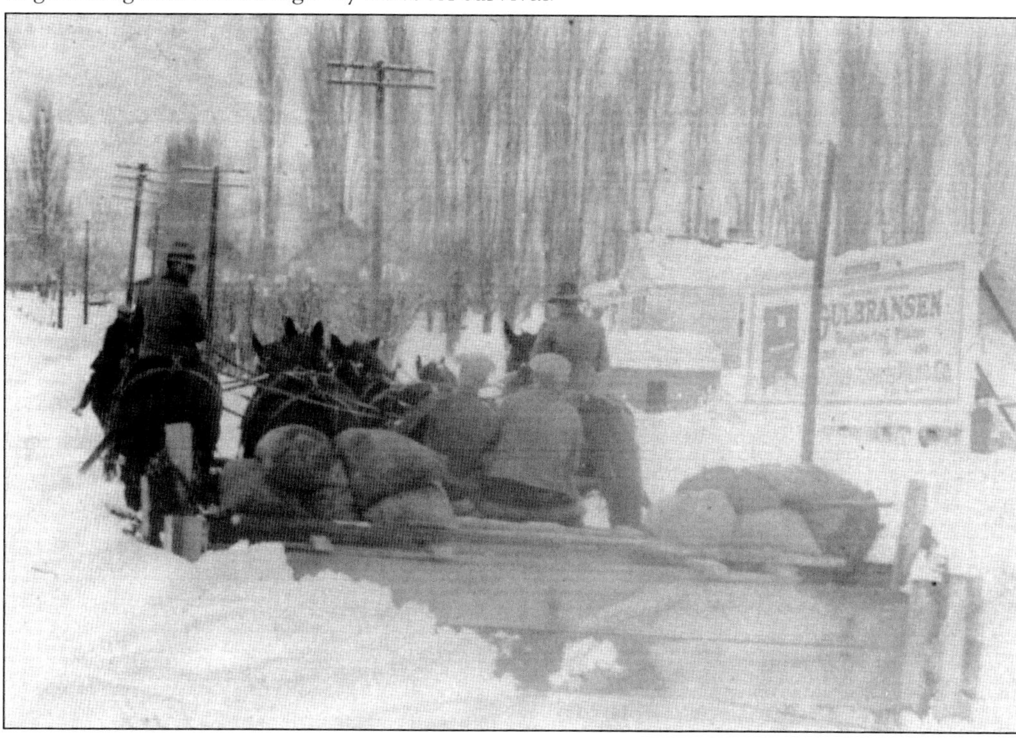

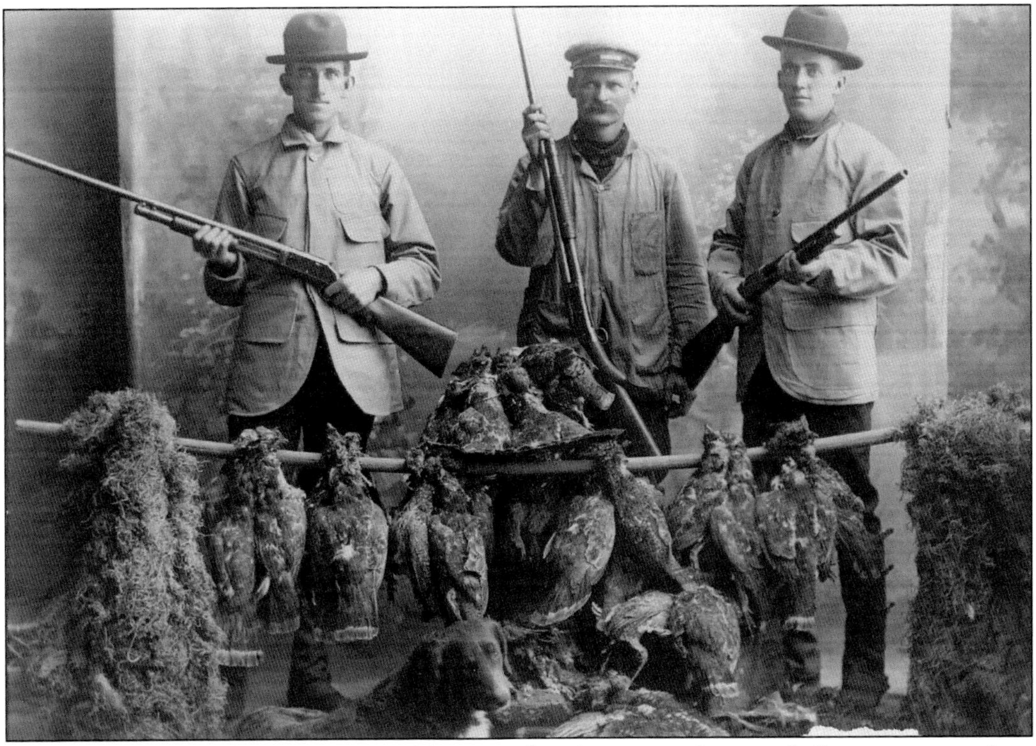

Pioneers participated in trapping and hunting for pleasure and survival. Bears, coyotes, deer, ducks, pheasants, and sage hens provided food and sport. Other animals were trapped, and the pelts were sold or used for clothing and other necessities. Pictured above in 1915 from left to right are hunters George Roylance, Chris Lind, and Charles Jones. Below is Wayne Barker with his hunting trophies and his enthusiastic dog in the 1950s. Early pioneers formed hunting parties to rid the area of bears, bobcats, wolves, foxes, and wolverines, which were considered pests. These hunts helped protect the farmers' families, poultry, and livestock.

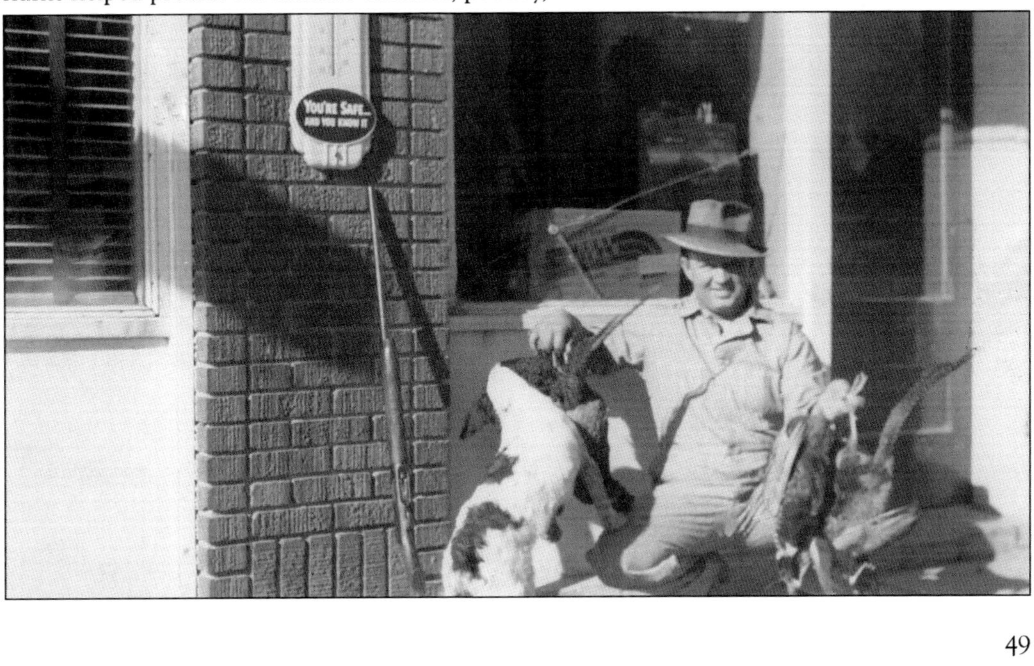

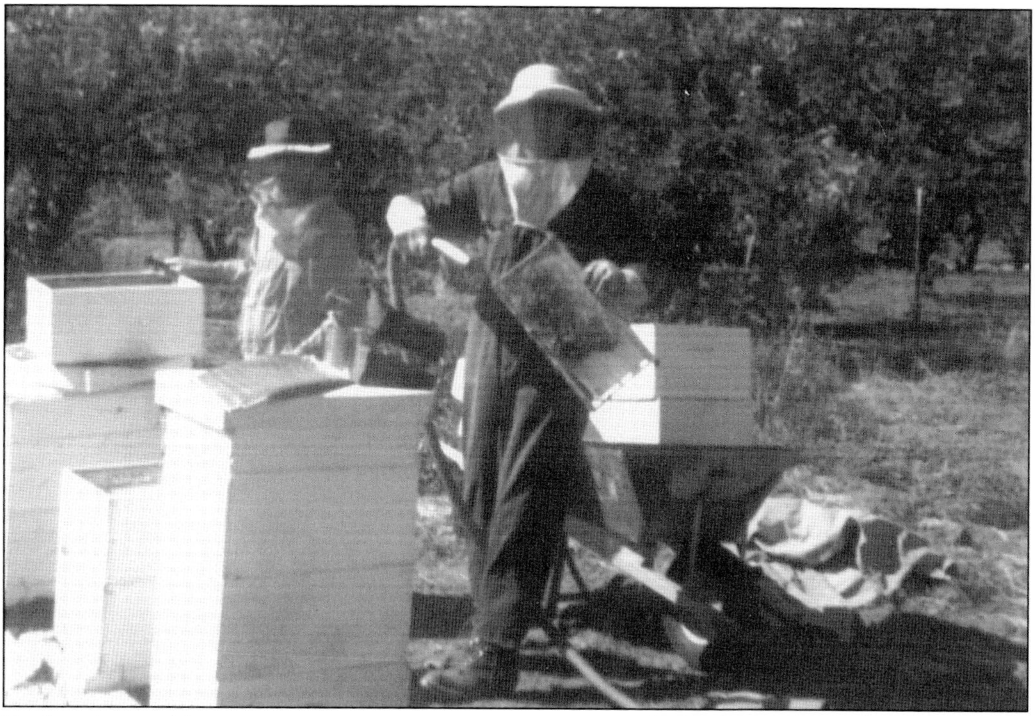

Beekeeping and honey extraction were necessary to provide food sweetener and to pollinate the orchards and crops. Elijah and Louise Shaw, some of the first apiarists in the area, sold their colonies to their son Lige in 1904. Honey sold for $1 per gallon in the early 1900s. Pictured are Wilford and Jerald Shaw collecting honey. Other apiarists were Tom Storey, Charles Pettigrew, Parley Shupe, Joseph Barker, and Oliver Miller.

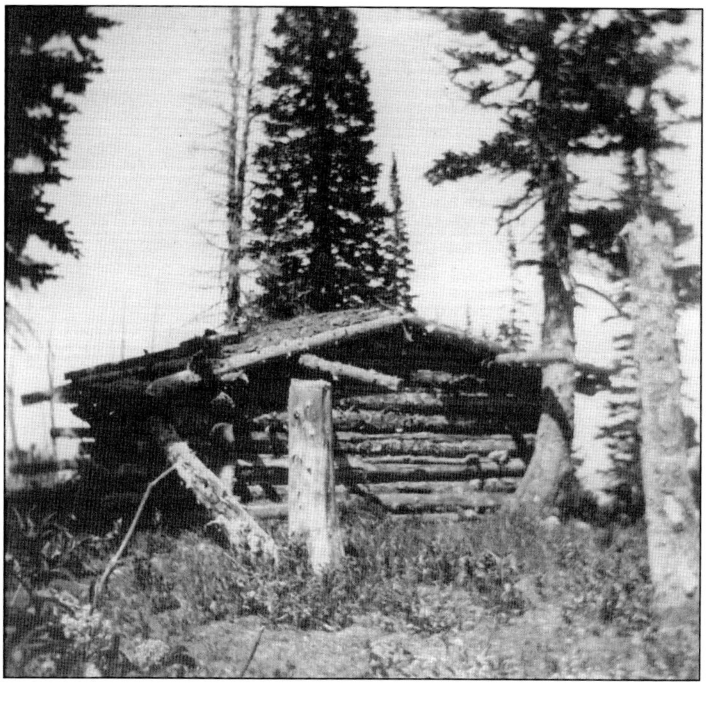

The Lone Tree Mine and Cabin were located in Cutler Canyon behind Ben Lomond Peak. This photograph of the cabin was taken around 1920. John Jones and his sons owned several mines. Their mining work started in the winter each year after the crops had been harvested. The winter treks were precarious, and when they finally reached their destination, they built a fire to signal their families that they had arrived safely.

Four

Education
Reading, Writing, and Arithmetic

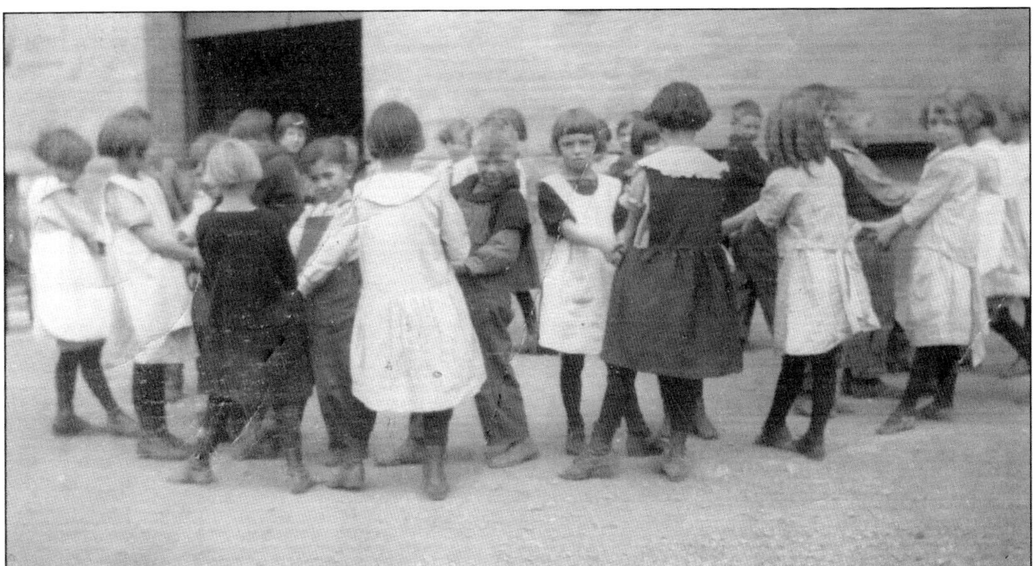

Second graders are participating in a group dance activity outside the North Ogden Central School in 1929. John Spackman is the fourth child from the left, looking outward. This image evokes memories of elementary school days and of learning dances and songs like "You Put Your Left Foot In."

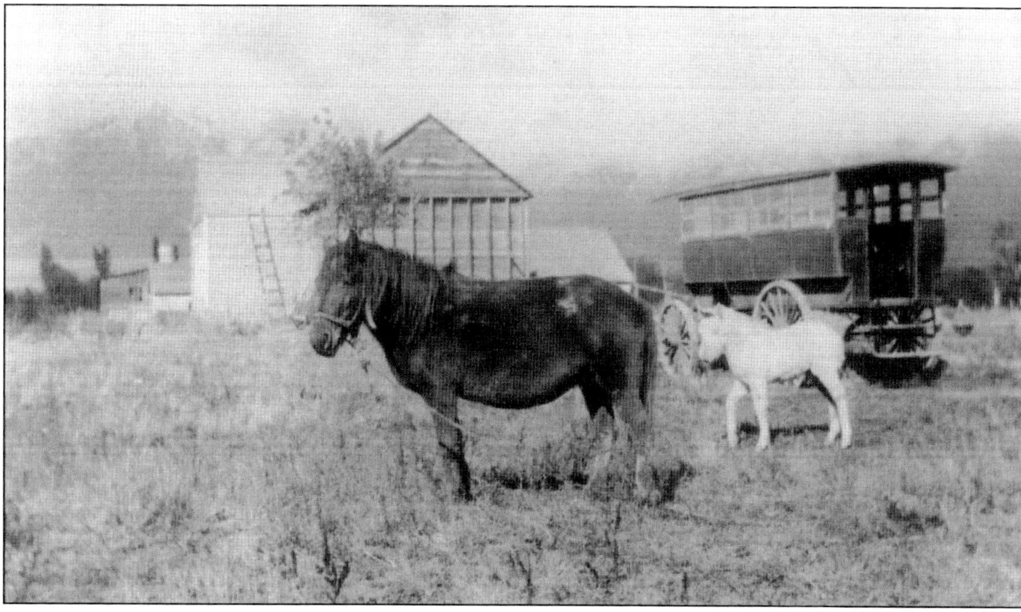

The "Push" (sometimes called the "Hack") was a wagon pulled by a team of horses that transported children to and from school. The earliest school buses were modified farm wagons covered with canvas tarpaulins, as shown below. A wooden roof and windows increased comfort levels, as shown above at the right. In the winter the children rode in a horse-drawn sleigh with bells jingling merrily. The route traveled each day was from the Sage Brush Academy at 1540 North Mountain Road to the Adobe Schoolhouse at 646 East 2600 North, and then down to the South Washington School at 2022 North 400 East.

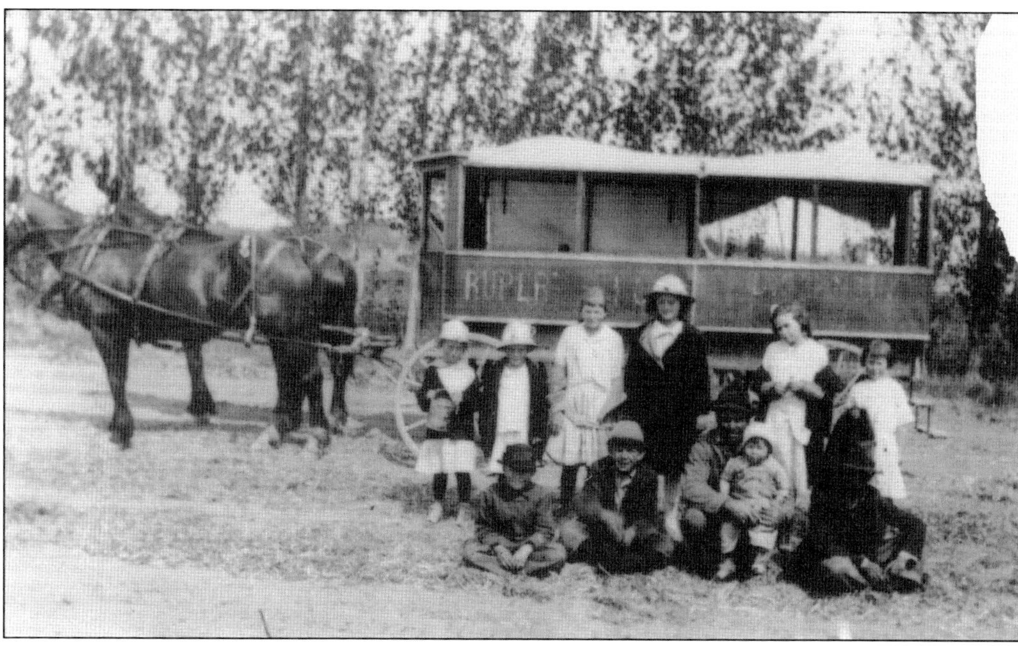

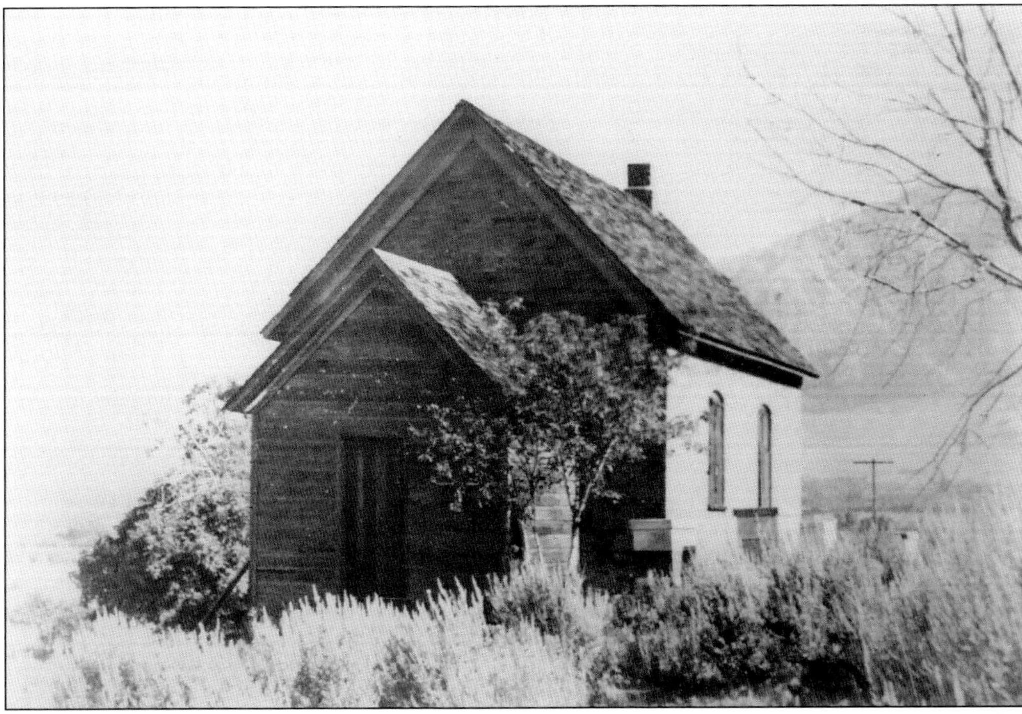

The Sage Brush Academy was a one-room school constructed at 1540 North Mountain Road in 1882. The students had to watch out for mountain lions, coyotes, and rattlesnakes. Slates were used for practice work, and they were cleaned by spitting on them, then wiping them with a cloth. A typical lunch was a slice of bread, hard-boiled egg, and salt wrapped in paper. Watercress and wild sego lily bulbs were gathered to eat.

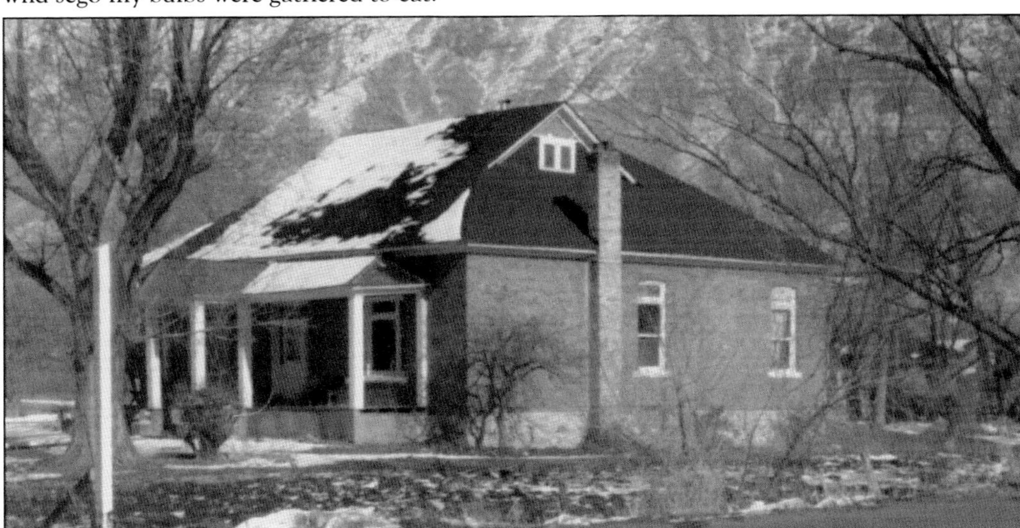

The earliest North Ogden schoolhouse was a one-room log building erected in 1851 near Montgomery Mound, and later moved inside the fort wall. In 1855, a larger adobe brick school was built at 646 East 2600 North. The South Washington schoolhouse, pictured above, was constructed in 1903 to help reduce overcrowding at the Adobe School and the Sage Brush Academy. The location of the two-room school was 2022 North 400 East.

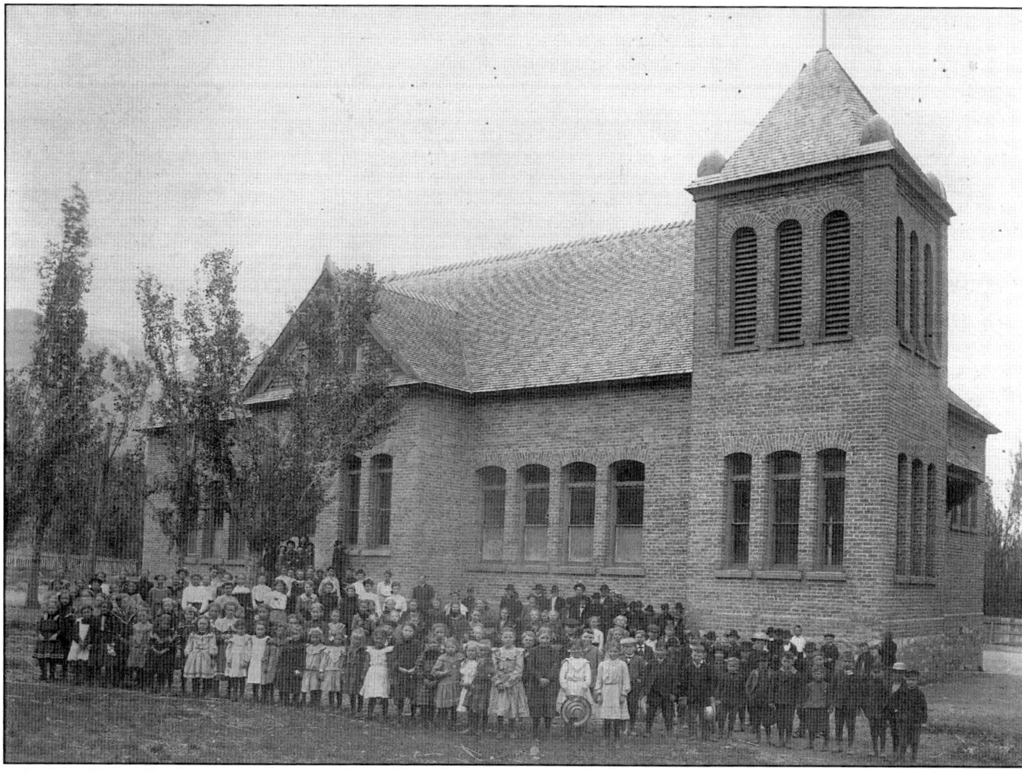

The Red Brick School, located at 626 East 2600 North, was constructed in 1890, replacing the Adobe Schoolhouse. The $3,500 building featured a bell tower, a library, an office, and three classrooms. Early students remembered some stern discipline at school, such as the teacher who flattened a coal scuttle on a boy's rear end.

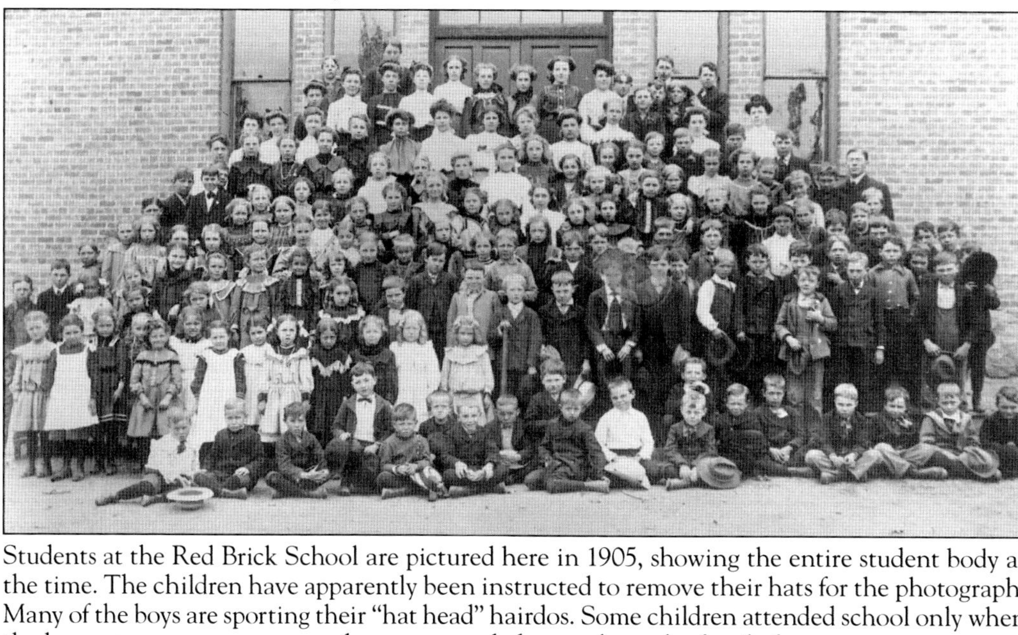

Students at the Red Brick School are pictured here in 1905, showing the entire student body at the time. The children have apparently been instructed to remove their hats for the photograph. Many of the boys are sporting their "hat head" hairdos. Some children attended school only when the harvest season was over, as they were needed to work on the family farms.

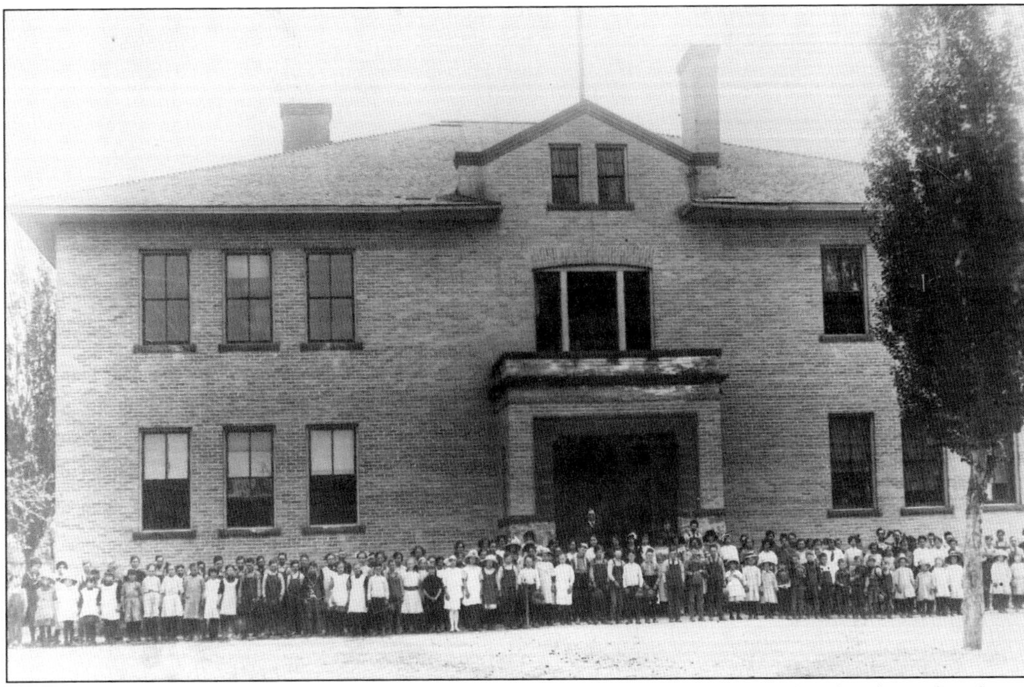

North Ogden Central School was referred to as the Yellow Brick School. The school was constructed in 1908 to replace the Red Brick School at a cost of $13,179. This photograph of the student body was taken around 1920. The school was a two-story building with eight classrooms. Restrooms were added later in the basement, and outside were teeter-totters, swings, a slide, and basketball standards.

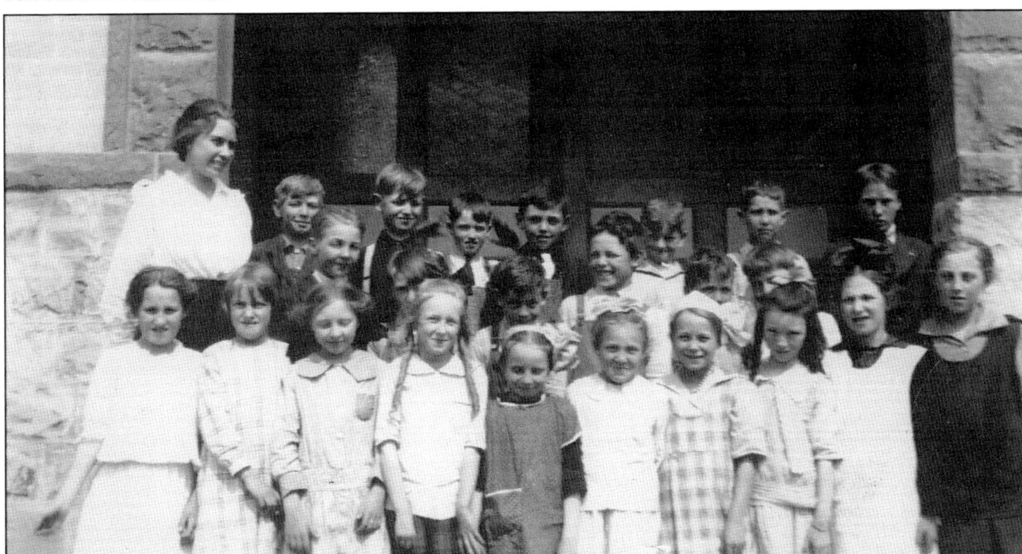

Shown in 1915 are Miss Kasius's students at North Ogden Central School. During this era female teachers had to comply with strict regulations. They were not allowed to date or marry, leave the city limits, or wear bright colors. Teachers were also required to wear at least two petticoats, with their skirt's hemline no more than two inches above the ankle, and were expected to remain in their home between the hours of 8:00 p.m. and 6:00 a.m.

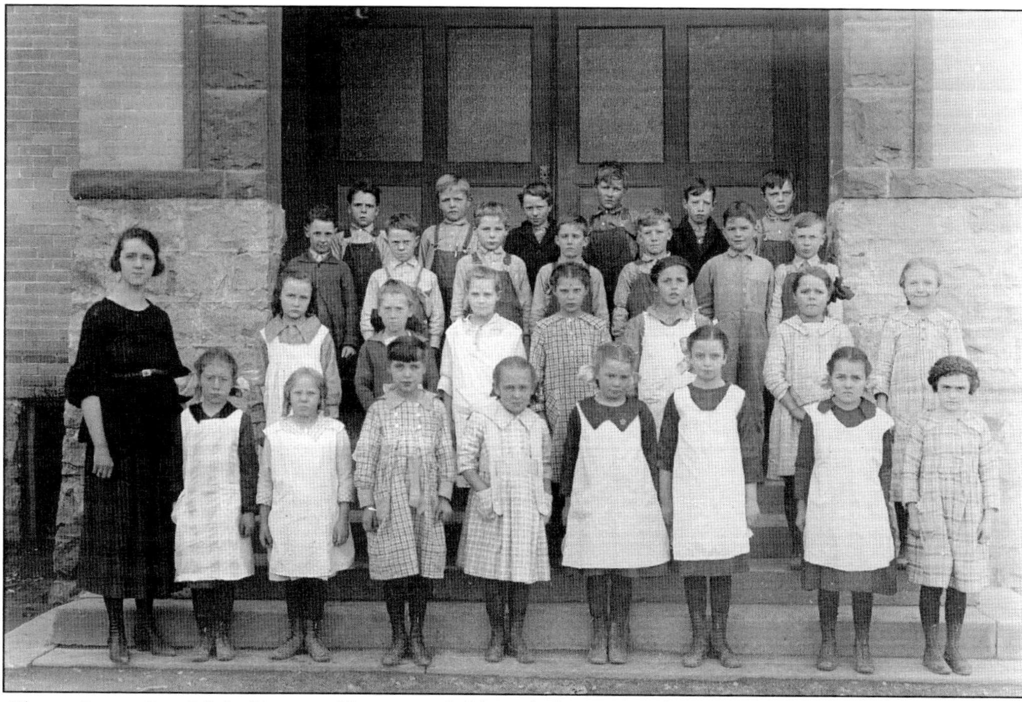

Above is teacher Veda Berrett (first row, left) with her 1919 third grade class at North Central School. Students pictured from left to right are (first row) Fern Chadwick, Ellen Garner, Anna Brown, Thelma Roylance, Jetta Barker, Annis Brown, Allene Orton, and Gwen Shupe; (second row) Alice Shaw, Clara Casperson, Bernice Staley, Eva Warren, Florence Campbell, Dora Briant, and Eva Hill; (third row) Walter Bailey, Vernon Holmes, Walter Montgomery, Volney Shaw, Wells Montgomery, Lowell Barker, and Lloyd Alvord; (fourth row) Morris Farr, Harland Draper, unidentified, Walter Briant, Hubert Bailey, and Joe Chandler. In the 1928 photograph below, the teachers at the North Ogden Central School are, from left to right, (first row) Anna Beth Rhees, Carma Thatcher, Elsie Gibson, and Melva Bybee; (second row) R. C. Metcalf, Maggie Taggart, Veda Berrett, Florence Manning, and Victor Hancock.

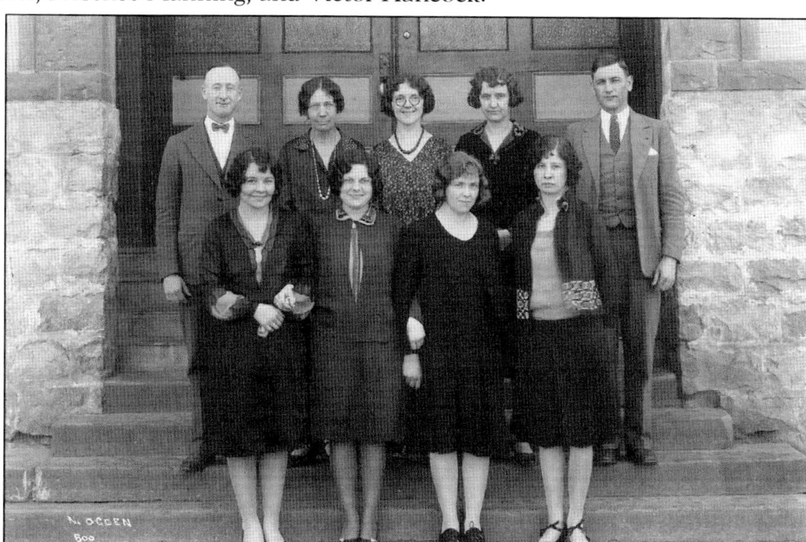

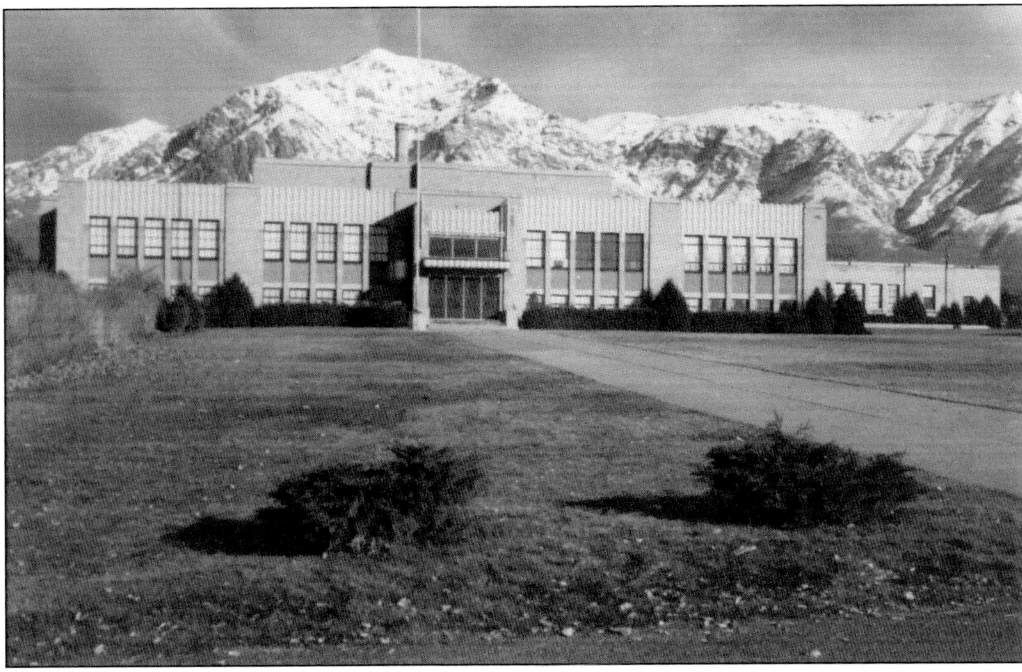

North Ogden Elementary School was constructed and dedicated in May 1937 at 474 East 2650 North. The yellow brick art deco–style school was designed by Leslie Hodgson (designer of Ogden High School) and built at a cost of $150,000. It originally housed all classes through 10th grade, and after 1950, through sixth grade. The playground had swings, a slide, monkey bars, foursquare, hopscotch, dodgeball areas, and a baseball diamond with bleachers. In 1945, a cafeteria was added to provide hot lunches. The school was demolished in 2009. A new elementary school was constructed to the east of the old site at a cost of $13.6 million. Below is one of the early classrooms in the old school, showing the third grade class of Lulu Richards in 1950.

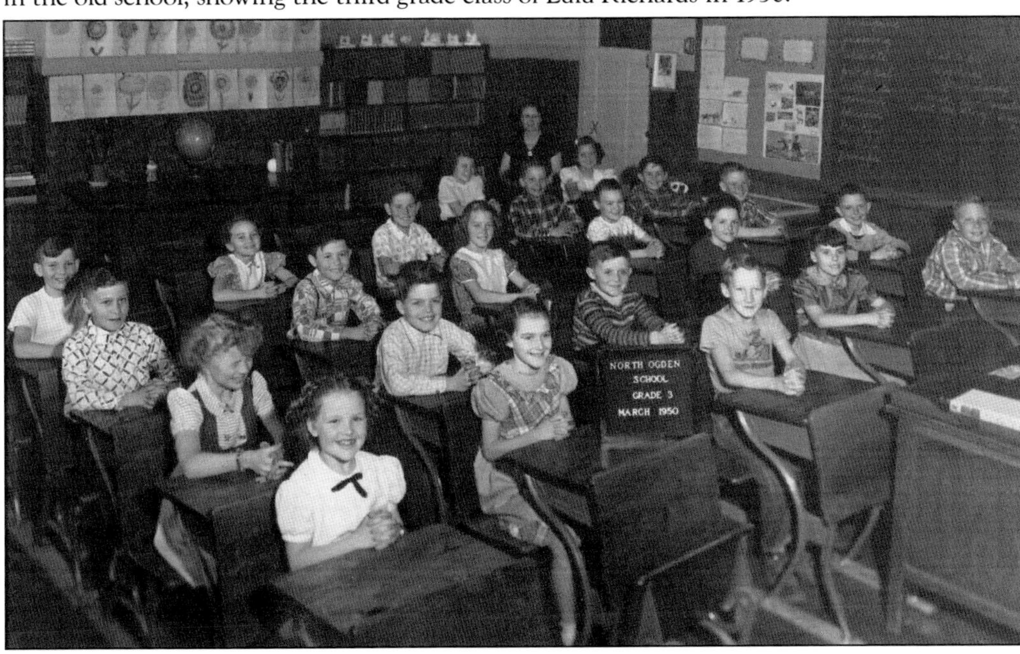

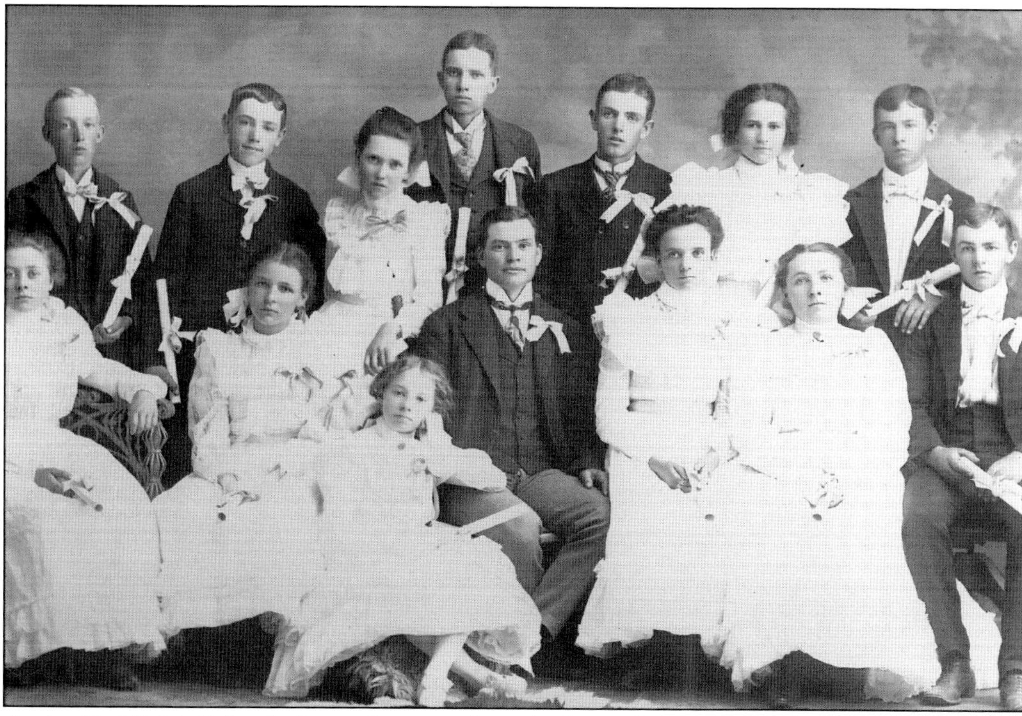

At the Red Brick School, the students graduated after eighth grade, and many later attended the Weber Academy, now known as Weber State University. Pictured above are the graduates of 1901 with their principal. From left to right are (first row) Esther Ellis (Andrews), Ann Barker (Clifford), Inez Dean (Spackman), Frederick Barker (principal), Florence Montgomery (Snooks), Maude Zimmerman, and Charles Barker; (second row) Earnest Daniels, Nephi Brown, Lottie Jones (Bailey), Lorin Williams, John Storey, Mary Ann Norris (Hill), and Clarence Barker. Below, the graduates of 1902 are pictured with their principal. From left to right are (first row) Lizzie Walker, Eva McBride, Levi Walker, and Jane Graham; (second row) Ella Fuller, Aleida Shupe, Riley Cain (principal), Annabel Fuller, and Myrtle Ririe. They have each earned a diploma and a ribbon, which has been pinned to their clothing for graduation.

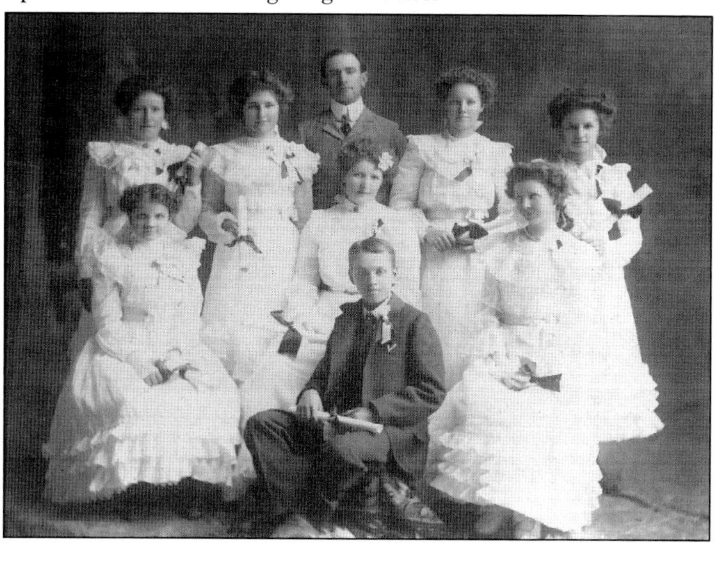

An eighth-grade diploma is shown for Harvey Chandler, who graduated in 1920 from the North Ogden Central School. His name is written in Spenserian-style script with a pen that has been dipped in ink. Children's inkwells at school were placed in the top right corner of each desk and used for penmanship practice. Often mischievous boys would secretly dip girls' braided hair into the ink.

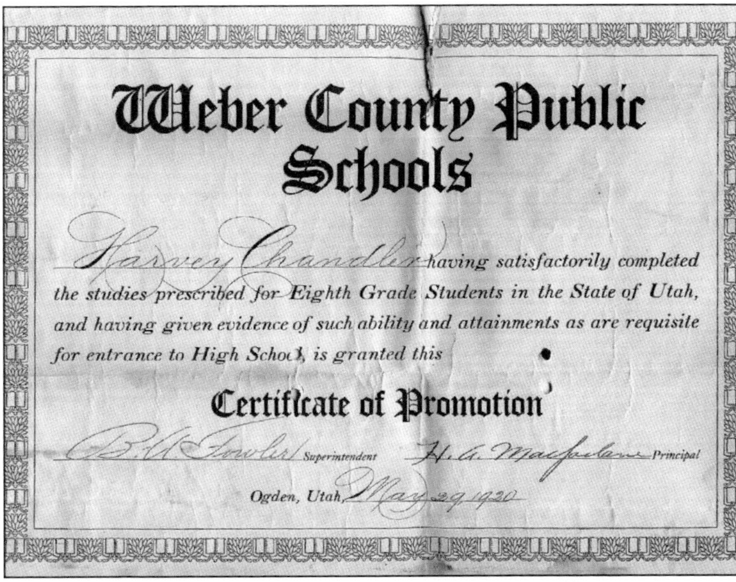

Weber County Public Schools

Harvey Chandler having satisfactorily completed the studies prescribed for Eighth Grade Students in the State of Utah, and having given evidence of such ability and attainments as are requisite for entrance to High School, is granted this

Certificate of Promotion

B. W. Fowler Superintendent H. A. Macfarlane Principal

Ogden, Utah, May 29 1920

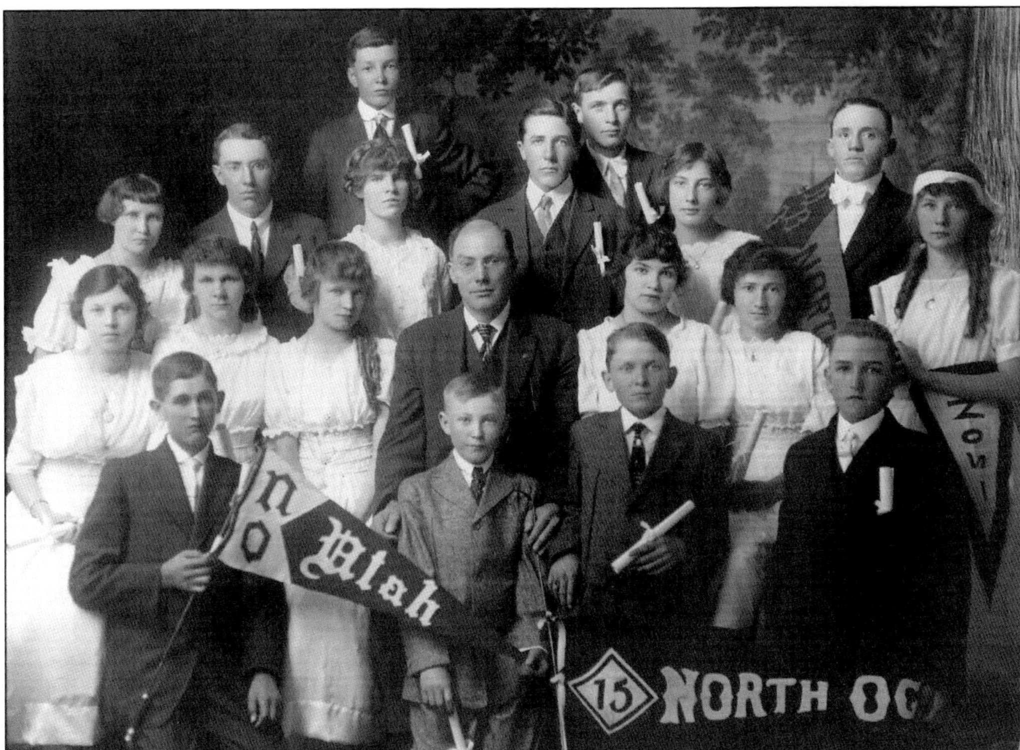

In 1915, the annual commencement exercises of the county schools were held. The pupils receiving certificates of graduation are listed as Bernice Randall, Benjamin Norris, Fawn Wilson, Lester Casteel, Sarah Jones, Floyd Campbell, Robert Ellis, Bertha Brown, Karl Storey, Byron Chadwick, Reta May Randall, Horace Dudman, Ellen Orton, William Berrett, Martha Chatelain, Mabel Huband, Elizabeth Casteel, and Victor Clyde Rogers. Principal and teacher John Q. Blaylock is in the center.

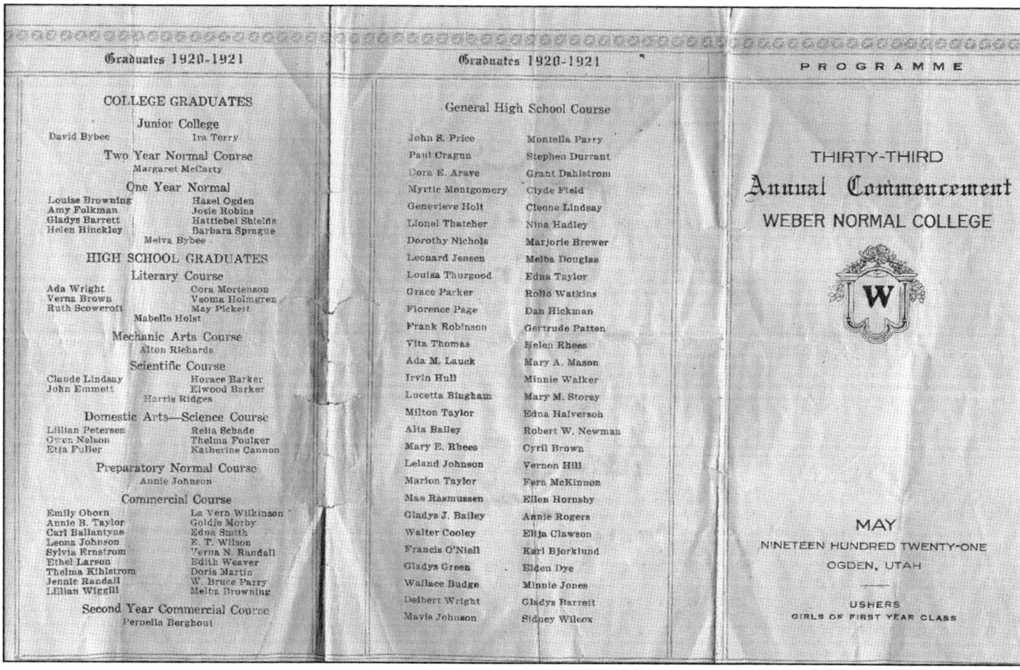

Graduates 1920-1921

COLLEGE GRADUATES

Junior College

David Bybee
Ira Terry

Two Year Normal Course

Margaret McCarty

One Year Normal

Louise Browning
Hazel Ogden
Amy Folkman
Josie Robins
Gladys Barrett
Hattiebel Shields
Helen Hinckley
Barbara Sprague
Melva Bybee

HIGH SCHOOL GRADUATES

Literary Course

Ada Wright
Cora Mortenson
Verna Brown
Veoma Holmgren
Ruth Scowcroft
May Pickett
Mabelle Holst

Mechanic Arts Course

Alton Richards

Scientific Course

Claude Lindsay
Horace Barker
John Emmett
Elwood Barker
Harris Ridges

Domestic Arts—Science Course

Lillian Petersen
Relia Schade
Gwen Nelson
Thelma Foulger
Etta Fuller
Katherine Cannon

Preparatory Normal Course

Annie Johnson

Commercial Course

Emily Oborn
La Vern Wilkinson
Annie B. Taylor
Goldie Morby
Carl Ballantyne
Edna Smith
Leona Johnson
E. T. Wilson
Sylvia Ernstrom
Verna N. Randall
Ethel Larson
Edith Weaver
Thelma Kihlstrom
Doris Martin
Jennie Randall
W. Bruce Parry
Lillian Wiggill
Melba Browning

Second Year Commercial Course

Pernella Berghout

Graduates 1920-1921

General High School Course

John S. Price
Montella Parry
Paul Cragun
Stephen Durrant
Dora E. Arave
Grant Dahlstrom
Myrtle Montgomery
Clyde Field
Genevieve Holt
Cleone Lindsay
Lionel Thatcher
Nina Hadley
Dorothy Nichols
Marjorie Brewer
Leonard Jensen
Melba Douglas
Louisa Thurgood
Edna Taylor
Grace Parker
Rollo Watkins
Florence Page
Dan Hickman
Frank Robinson
Gertrude Patten
Vita Thomas
Helen Rhees
Ada M. Lauck
Mary A. Mason
Irvin Hull
Minnie Walker
Lucetta Bingham
Mary M. Storey
Milton Taylor
Edna Halverson
Alta Bailey
Robert W. Newman
Mary E. Rhees
Cyril Brown
Leland Johnson
Vernon Hill
Marion Taylor
Fern McKinnon
Mae Rasmussen
Ellen Hornsby
Gladys J. Bailey
Annie Rogers
Walter Cooley
Elija Clawson
Francis O'Niell
Karl Bjorklund
Gladys Green
Elden Dye
Wallace Budge
Minnie Jones
Delbert Wright
Gladys Barrett
Mavis Johnson
Sidney Wilcox

PROGRAMME

THIRTY-THIRD
Annual Commencement
WEBER NORMAL COLLEGE

W

MAY
NINETEEN HUNDRED TWENTY-ONE
OGDEN, UTAH

USHERS
GIRLS OF FIRST YEAR CLASS

The 33rd annual commencement program for Weber Normal College is pictured for May 1921. The list of events includes a college day, an alumni banquet, a senior day, and a field day at Lorin Farr Park. The ceremony included selections from the college orchestra and the choir. Also on the program were the Girls' Glee Club, a string quartet, poetry readings, and solos.

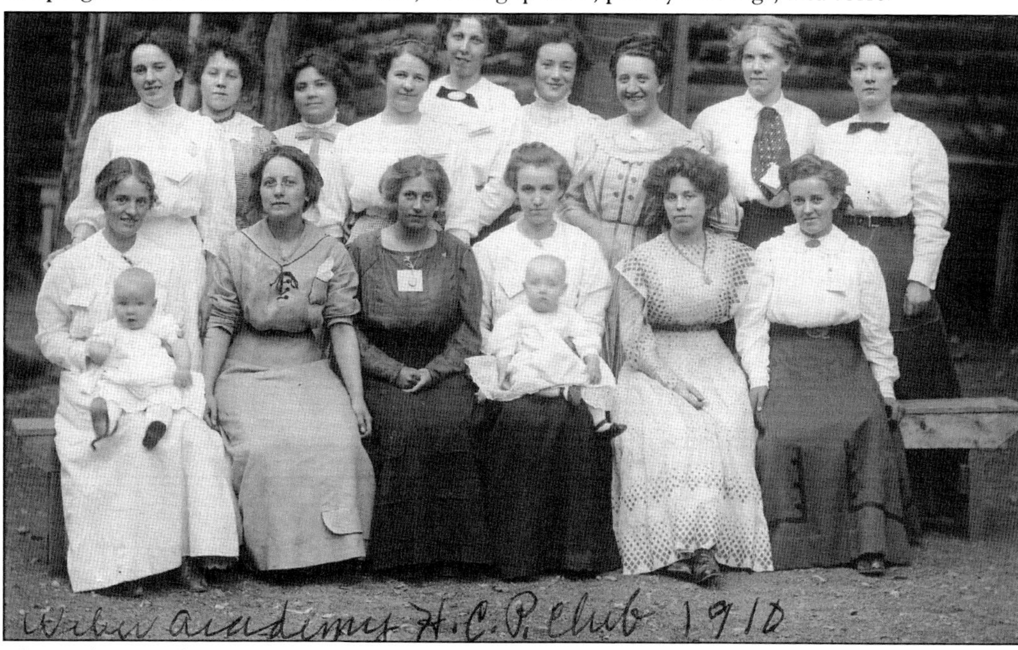

The Weber Academy HCP Club was a literary society for junior and senior college women from 1908 to 1910. They read books from many great authors, including Oliver Wendell Holmes, James Russell Lowell, and George Eliot. They met regularly to discuss the books and also had a few dinner parties each year.

Five

Transportation
Conveying, Carrying, and Carting

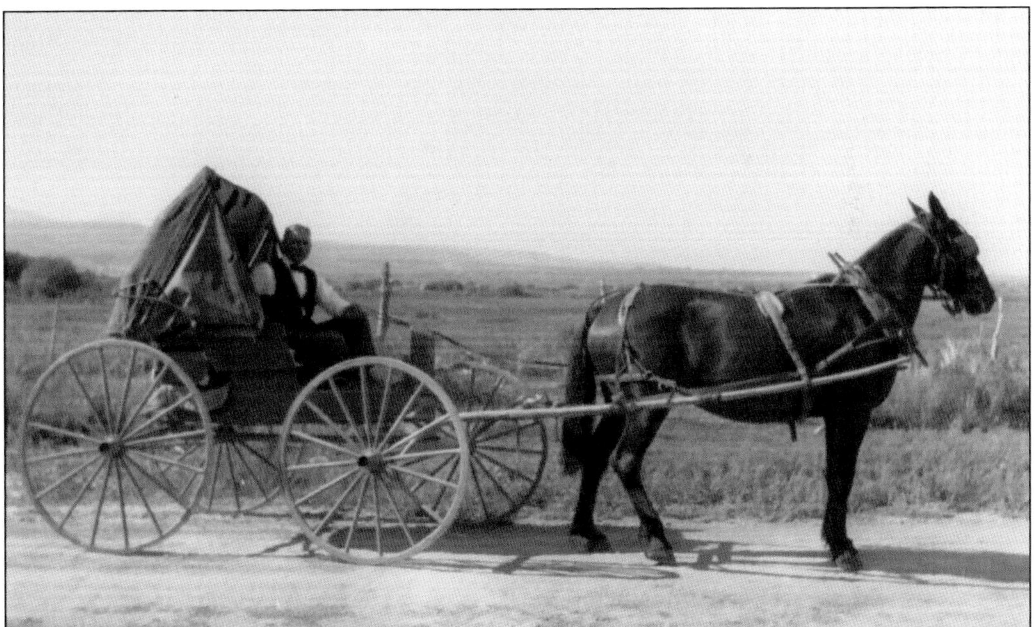

In this photograph from around 1910, Emil Chatelain is at the reins of the horse and buggy. The Stanhope buggy had a closed-in back and wooden sidebars that attached to the horse. The horse and buggy was the primary mode of short-distance transportation between 1865 and 1915. The buggy, which cost between $25 and $50, could easily be hitched and driven by untrained women or children. A buggy whip had a small tasseled tip called a snapper.

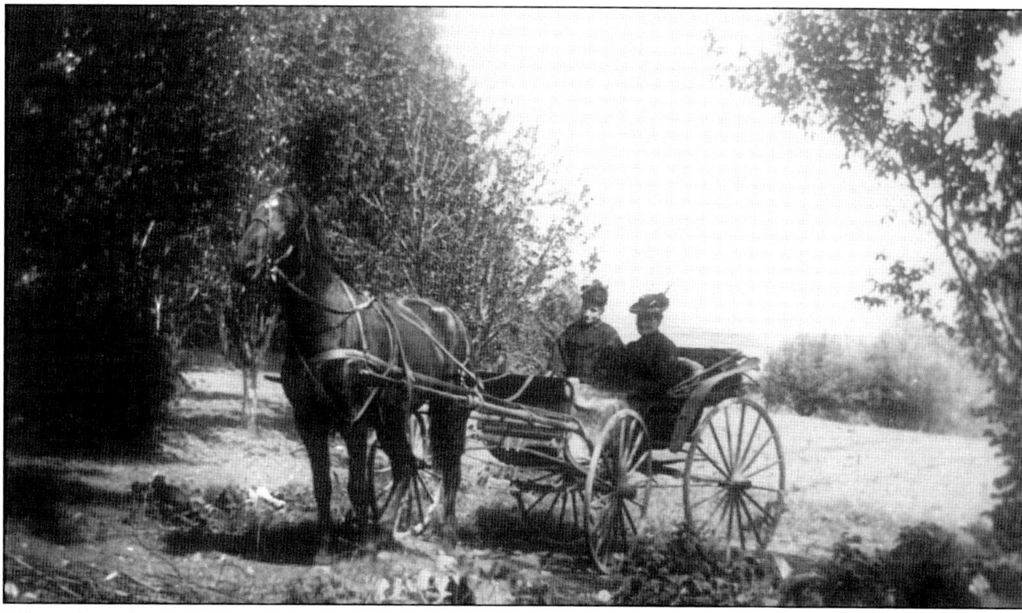

Close friends Hannah S. Randall and Margaret Storey hitched up the horse "Old Fan" to the buggy on Sundays. They traveled around town to gather eggs that townspeople had saved for them. The money they earned from the sale of the eggs was donated to help build the LDS Relief Society building.

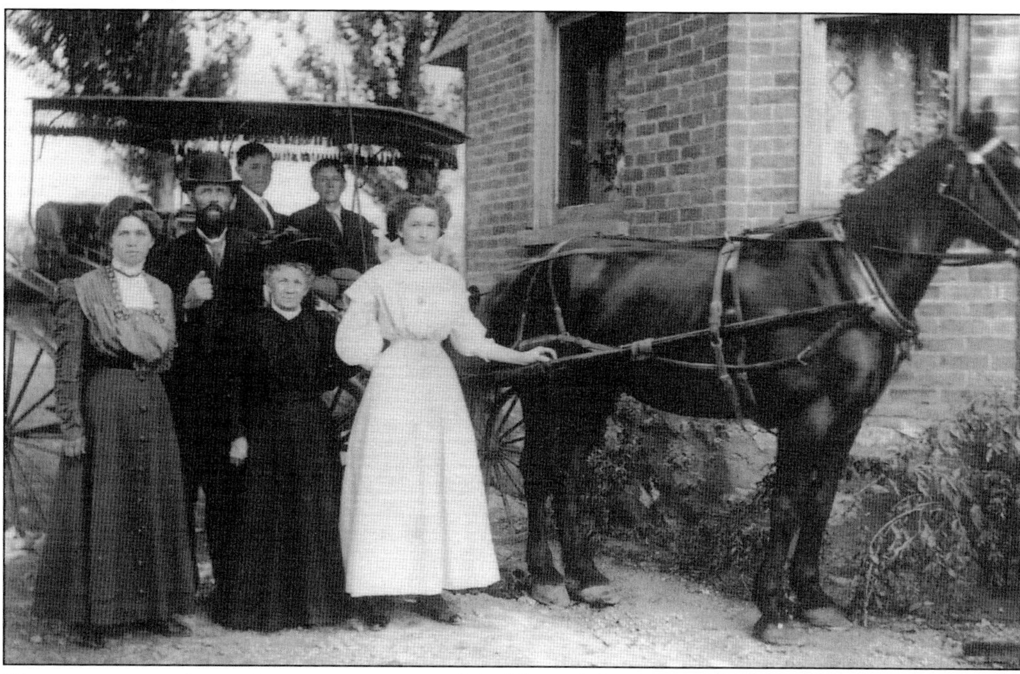

The surrey was a horse-drawn carriage used for "fancy" driving to church or town. Pictured here around 1900 is the Hall family. From left to right are (first row) Annie Jesse, John Sr., Annie (Parratt), and Eliza (Higgins); (second row) John Thomas and William George. Their brick home was constructed in 1890 near 825 East 2750 North. Electricity, running water, and a telephone were installed by 1916. A bathroom was added in 1927, eliminating cold trips to the outhouse.

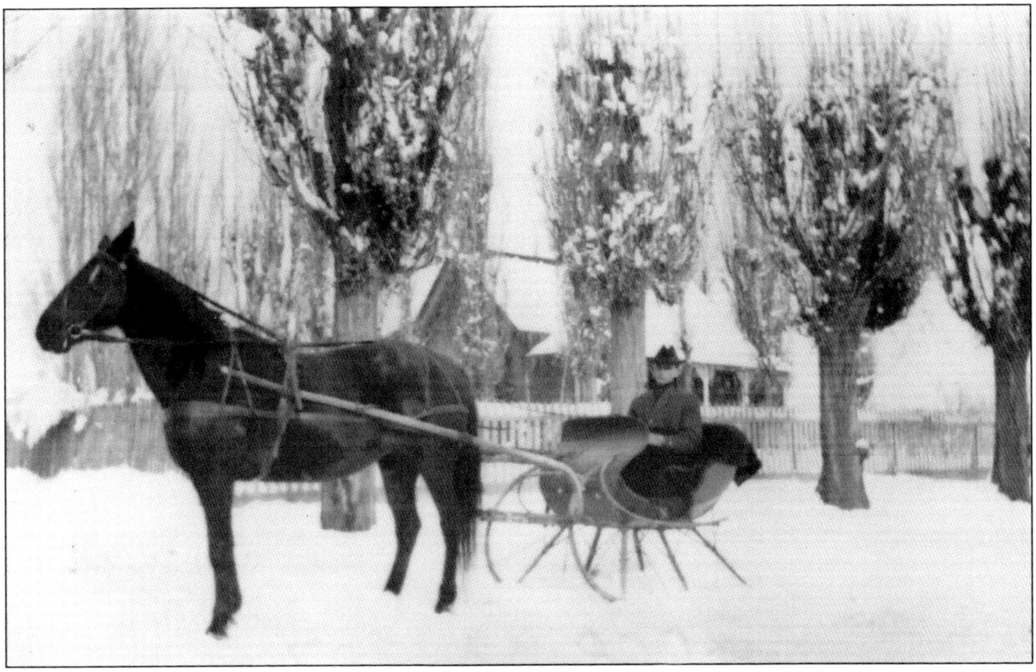

LeRoy Snooks is riding in a one-horse sleigh or cutter, a sleek vessel made of wood with curved, metal blades that allowed travel through snow-covered fields and country roads. Portland cutters were developed in the mid-1800s. Fancy cutters trimmed with silk and silver cost about $150, but by 1910, plain cutters were available for about $20.

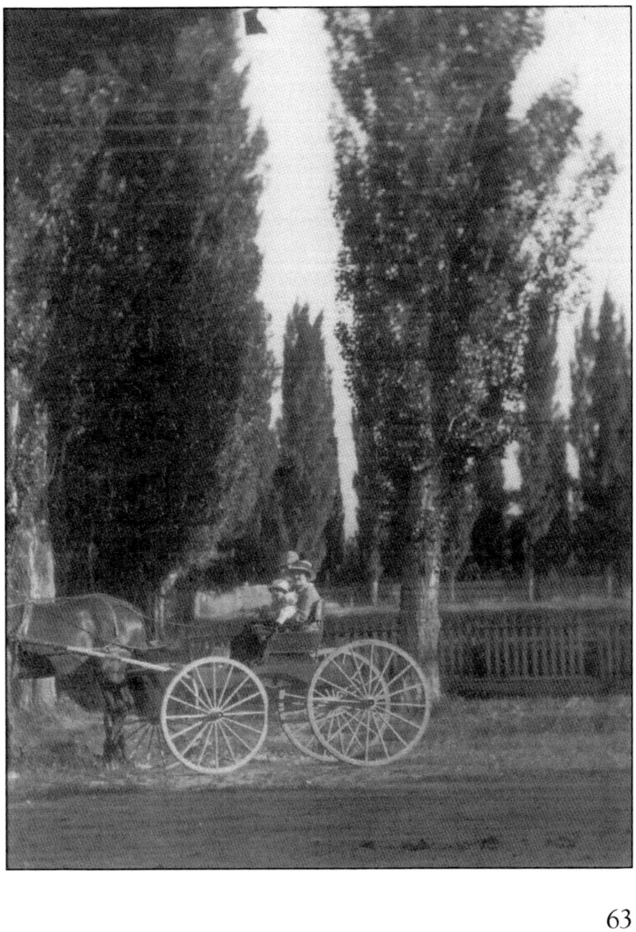

Charles and Elsie Jones ride in a horse-drawn buggy with Eleanor Redfield around 1900. Charles, Elsie, and 10 more children grew up in a log house on "Cat Claim" property. Their grandfather, Richard Jones, relinquished the family's pet cat in 1863 to Native Americans in exchange for land. Being fascinated by the unfamiliar tame cat, the Native Americans agreed to give up their squatter's rights to the eastern North Ogden land.

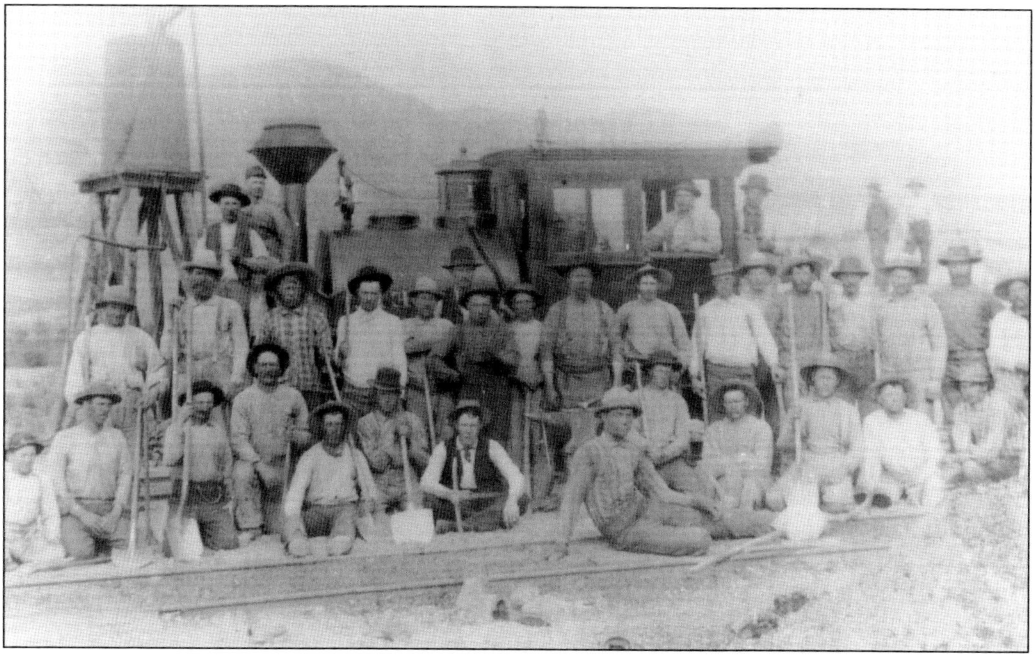

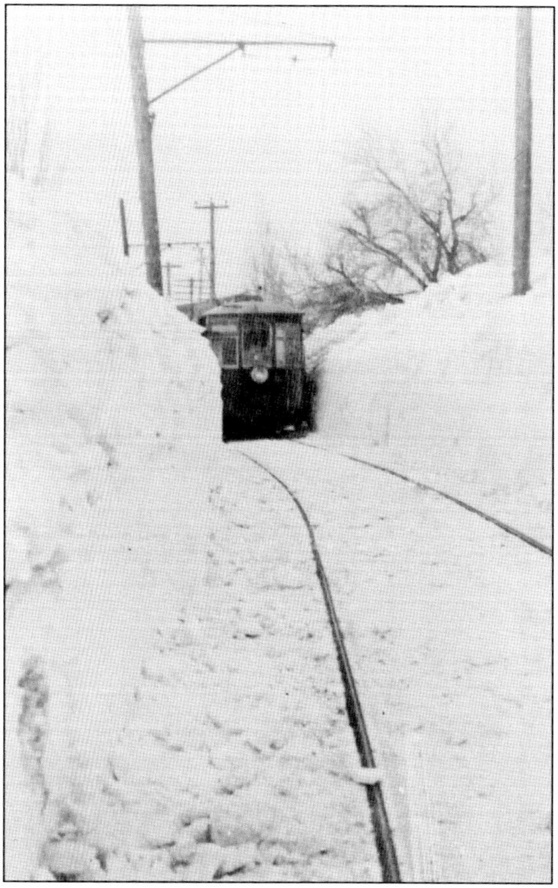

The crew laying the track for the dummy line paused for the photograph above. This section of track was constructed in 1887, completing the stretch from North Ogden to Hot Springs Resort. By 1909, dummy engines (so-called because of the closed-in engine) replaced mule power in the railway system. The dummy line was developed as a branch line of the Ogden City Railroad. It ran from downtown Ogden through North Ogden and Pleasant View and continued on to Hot Springs Resort, a popular recreational destination. The small locomotive was powered by a steam-producing coal engine, which pulled two passenger cars. An electric streetcar later replaced the dummy, traveling along the same route. At left, the streetcar is shown in 1919 traveling through deep snow in an area called "the cut."

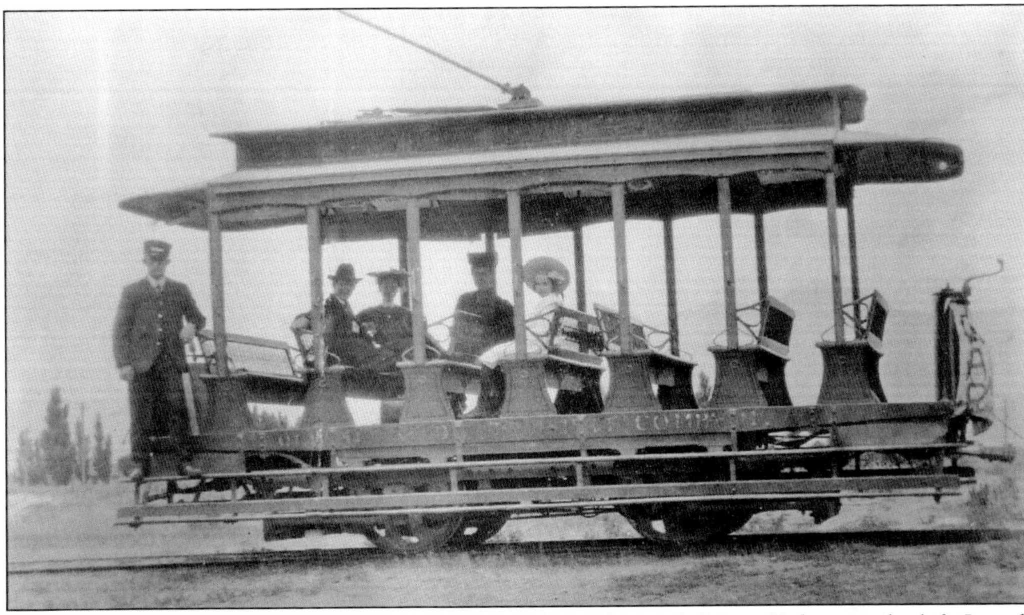

The electric streetcar is pictured above in 1907 with conductor LaMoni Holmes at the left. Joseph Ballif is standing in front of a later version of the closed-in streetcar below in 1920. The streetcar carried passengers, supplies, students attending Weber Academy, and carloads of fruit and produce exported by local farmers. The 7¢ fare was dropped into a secure metal container, and the 10-mile round trip took about an hour. Surges of electrical power caused the train to lurch forward, and then it screeched and groaned to a stop as the brakes were applied. Sand was dropped on the tracks in front of the wheels to facilitate stopping. Young pranksters often greased the tracks to make the train slide past designated stops. They also played tunes on the signal cord, to the great annoyance of the conductor.

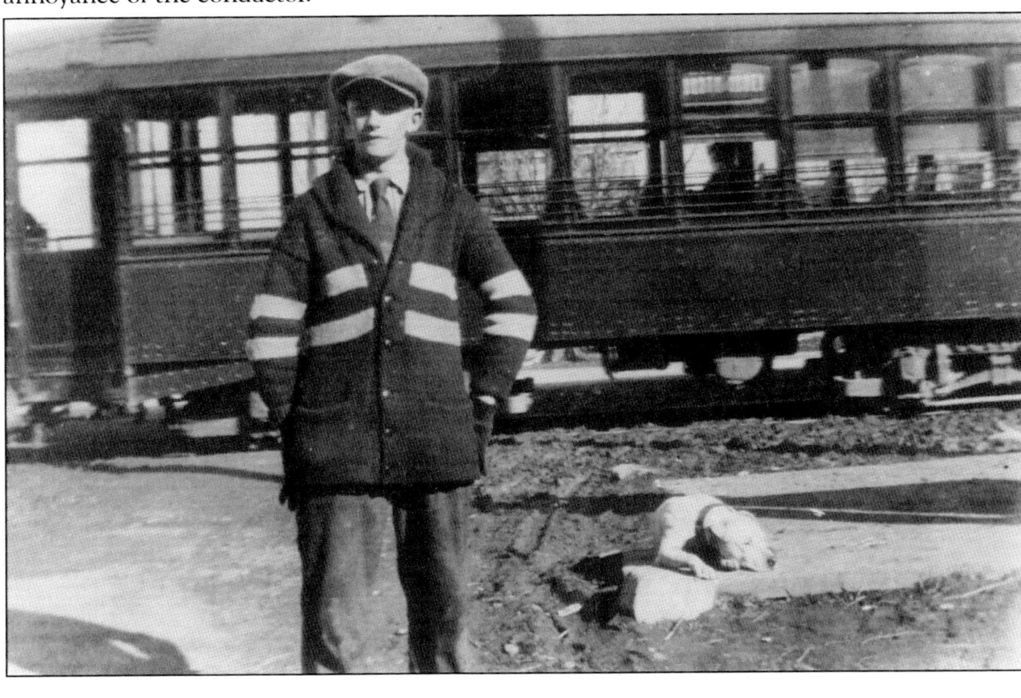

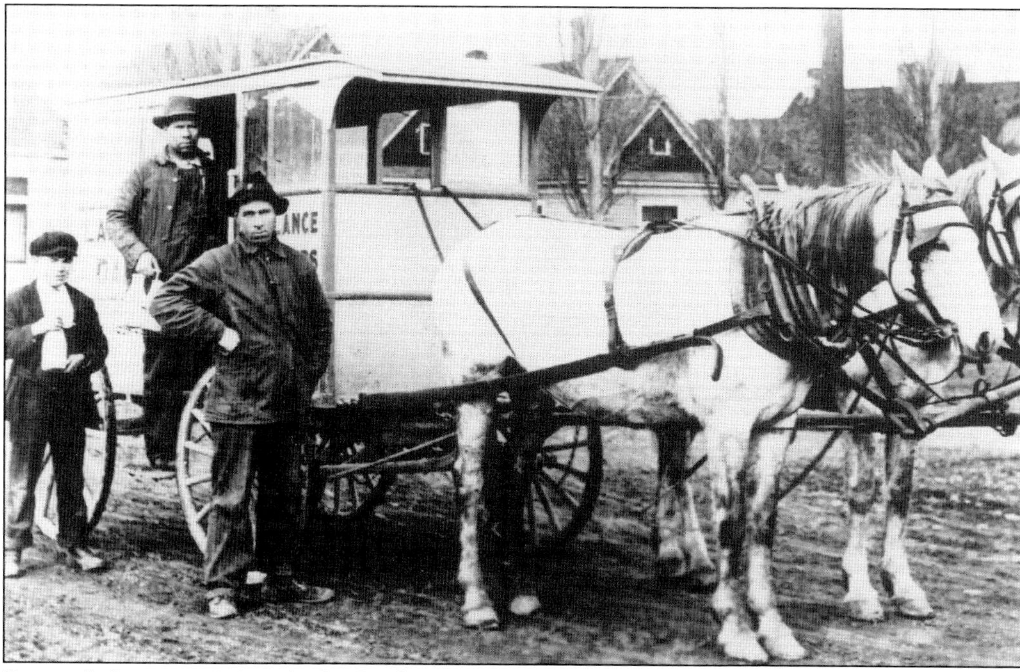

Pictured above in 1912 with the Roylance Dairy delivery wagon are "Buz" Wallen (left), Alma Roylance (center), and Heber T. Roylance. Below is Will Linford with the Lakeview Dairy delivery wagon. The horse-drawn delivery wagons transported milk, cream, and butter to customers in the area every day. The milk was first cooled in the North Ogden canal or in artesian well water, and it was kept cool for delivery with water-soaked gunnysacks placed on top of the cans. The milk was measured out with a quart or gallon can and poured directly into the housewives' containers. When the wagon stopped at a home to make a delivery, a round stop weight was placed on the ground and tied to the horses' bridles to keep the team from running away.

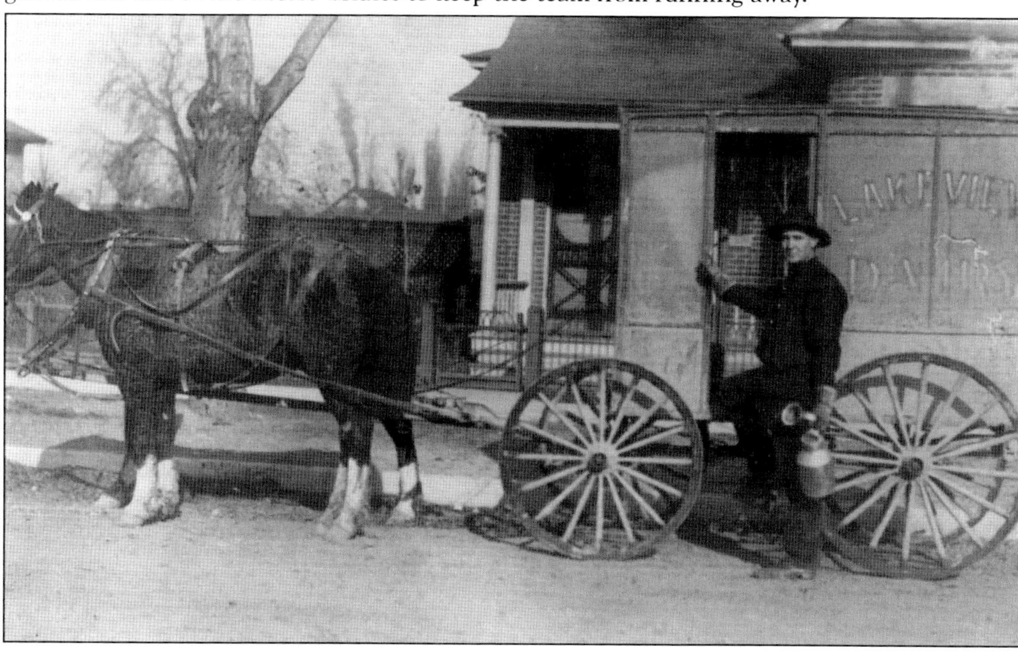

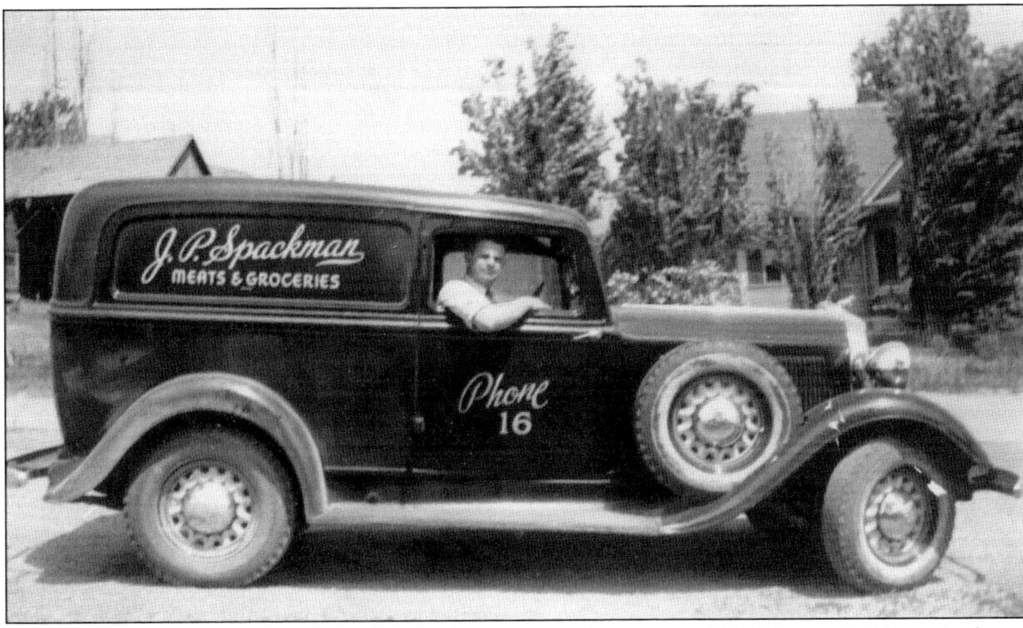

J. Parley Spackman delivered goods from his mercantile store at 2596 North 400 East. Delivery trucks, like the 1935 Ford pictured above, were commonly used during this era. Early telephone numbers were only two digits, as shown on the truck's door. Parley and his wife, Inez, opened the store in 1922. They sold groceries, fabric, tobacco, hardware, and farming supplies, and also bartered for items the farmers needed, trading for produce and eggs.

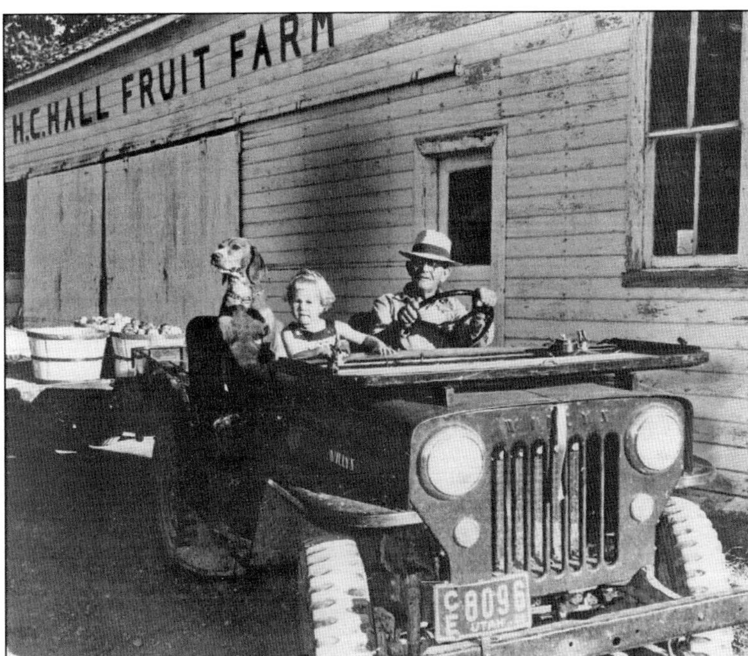

With over 100 acres of land, Henry Charles Hall was one of North Ogden's most prominent fruit growers. He is pictured driving a Jeep with his granddaughter Cherie and their dog Ike around the 1950s. Henry C. passed the farm down to his sons, Henry R. and George E. Hall. The Hall Fruit Farm, located near 807 East 2750 North, was the longest to survive the encroaching subdivisions.

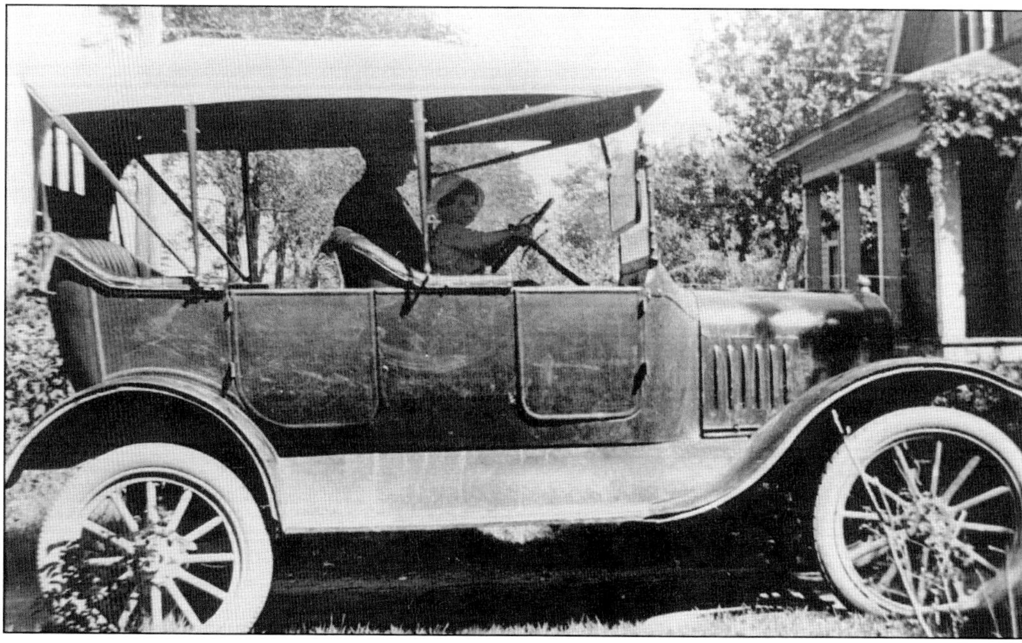

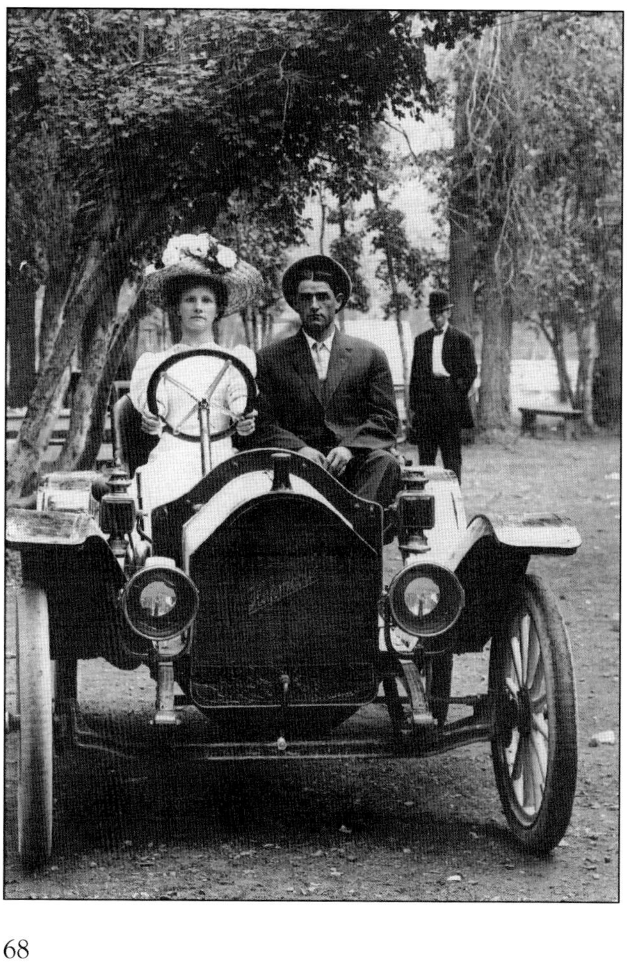

The 1919 Model T Ford above was one of the first automobiles in North Ogden. Grace Montgomery and William Orton are shown at left in a Model T Ford in 1920. An account from Claude Ellis states that he courted his wife-to-be in a horse-drawn rubber-tired buggy for three years starting in 1914, when there were only two automobiles in North Ogden. The nickname for the Model T was "Tin Lizzie." Lizzie was a common name for horses at the time, and people had never seen anything quite like the car, so it was thought of as a metal horse. A Model T sold in 1908 for $825, and more than 15 million cars were manufactured with very few changes to the design from 1909 to 1927. The car's top speed was 45 miles per hour.

Six

Social Life
Orchestrate, Meditate, and Celebrate

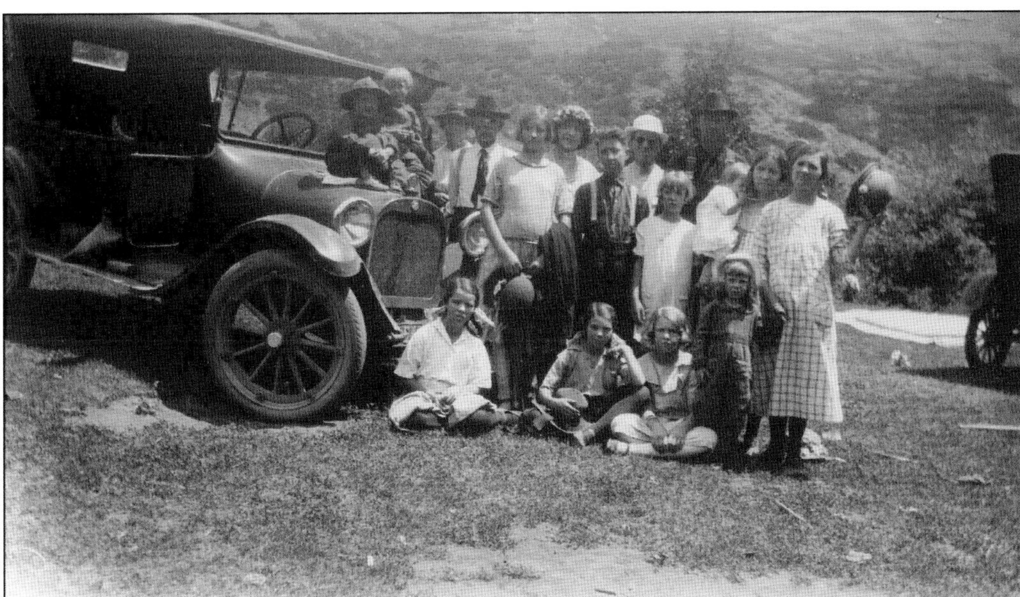

With the availability of automobiles came more family outings. The Elihu Warren family piled into Clyde Campbell's Dodge and headed out for a camping trip around 1923. The campers are, from left to right, (first row) Lucille, Vera, Bernice, and June Clark; (second row) Lula, Donald, and Erma Chadwick; (third row) Jay, Mildred, Clyde and Mabel Campbell, Elihu Nathan, Norma and Covel Woody, Lewis and Myrtle Chadwick holding son Max, and Lettie Clark.

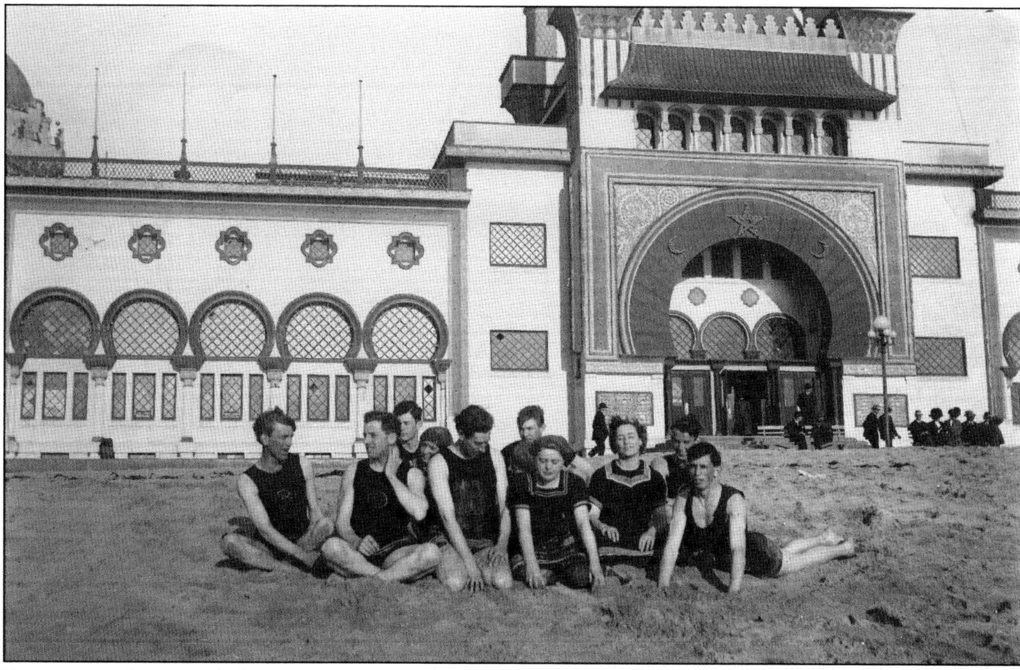

Some popular travel destinations were Saltair Resort at the Great Salt Lake and Yellowstone National Park. In the photograph above, Florence Montgomery and her friends are enjoying the sun at Saltair in 1904. The popular recreation site was reached by train and its main attraction was swimming in the lake, which was likened to bobbing about like corks because of the water's 25 percent salt content. Also available were rides, games, vaudeville shows, hot-air balloons, fireworks, and "the world's largest dance floor." Below in the 1933 photograph are, from left to right, Wilford and Lucille Shaw, and Beatrice and Ralph Garner near Mammoth Hot Springs in Yellowstone. The park was a sightseer's paradise with its geysers, thick forests, and abundant wildlife. In the 1930s, bears wandered up to tourists' cars begging for food, and there were no restrictions for hikers around the dangerous thermal areas.

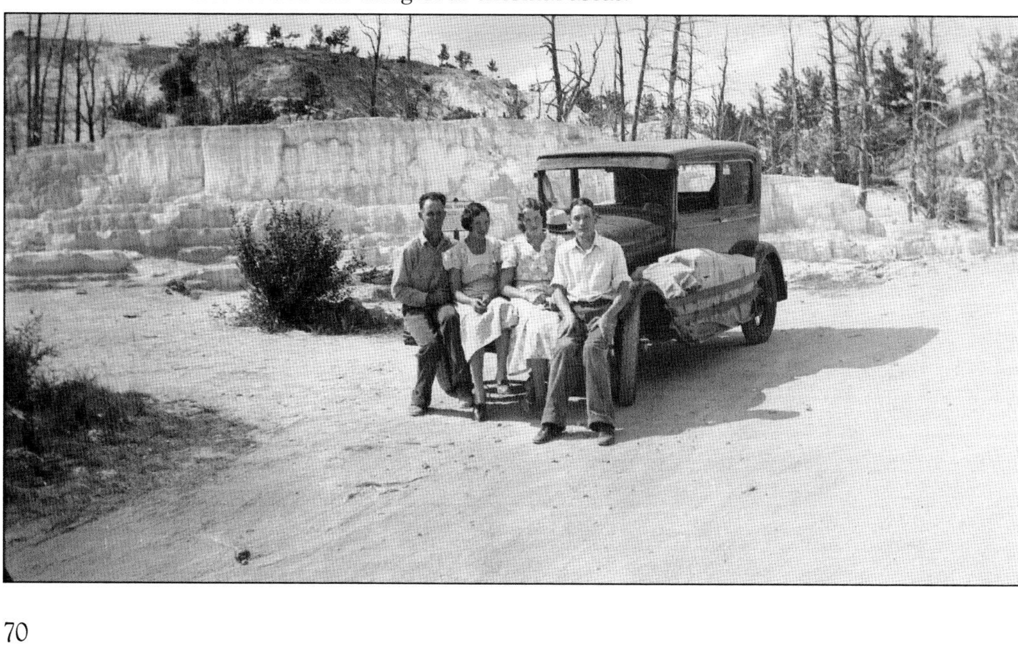

After their graduation in 1936, these North Ogden friends posed for a photograph while on vacation in California. The cool guys are, from left to right, Jack Deamer, Bill Bailey, Verle Barker, and Lowell Shupe. Local photographers often used staged settings for these snapshots of tourists, as it was a profitable source of income.

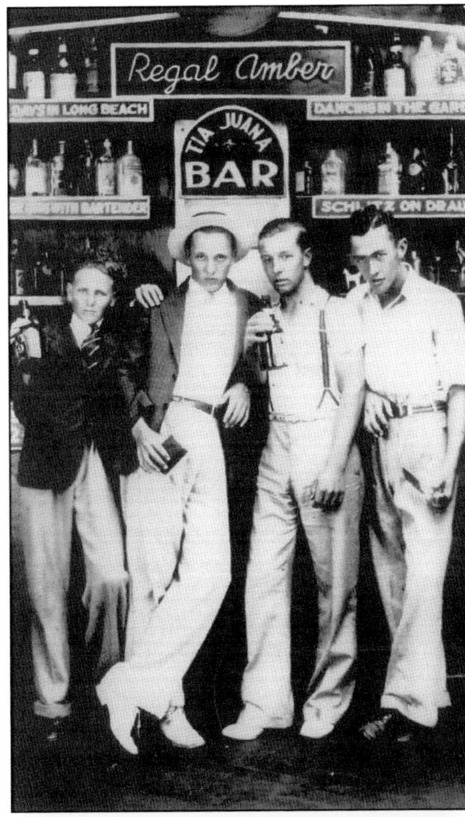

Good friends Wilford Shaw and Rulon Orton stroll down 2550 North Street, also known as Poplar Street, sharing cotton candy from Chandler's Candy Store in 1927. The street was lined with poplar trees during North Ogden's early days. The fast-growing trees were often used as a windbreak. The "Yellow Brick School" with its rock foundation is visible at the right.

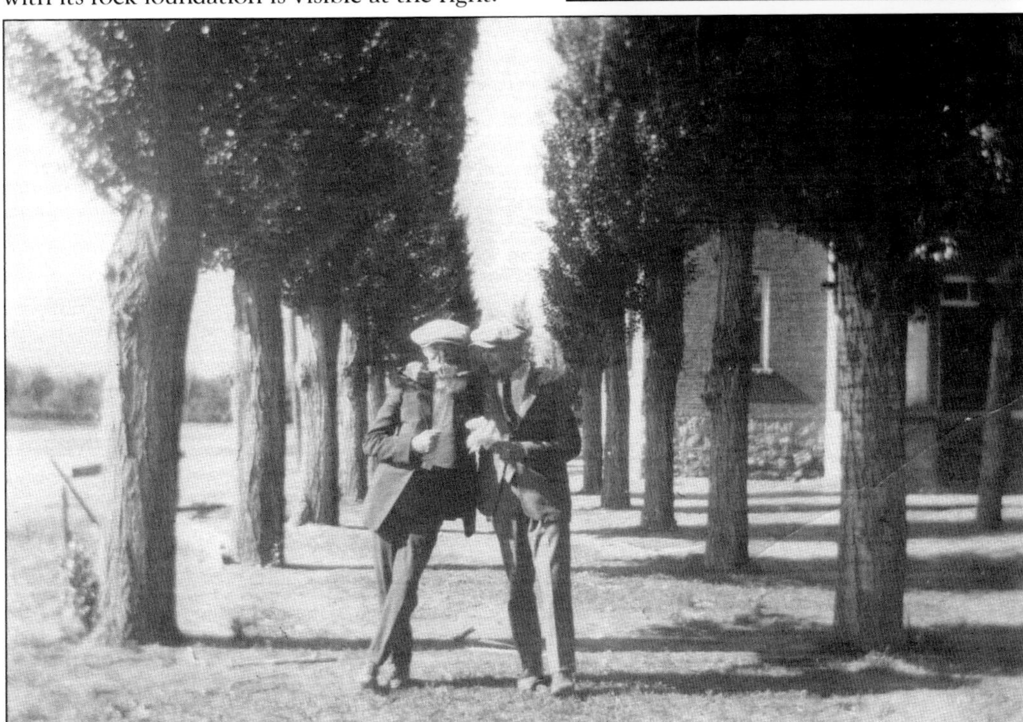

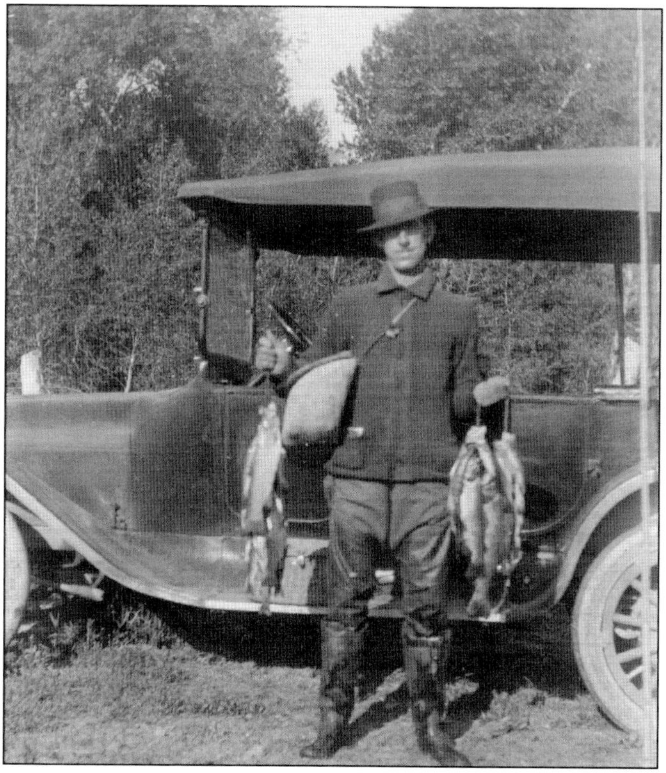

Fishing has been a favorite activity for many years. Pictured at left in the 1920s is Victor Roylance with his catch of the day. If a day's fishing was not productive, one could stop at the trout farm on the way home. Barker's Cold Springs Trout Farm was developed in 1924 near 2284 North Fruitland Drive, where a spring bubbled out of the ground at a constant 50 degrees. The business was abandoned during the 1930s because Depression-hungry folk stole the fish. In the early 1940s, the unique business was revived by Lyman Barker's sons, Ward and Ross. The ponds were cleaned out after a flood, and a new hatchery and rearing ponds were constructed. Robyn Barker is pictured below catching a fish at the trout farm.

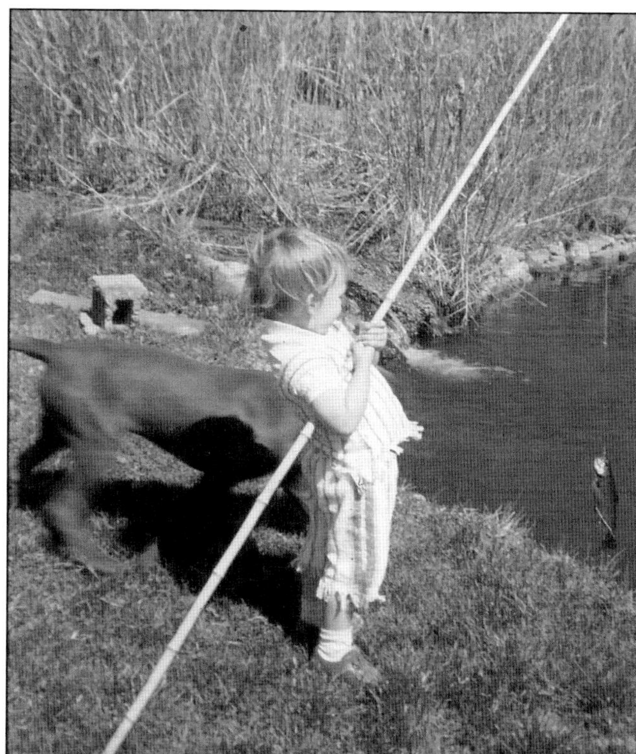

Hiking, horseback riding, and picnicking were favorite pastimes for the families of North Ogden. At right, a trip to Ben Lomond Peak was accomplished on horseback in 1927. The adventurers are, from left to right, Lucille (Bingham) and Wilford Shaw, and Della (Shaw) Chandler. Harry Chandler took the photograph. Traditional picnics were taken in the foothills of North Ogden on the Saturday before Easter. One of the annual Easter picnics at Frog Rock, a rock formation resembling an open-mouthed frog, is shown below in 1946. Pictured from left to right are Wilford, Jerald, Marvin, and LaVern Shaw; Paula Butcher; LaRaine Montgomery; and LouJean Shaw. Another yearly trek to the foothills was taken in May to gather wildflowers for Memorial Day.

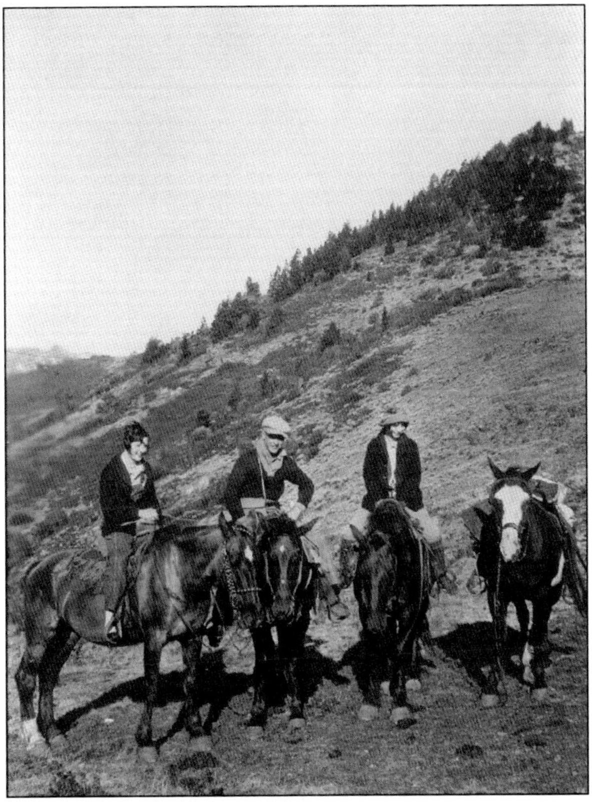

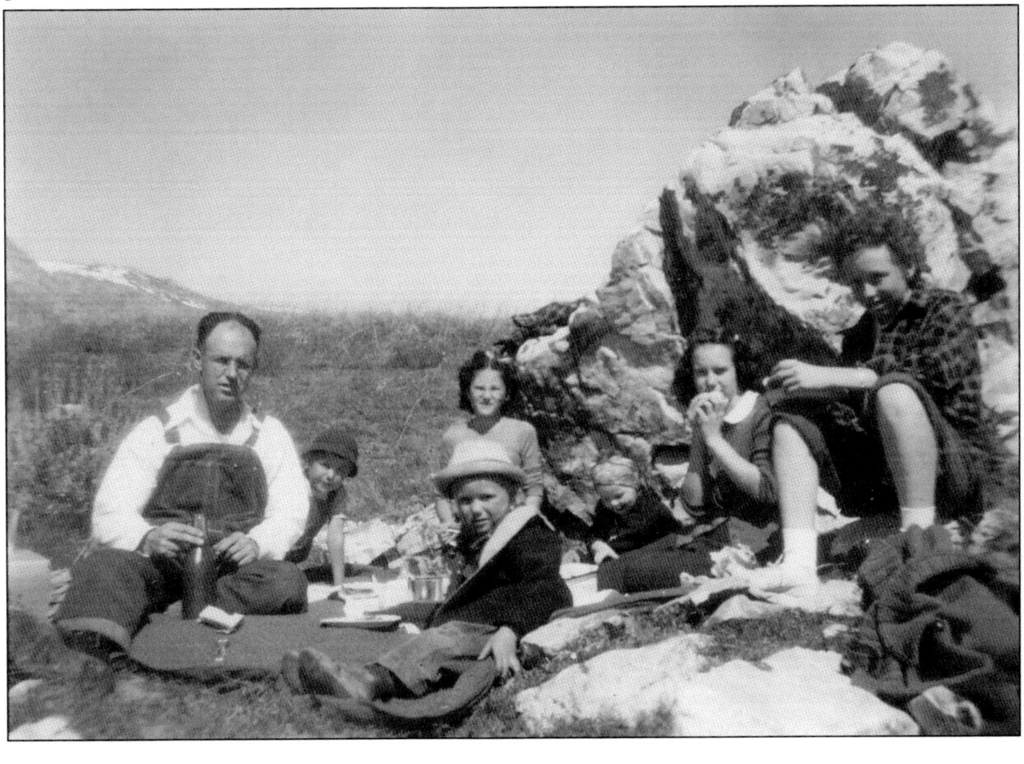

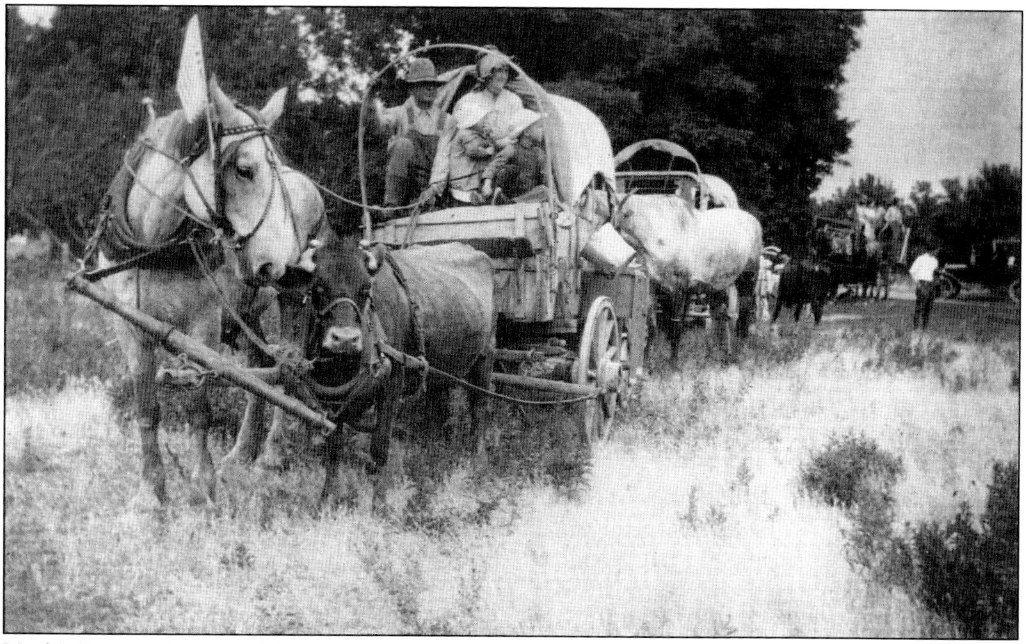

Utah's Pioneer Day is celebrated on July 24, commemorating the first group of Mormon pioneers to reach the Salt Lake Valley in 1847. The pioneers immigrated to Utah from the eastern states, using handcarts and covered wagons to carry their supplies. The treacherous 1,000-mile journey was made to seek refuge from religious persecution. Commemorative parades and celebrations are held yearly throughout the state. In the photograph above is an early parade display of a covered wagon around 1900. A mule and a cow are hitched together to pull the wagon, and a Model T car is parked in the distance. Below, a tractor pulls a makeshift float carrying a group of square dancers. Note the wind-up phonograph in the left corner that played their dance music.

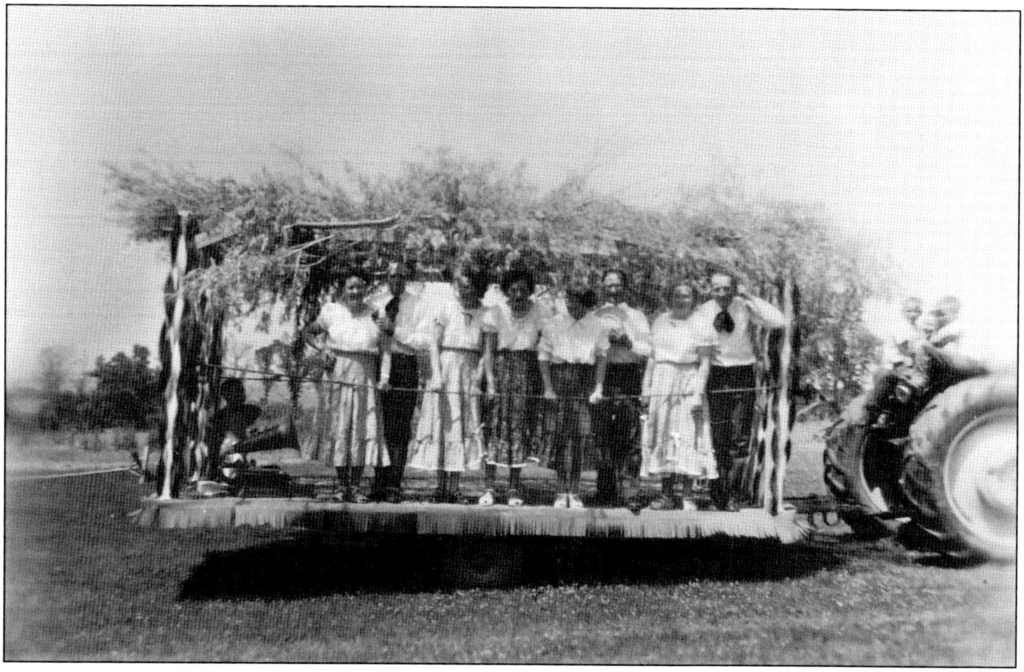

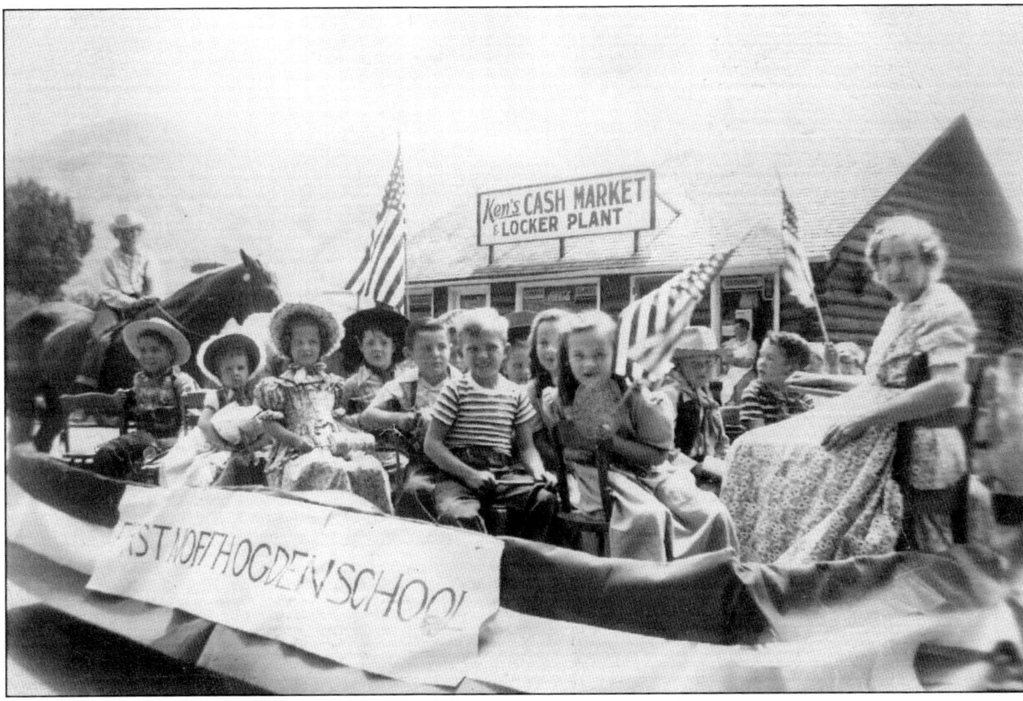

Children's parades have always been a big part of the annual North Ogden Cherry Days celebrations. Local children decorated their bicycles and tricycles with patriotic-colored crepe paper, flags, and streamers to participate in the parade, seen below around 1945. Above, a class of first-graders from North Ogden School rides on a float with their teacher, Florence Manning, with flags waving. At the North Ogden Park after the parade, the children were enticed by concession stands for hot dogs, ice cream, cold drinks, popcorn, cotton candy, and game booths. Bags of free cherries were a favorite with the crowds in the early years. Baseball games, boxing matches, and horse pulling contests were also popular attractions.

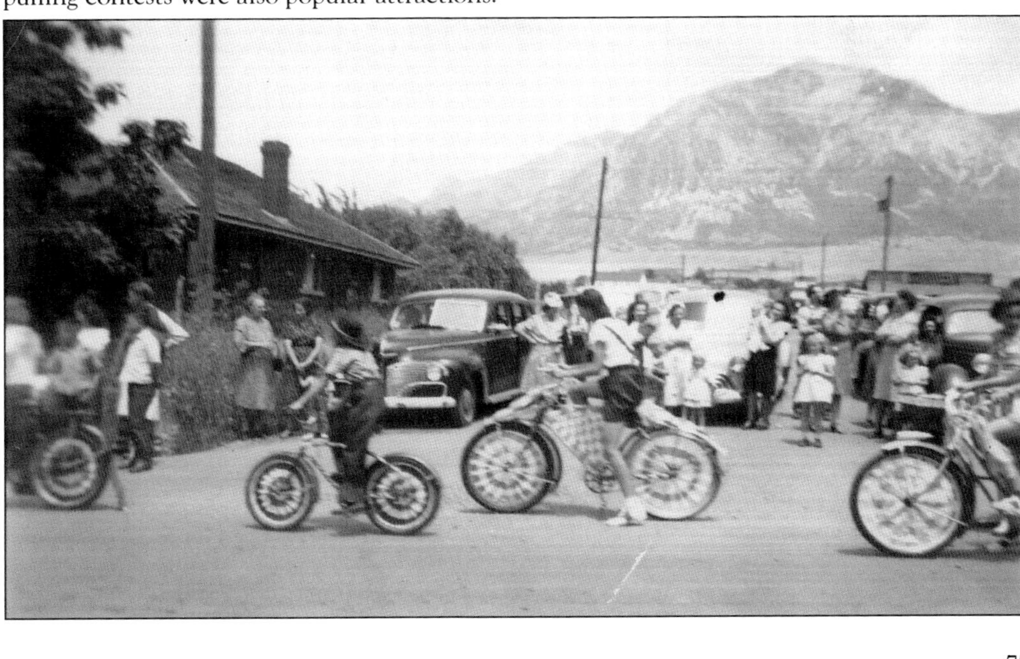

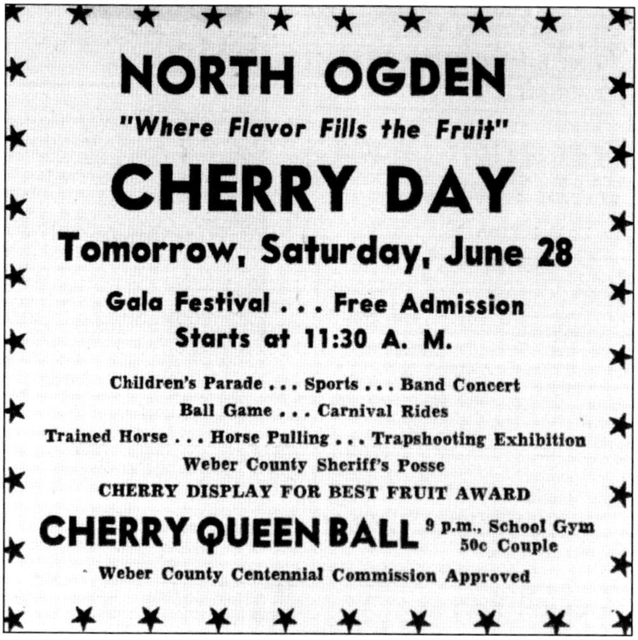
NORTH OGDEN
"Where Flavor Fills the Fruit"
CHERRY DAY
Tomorrow, Saturday, June 28
Gala Festival . . . Free Admission
Starts at 11:30 A. M.
Children's Parade . . . Sports . . . Band Concert
Ball Game . . . Carnival Rides
Trained Horse . . . Horse Pulling . . . Trapshooting Exhibition
Weber County Sheriff's Posse
CHERRY DISPLAY FOR BEST FRUIT AWARD
CHERRY QUEEN BALL 9 p.m., School Gym 50c Couple
Weber County Centennial Commission Approved

The first North Ogden Cherry Days celebration was held on July 14, 1932. A committee was formed with the intention of expanding the cherry market throughout the states. The celebration was a yearly tradition afterwards. Colorful displays of cherries, parades, and dances were common. Florence (Warren) Campbell won a slogan contest with "North Ogden, Where Flavor Fills the Fruit," as shown in the advertisement to the left on June 27, 1947. Below is a 1954 parade float showcasing the Cherry Days royalty. Queen Julia Campbell is sitting at the top. Her attendants are Marilyn Brown (left), Renee Heiner (center), and Eleanor Randall.

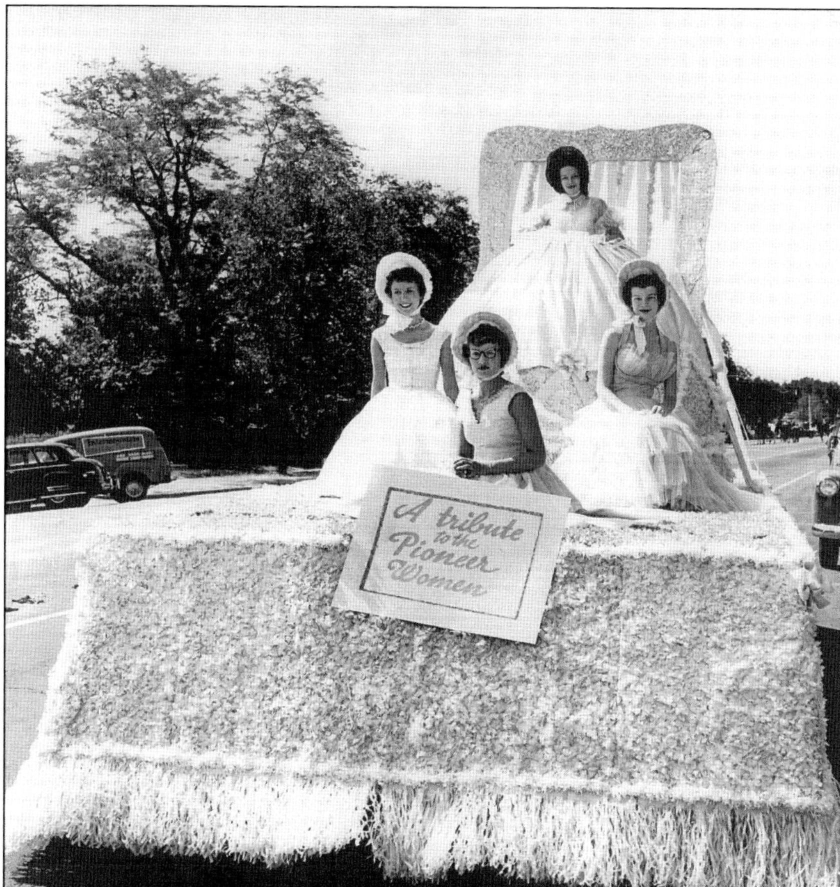

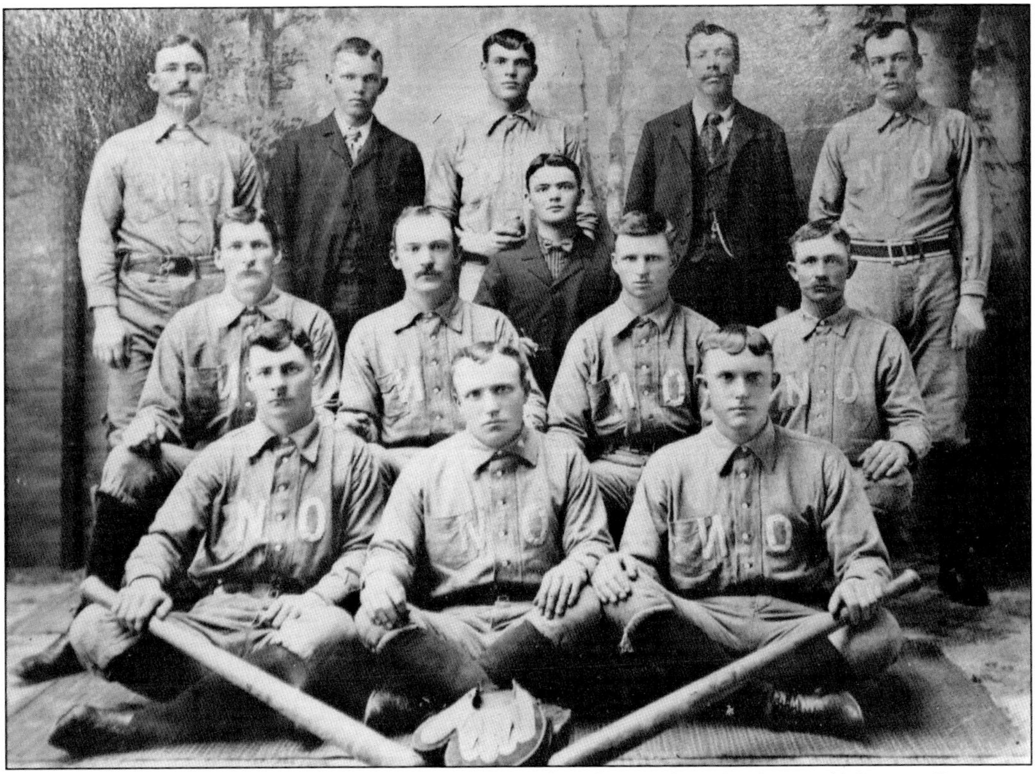

In 1893, North Ogden's first known baseball team played in Weber, Cache, and Morgan Counties. The team was transported to their games by horse and buggy. From left to right are (first row) George Randall, Solomon Shupe, and Lamoni Holmes; (second row) Enoch Randall, Milton Holmes, Andrew Clark, Heber Randall, and Will Cazier; (third row) Joe Cazier, Harry Chandler, Joseph Godfrey, Wiltz Bailey, and Nattie Montgomery.

This North Ogden baseball team won the city's first known championship in 1910. The players, from left to right, are (first row) David Randall and W. Nathan Barker; (second row) Joe Storey, Heber Randall, LeRoy Chadwick, LeRoy Snooks, William Deamer, and Parley Shupe; (third row) Eddie Marshall, Lewis Randall, Tom Brown, David Spackman, Charles Shaw, and George Randall. In 1901, a baseball diamond and grandstand were constructed to accommodate the games.

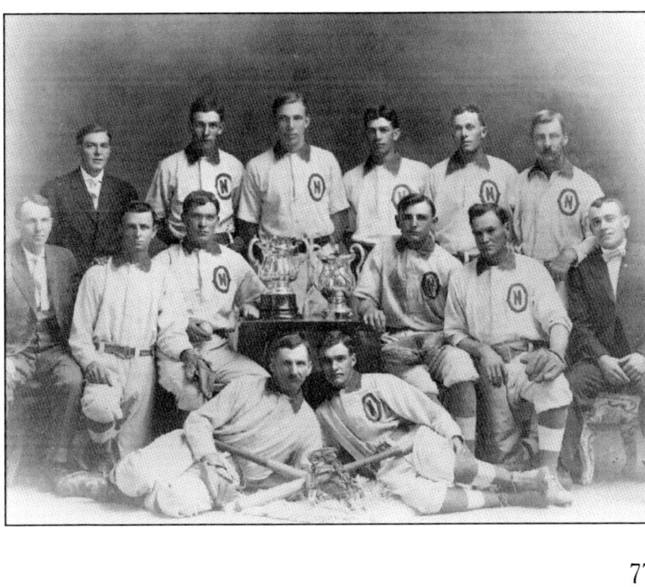

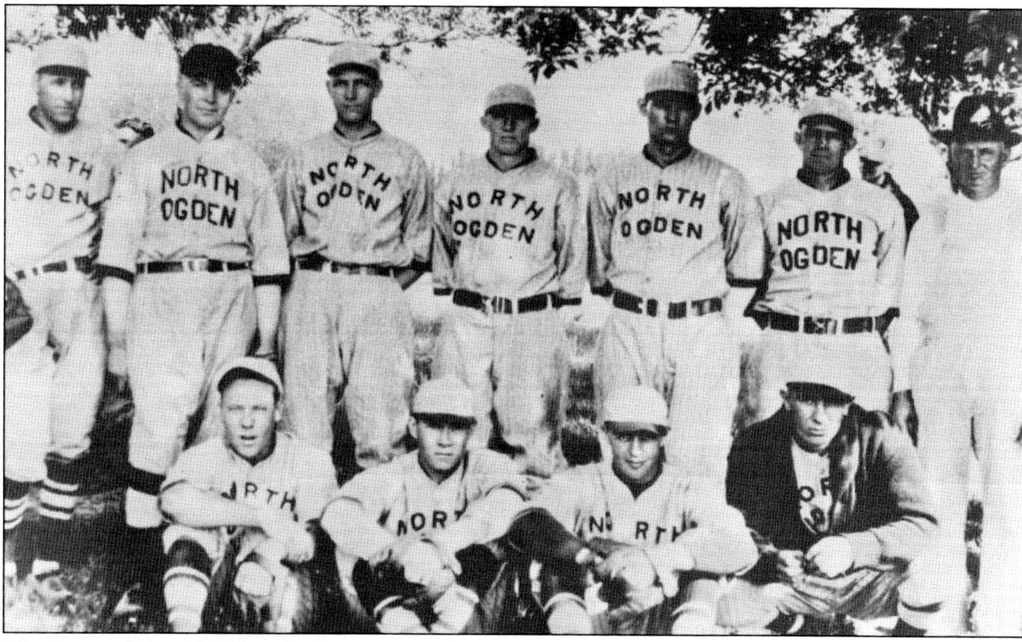

Members of the 1926 baseball team are shown in this image. From left to right are (first row) second baseman James Garner, shortstop Charles Berrett, catcher Art Rawson, and pitcher Boyd Highfield; (second row) pitcher Charles Randall, center fielder John Campbell, right fielder Clarence Randall, third baseman William Berrett, left fielder Lloyd Highfield, coach James Spackman, and manager Heber Randall. The team defeated Roy during an exhibition game for the Sixth Annual Farm Bureau celebration.

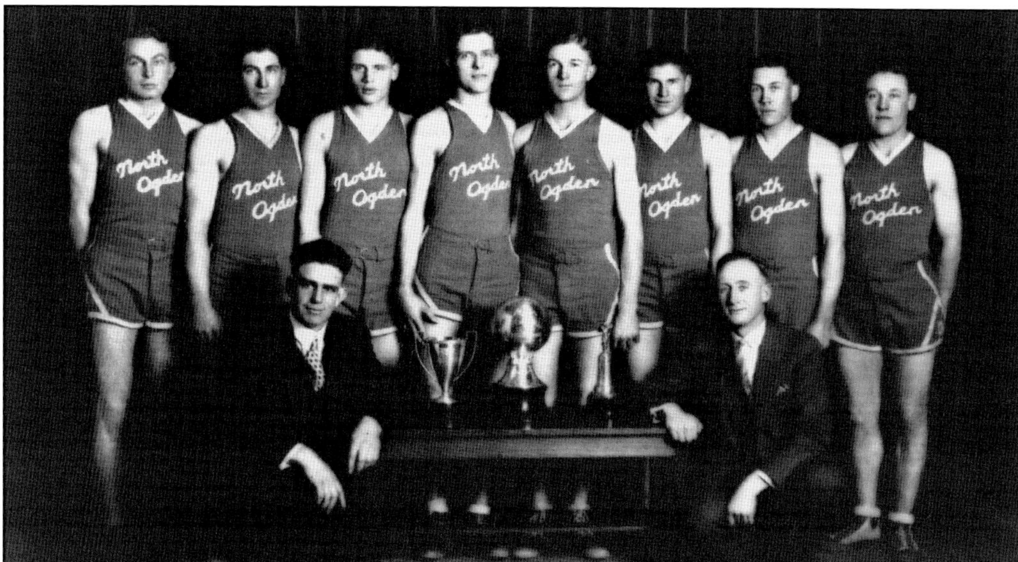

In 1927, North Ogden won the LDS church basketball championship, defeating a more polished and favored North Davis team. Pictured from left to right are (first row) James Spackman and Roy Metcalf; (second row) Harvey Chandler, Elihu Warren, Lewis Brown, Clarence Randall, Doral Campbell, Allen Warren, Charles Berrett, and James Garner. The team became the permanent owners of a traveling trophy after winning the third consecutive year.

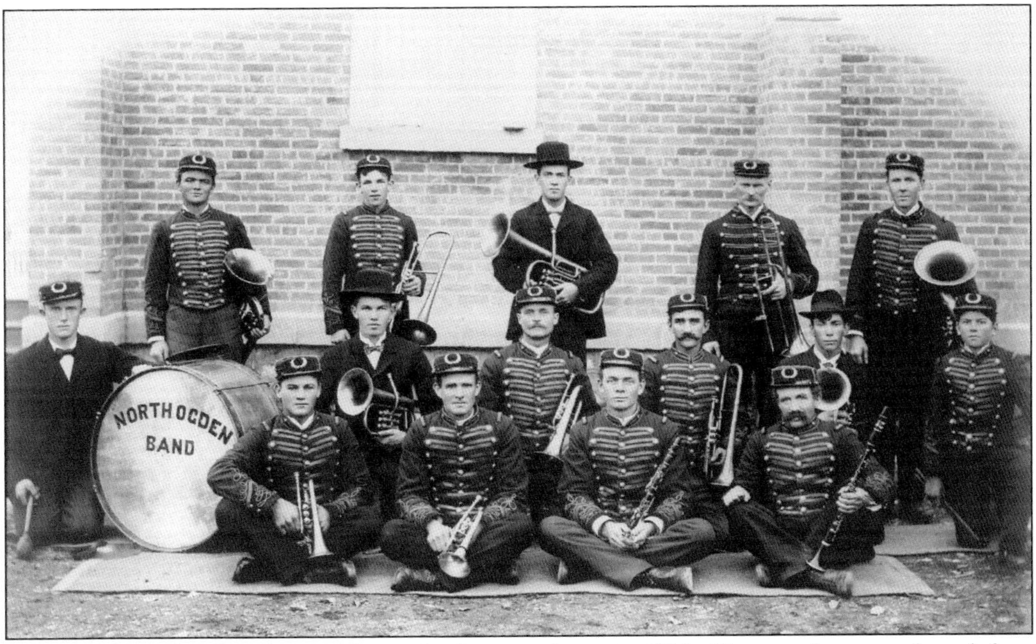

The North Ogden Band wore blue and white uniforms in 1912. The members are, from left to right, (first row) William Deamer, Thomas Storey, Charles Ellis, and Charles Storey; (second row) Lamoni Holmes, Harry Chandler, Freddie Ellis, Jimmy Dudman, Mason Blaylock, and Joseph Ellis; (third row) Andrew Clark, Joseph Storey, Charles Jones, Chris Lind, and Arthur Berrett. The early bands often serenaded the townspeople from a horse-drawn wagon.

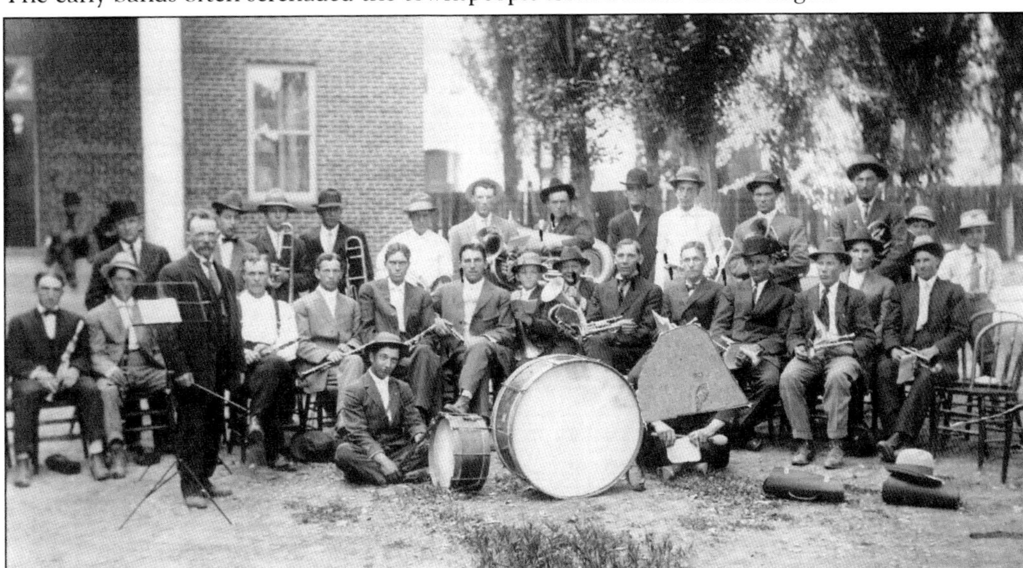

The 1914 North Ogden Band members are, from left to right, (first row) Charles Storey, Clyde Campbell, and Bill Deamer; (second row) Joe Orton, unidentified, Elijah Shaw, Clarence Barker, Lorin Williams, Thomas Orton, two unidentified boys, Ed Berrett, Lewis Randall, two unidentified men, Will Orton, and Will Warren; (third row) Leon Orton, Harold Campbell, Gilbert Randall, Joseph Chadwick, unidentified, Henry Storey, Earl Chadwick, Charles Jones, unidentified, LeRoy Chadwick, Lewis Chadwick, and two unidentified boys.

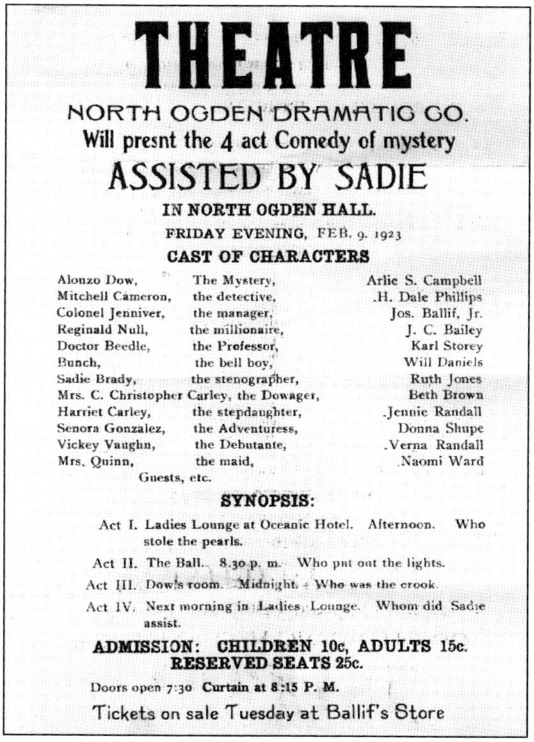
THEATRE

NORTH OGDEN DRAMATIC CO.
Will presnt the 4 act Comedy of mystery

ASSISTED BY SADIE

IN NORTH OGDEN HALL.

FRIDAY EVENING, FEB. 9. 1923

CAST OF CHARACTERS

Alonzo Dow,	The Mystery,	Arlie S. Campbell
Mitchell Cameron,	the detective,	.H. Dale Phillips
Colonel Jenniver,	the manager,	Jos. Ballif, Jr.
Reginald Null,	the millionaire,	J. C. Bailey
Doctor Beedle,	the Professor,	Karl Storey
Bunch,	the bell boy,	Will Daniels
Sadie Brady,	the stenographer,	Ruth Jones
Mrs. C. Christopher Carley,	the Dowager,	Beth Brown
Harriet Carley,	the stepdaughter,	.Jennie Randall
Senora Gonzalez,	the Adventuress,	Donna Shupe
Vickey Vaughn,	the Debutante,	.Verna Randall
Mrs. Quinn,	the maid,	.Naomi Ward

Guests, etc.

SYNOPSIS:

Act I. Ladies Lounge at Oceanic Hotel. Afternoon. Who stole the pearls.

Act II. The Ball. 8.30 p. m. Who put out the lights.

Act III. Dow's room. Midnight. Who was the crook.

Act IV. Next morning in Ladies Lounge. Whom did Sadie assist.

**ADMISSION: CHILDREN 10c, ADULTS 15c.
RESERVED SEATS 25c.**

Doors open 7:30 **Curtain at 8:15 P. M.**

Tickets on sale Tuesday at Ballif's Store

Early entertainment consisted of dances, plays, band concerts, and vaudeville or lantern shows. A lantern show told a story with the help of cut-out figures and scenes that were inserted into a large lantern to create shadow images. The images were changed as the story progressed. Dances were held for everyone, sometimes lasting all night long. When the dance floor was crowded, numbers were drawn to take turns. Children were put to bed in another room while the dancing went on, and a potluck meal was served at midnight. At left is a theater playbill from 1923 advertising "Assisted by Sadie," a four-act comedy of mystery. The synopsis includes "Who stole the pearls, Who put out the lights, Who was the crook, and Whom did Sadie assist." Below is a tap-dancing group of children with Weldon Taggart in the center.

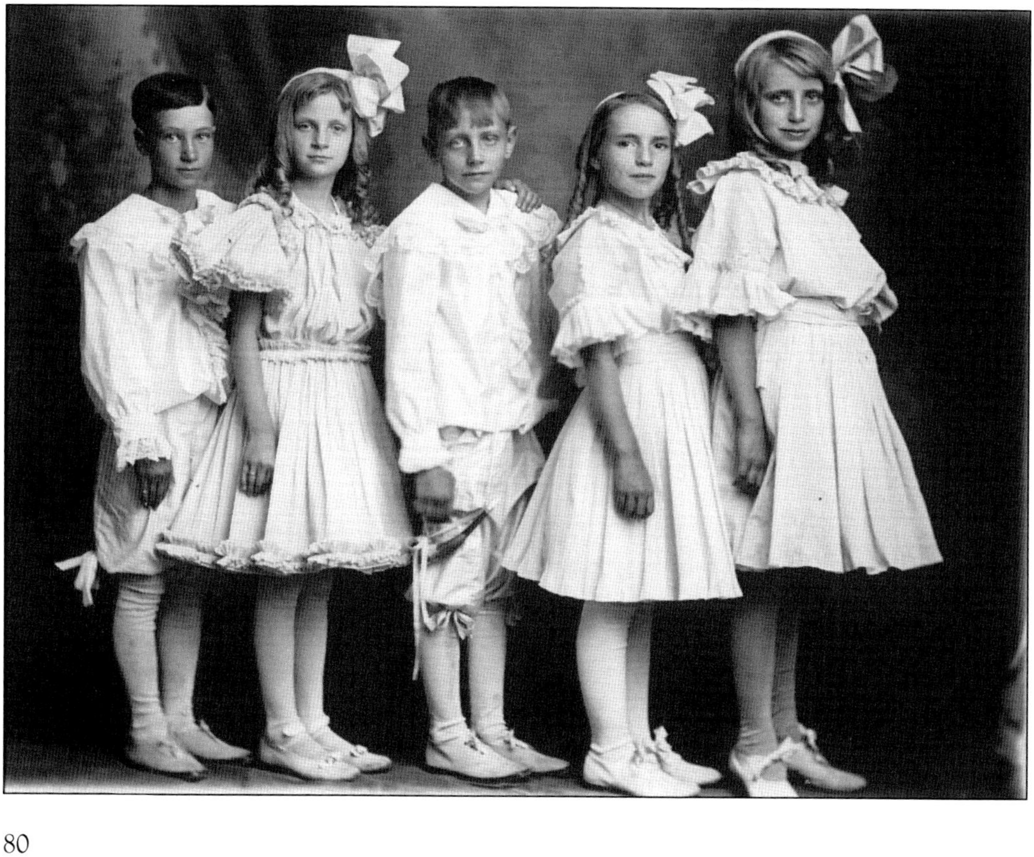

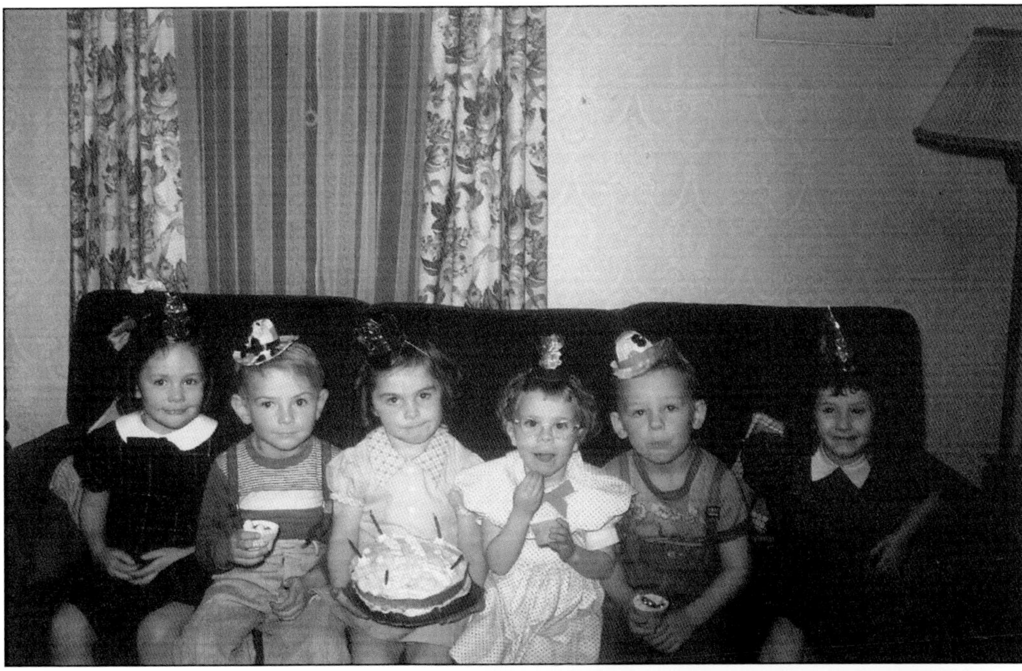

Birthday and Christmas celebrations have always been favorites. The photograph above shows Shauna Chandler's fifth birthday party in 1951. The partygoers are, from left to right, Diane Wyatt, Stephen Kendall, Shauna Chandler with her cake, cousin Carol Chandler, and two unidentified children. Each child has a personalized party hat. Grant Roylance, right, celebrates Christmas in 1951, having just opened gifts of a toy horse and ball. To his right, a horse pull-toy, complete with a cowboy, has already been opened. The expression on Grant's face illustrates the excitement of Christmas morning and triggers many fond memories.

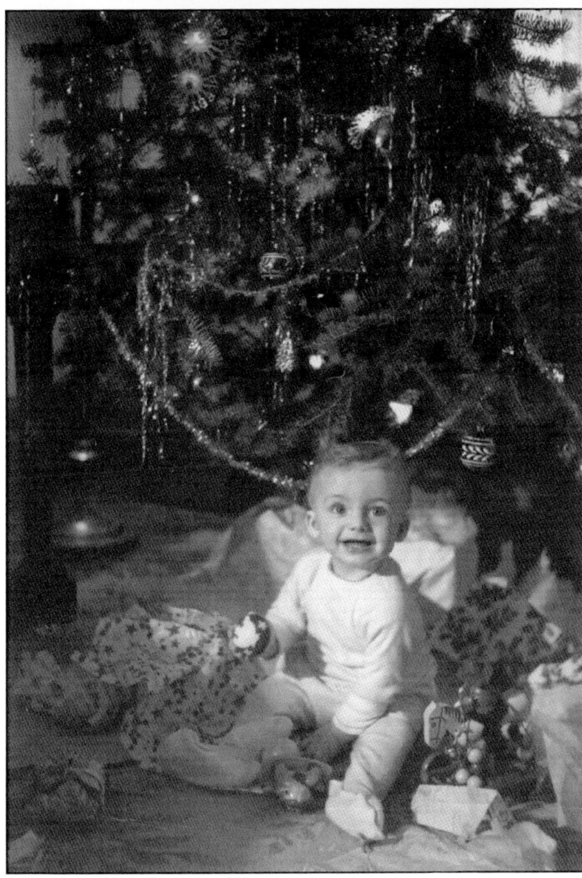

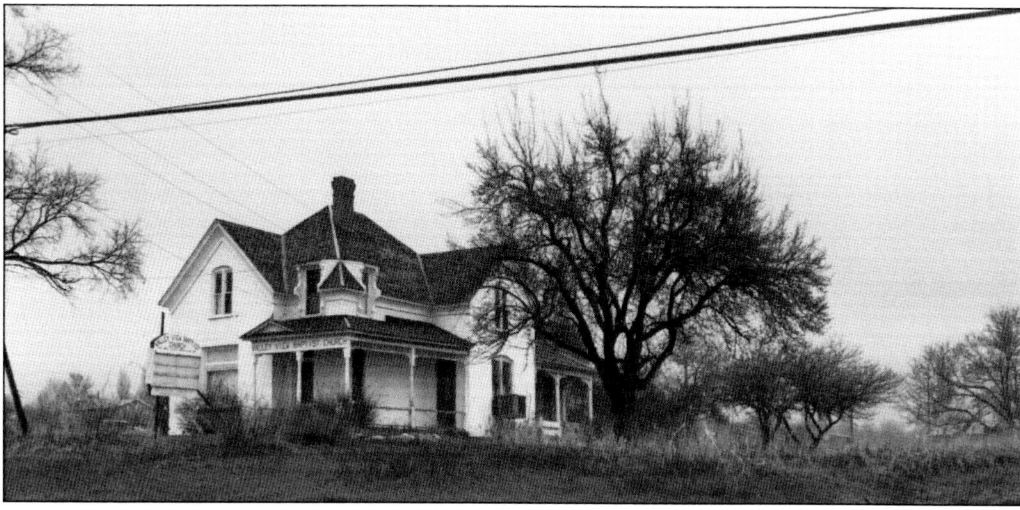

In 1964, the Valley View Baptist Church was established at 2712 North 400 East in a home built by James Storey in 1900. The church members initially held meetings in a local garage. Early pastors of the church were James Deguire, William Jones, and Beuford Hall. A new building, constructed on the site in 1984, contained a chapel, a fellowship hall, and classrooms. The old home was then demolished.

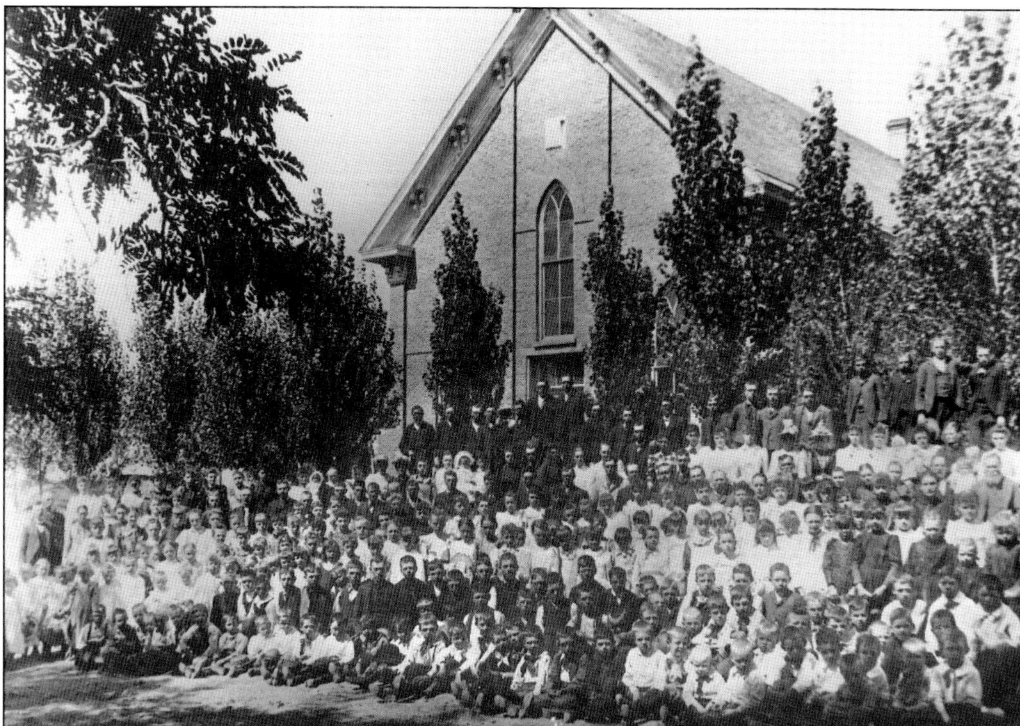

The North Ogden LDS church building was completed in 1895, and the proud members gathered for a photograph. Work on the building began before 1880 at 626 East 2600 North, with the estimated cost of $800, but the actual cost was much higher. The building was later remodeled and dedicated in 1910 by LDS church president Joseph F. Smith. An annex, a bishop's office, and eight classrooms were added.

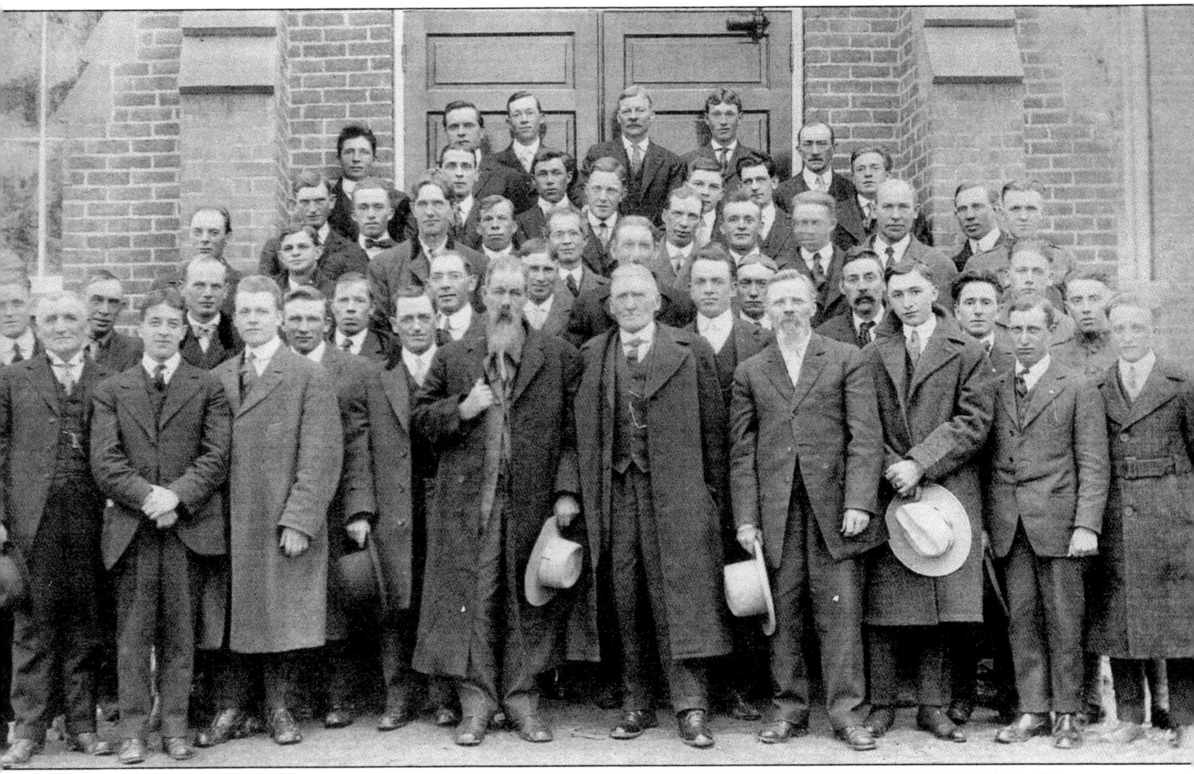

In 1918, the Fourth Quorum of Elders from the North Ogden and Pleasant View LDS church are pictured. From left to right are (first row) Alford Ford, Harold Campbell, Lee Barker, Franklin Campbell, Gideon Alvord, Heber Huband, Charles Norris, Clyde Campbell, and William Daniels; (second row) Claude Ellis, William Roylance, Henry Story, William Orton, Alma Roylance, Oliver Miller, Edward Berrett, William Warren, Enoch Randall, Hyrum Judkins, Parley Pickford, Lyman Barker, Conrad Chatelain, Angus Brown, and Robert Ellis; (third row) Nathanial Bailey, Parley Spackman, Joe Hill, Lorenzo Anderson, David Shupe, unidentified, Hyrum Bailey, John Storey, Aldro Barker, J. Martin Larsen, Thomas Brown, and Arzone Marshall; (fourth row) Elzy Brown, Lewis Chadwick, Albert Shaw, Hyrum Montgomery, Charles Orton, Floyd Hill, John Campbell, Mormon Cragun, Nephi Matthews, and Eddie Marshall; (fifth row) Charles A. Jones, Marlin Berrett, George Randall, and George Alvord. These men were among the first settlers of North Ogden.

THEATRE.

NORTH OGDEN SUNDAY SCHOOL
WILL PRESENT

AMONG THE BREAKERS.

A sterling drama in two acts.

IN NORTH OGDEN HALL.

Friday evening, Nov, 24th 1911.

CAST OF CHARACTERS

David Murray,	keeper of Fairpoint light,	Wm. Gibson
Larry Divine,	his assistant,	Frank Blaylock
Hon. Bruce Hunter,		Thomas Orton
Clarance Hunter,	his ward	N. J. Brown
Peter Paragraph,	a newspaper reporter,	D. E. Randall
Scud	Hunter's colored servant	Parley Reynolds
Minnie Daze,	Hunter's Niece,	Ora Marshall
Bess Starbright,	cast upon the waves,	Ella Garner
Mother Cary,	a reputed fortune teller,	Annie Barker
Biddy Bean,	an Irish girl,	Ada Chatelain

SYNOPSIS:

Act I. Interior of Murray's cottage, time evening. Mother Cary tells Dayids fortune. Scuds arrival.. Am de lady of de house disemgaged. The lion and the lamb under same roof. Murrays plot fails

Act II. Same as act one, time morning. Face to face. Away ere 'tis too late: 'tis too late now. "Repentance washes a soul and brings it nearer a merciful Father. The recognition, forgivness and reunion

Primary department sing between acts.

ADMISSION: CHILDREN 10c, ADULTS 15c.

RESERVED SEATS 25c.

Tickets on sale at store, Thursday morning, Nov. 23d 1911

Doors open at 7:30. Curtain. 8:10

This bill reads, "North Ogden Sunday School presents 'Among the Breakers,' a sterling drama in two acts." This program is dated November 24, 1911, and lists the cast of characters, the synopsis, and admission prices. The primary school children sang between acts. These types of presentations were commonly produced for community entertainment, and in addition, they usually taught a moral lesson.

The Retrenchment Association was founded as a young women's organization in 1869 by the LDS church. Young ladies were taught to abstain from extravagance in dress, eating, and speech. Pictured from left to right are (first row) Florence Snooks, Myrtle Chadwick, and Florence Chatelain; (second row) Ethel Caldwell, Stena Montgomery, Mary Woodfield, Susan Ellis, and Lucy Kofoed; (third row) Nettie Deamer, Luella Erickson, unidentified, Florence Manning, Naomi Rush, and Evelyn Orton.

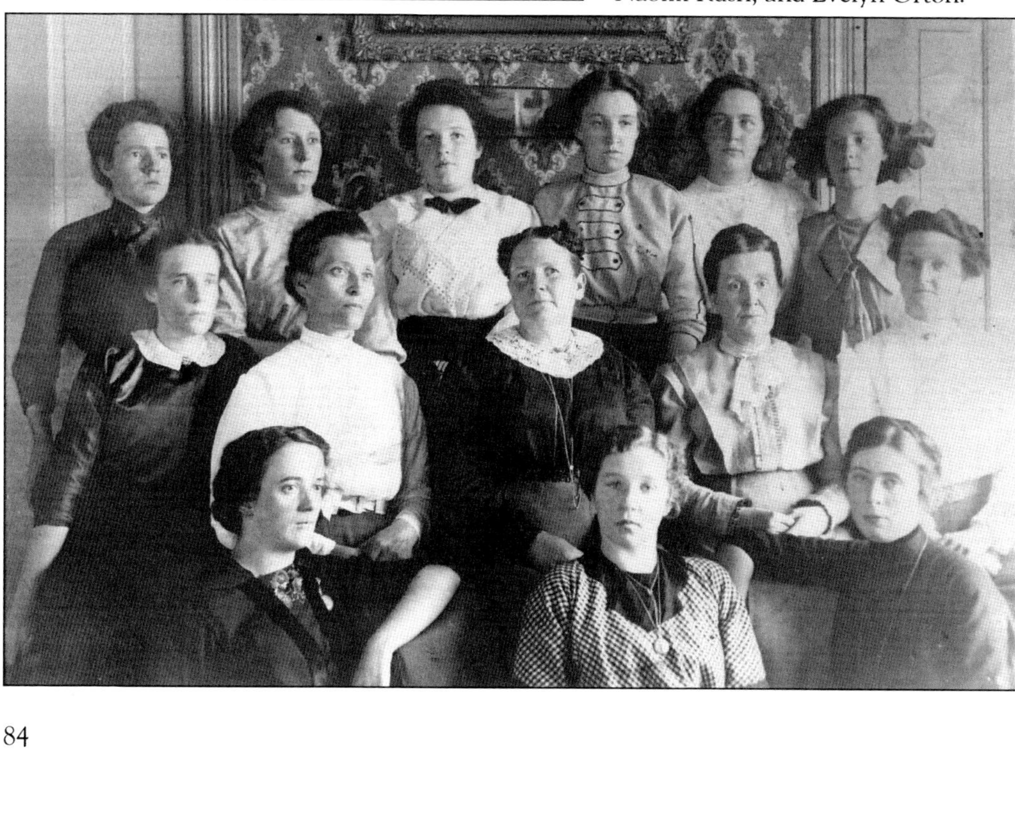

Women's fashion changed drastically over the years. Emma Spackman is pictured at right in the finery of 1910, when full-length dresses and hats were stylish. Undergarments included stiff petticoats, tight corsets, long stockings, and bloomers. Early pioneers in North Ogden attempted to establish a silk industry to harvest the thread for beautiful silk clothing. Silkworms and mulberry trees were imported from France around 1855. The industry failed, but some of the original mulberry trees can still be found in the area. In the 1950s, the teenagers wore poodle skirts, full-circle skirts that were popular because of their free-swinging shape. The blouse was tucked in at the waist and worn with short bobby socks and oxford shoes. Pictured below from left to right are Julia Campbell, Arnell Swenson, Margene Pulsipher, and LaVern Shaw.

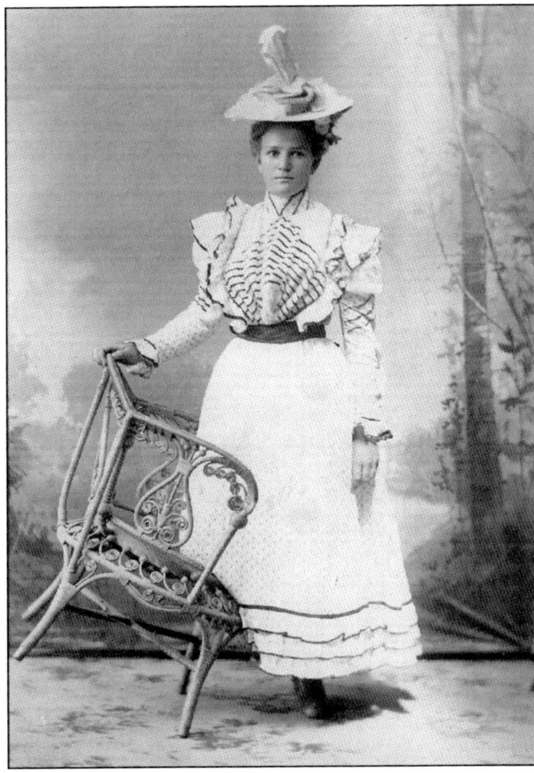

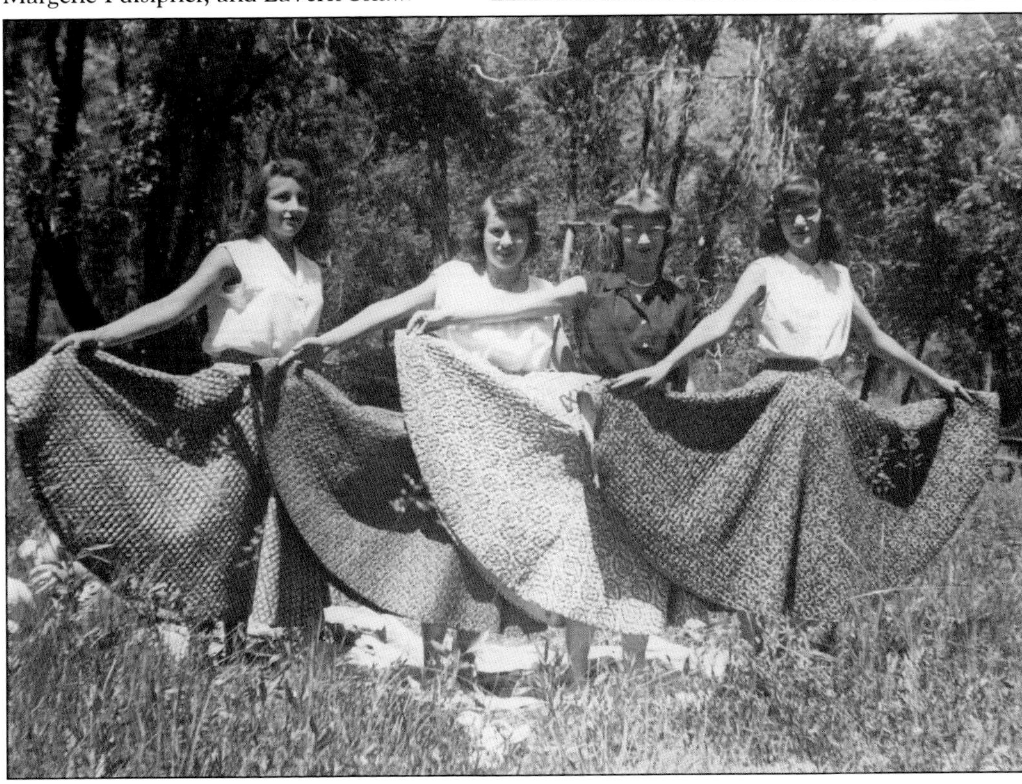

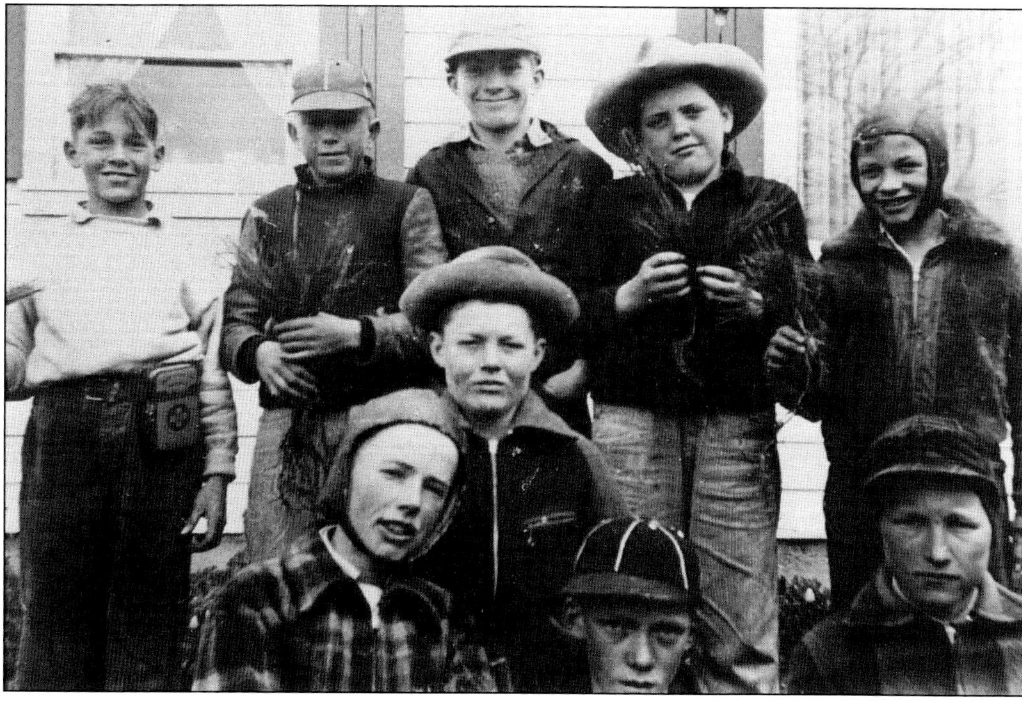

Boy Scouts from North Ogden Troop 28 are participating in the reforestation of North Ogden Canyon in April, 1942. Some of the boys are holding pine and spruce tree seedlings for the project. Pictured are, from left to right, (first row) Owen Gibson, Gerald Gibson, and Bill Tidwell; (second row) Junior Neuenschwander; (third row) Karl Allred, Richard Layton, Junior Bates, Alton Mathie, and Lavere "Bud" Campbell.

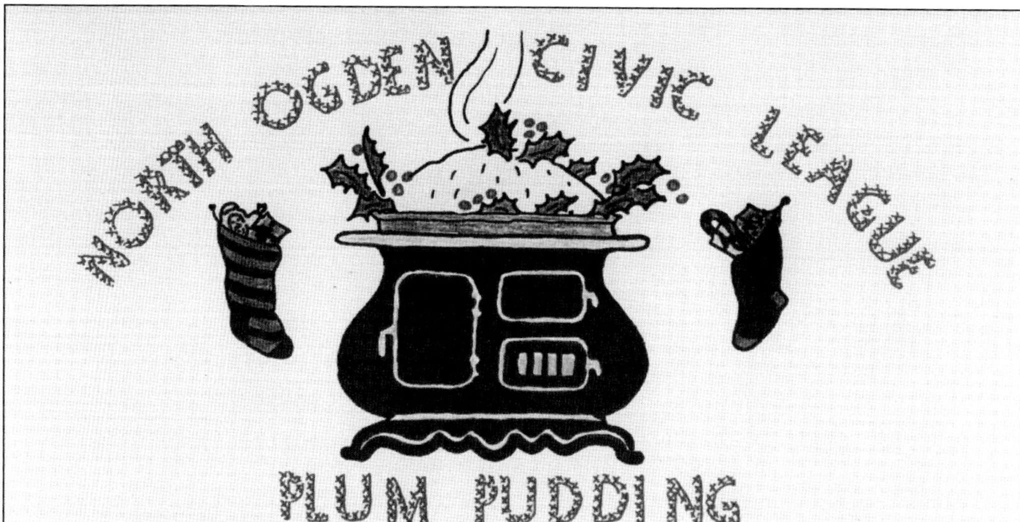

One of the North Ogden Civic League's most successful fund-raising projects was their popular canned plum pudding. The pudding label was designed by Helen Olsen. Peg Fjeldsted, the first president, originated the project, raising funds to help finance the development of the Ben Lomond Swimming Pool. The organization began in 1957, and has donated funds for many worthy causes, including covered pavilions, playgrounds, tennis courts, band uniforms, and fire equipment.

Seven

Accolades
Adorable, Admirable, and Awarding

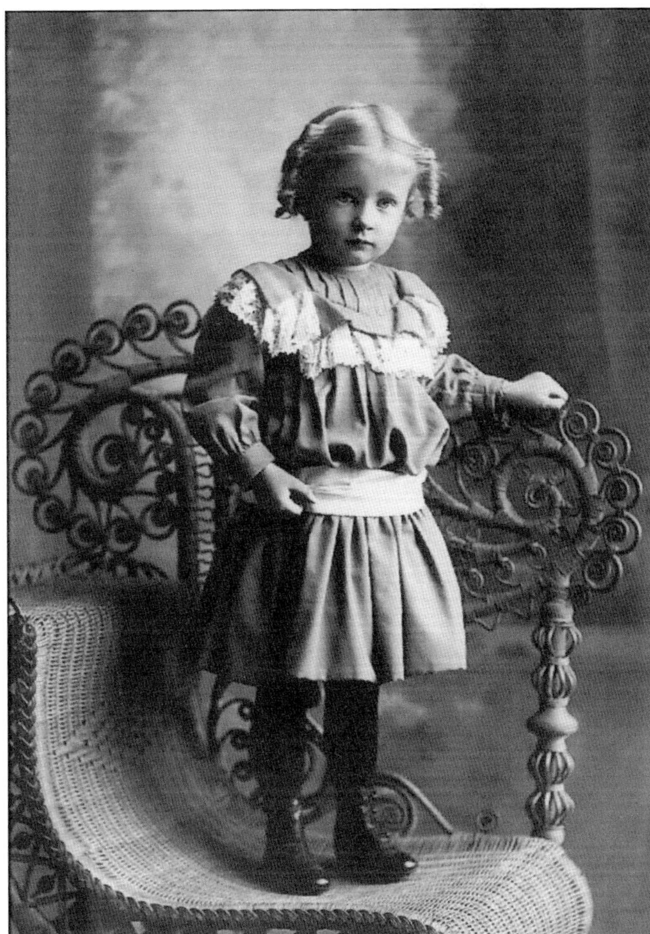

In 1906, Bernice Randall had her portrait taken on an ornate wicker chair, a prop known as a posing chair that was used by early photographers. The photographers often used hidden devices to help hold the child still for a photograph. Bernice's pretty dress, black stockings, and button-up shoes were typical of the time period. To help keep their dresses clean, girls usually wore pinafores.

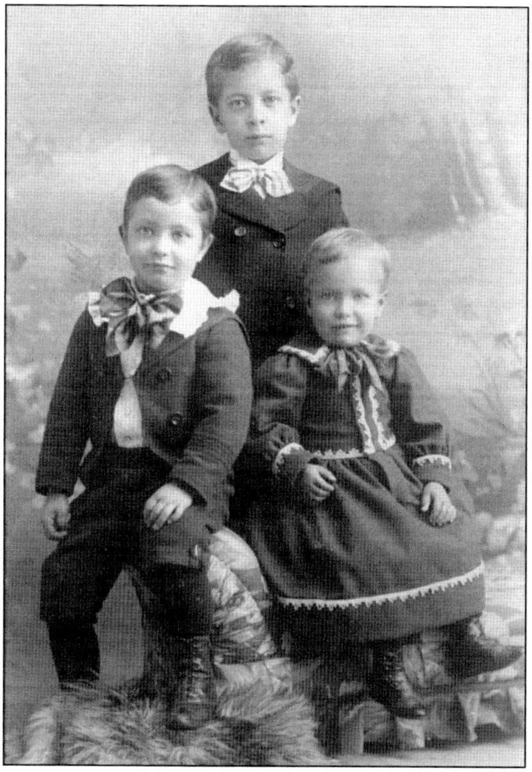

After completing their chores, pioneer children had time to play. Hide-and-seek in the sagebrush was a favorite game. Leapfrog and hoop rolling were also fun outdoor activities. Indoors the families read to each other, sang songs, and played games like Button, Button; Cat's Cradle; or Hunt the Thimble. Sometimes they made popcorn balls and pulled taffy. Pictured at left around 1900 are the sons of Scott W. and Lucinda Campbell—Clyde Strong (left), Harold Scott (center), and Arlie Sylvester. Shown below around 1898 are the children of Franklin Thomas and Caroline Campbell Clifford. From left to right are Franklin Alva, Golda Lurene, and Chloe Caroline Clifford. Baby boys were commonly clothed in gowns during the pioneer era.

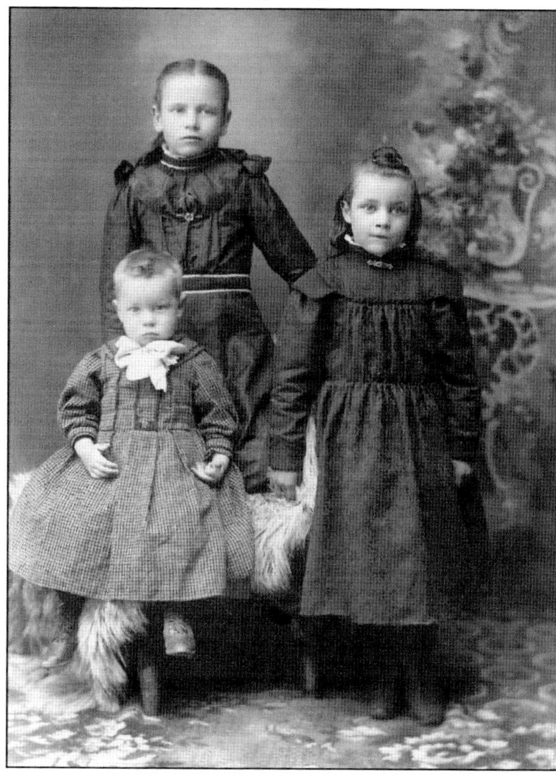

In the 1890s photograph at right are three of Elihu Nathan and Mary Priscilla (Bailey) Warren's children. They are, from left to right, Lettie Grace, Mabel Estella, and Myrtle Warren. The family had nine children born in North Ogden. Below in 1885 is Nettie Luella Deamer, daughter of James and Annie (Spackman) Deamer. Nettie had six brothers and sisters. Children's clothing was usually handmade by the mother of the family. For pioneer families, meeting the needs for shelter, food, and clothing was an endless task. The girls wore calico dresses in the summer, and all children went barefoot. In winter, the girls wore dresses made of a rough homespun fabric called linsey-woolsey. On cold days, boys wore trousers made of wool, with lighter fabrics in summer. On cold winter mornings, mothers would often warm their children's clothing on the stove.

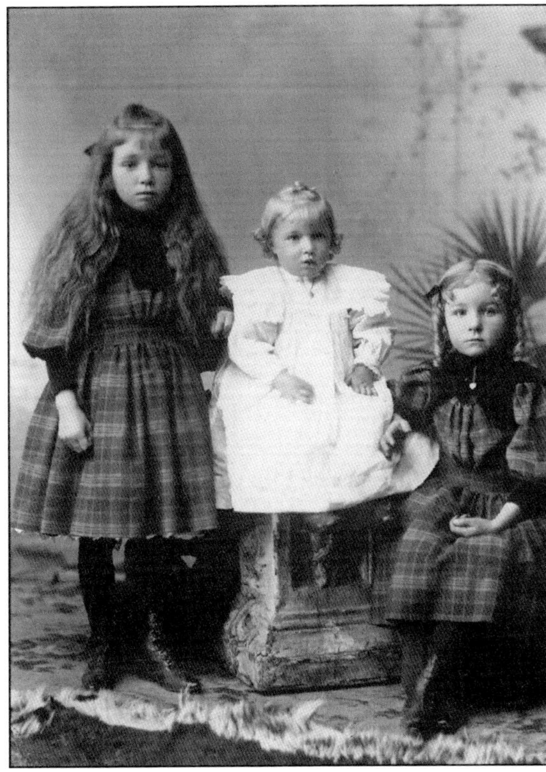

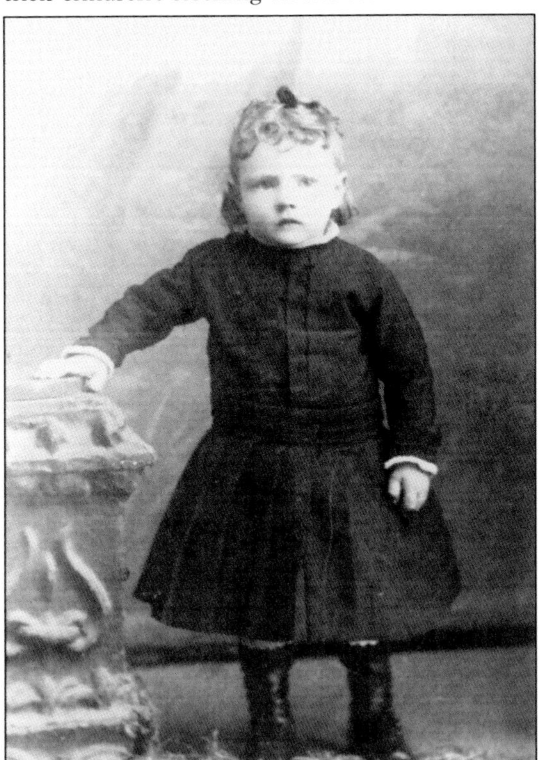

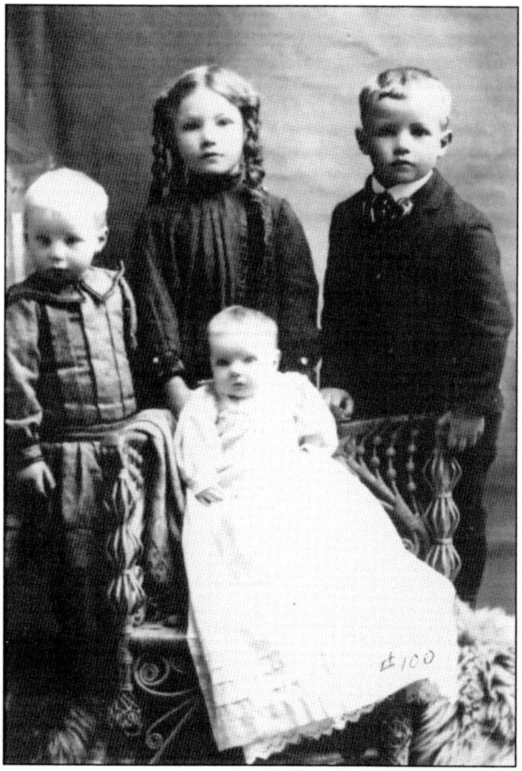

The first four children of John and Kate Ward are pictured at left around 1900. They are, from left to right, Thomas James, Celia Iness, and John Leo, with baby Harriet Jane in the center. Pioneer children were expected to help with chores. Girls learned needlework at an early age and helped with younger children, kitchen duties, and cleaning. Boys helped plant, harvest, milk cows, and hunt. Most children collected cow chips (dried dung) to be burned in the cook stove.

In 1945, Dennis (standing) and Robert Chamberlain are photographed with a metal toy airplane, a photographer's prop. The production of pedal cars began in the 1890s, and the ride-on toys were modeled after existing vehicles of the time. During the mid-1940s, that production came to a halt when metal was needed for the war effort. The cars became available again in the 1950s, and remain a classic 1950s toy.

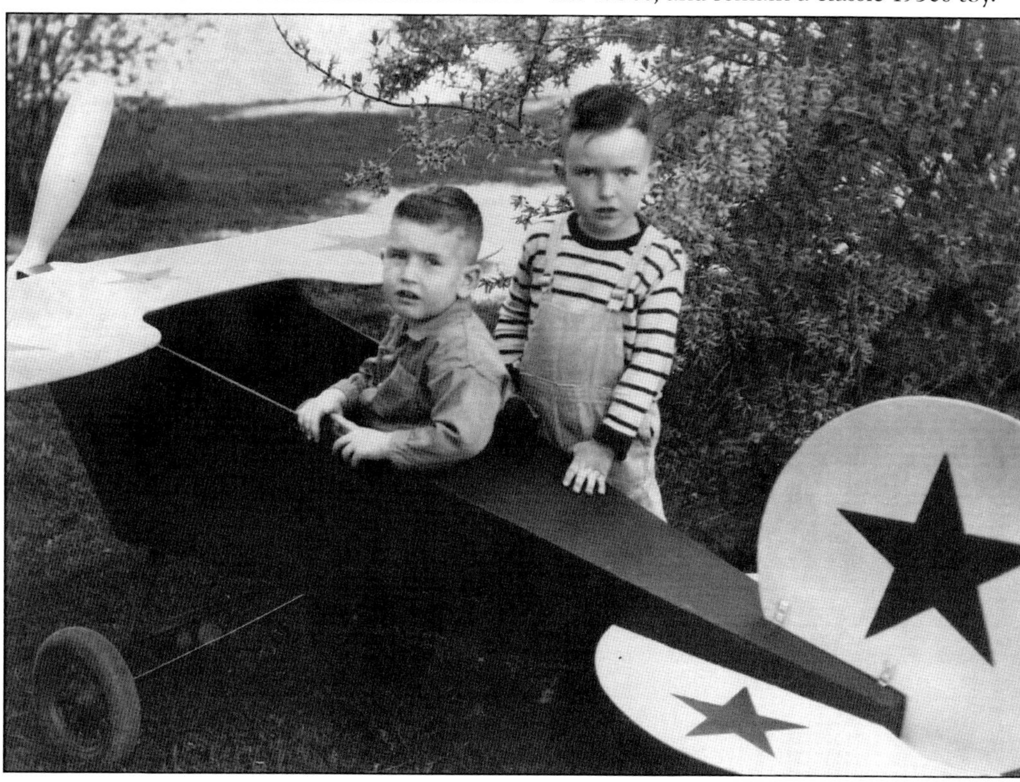

A proud Mildred Campbell is shown at right in the winter of 1921 with her snowman creation, complete with eyes of coal and a magical hat. North Ogden Canyon can be seen in the background. Sharon (left), Nancy (center), and Carol Roylance are pictured below with their toboggan, ready for some fun winter sleigh riding. Many of the winters in the region were unusually harsh, creating a winter wonderland for children.

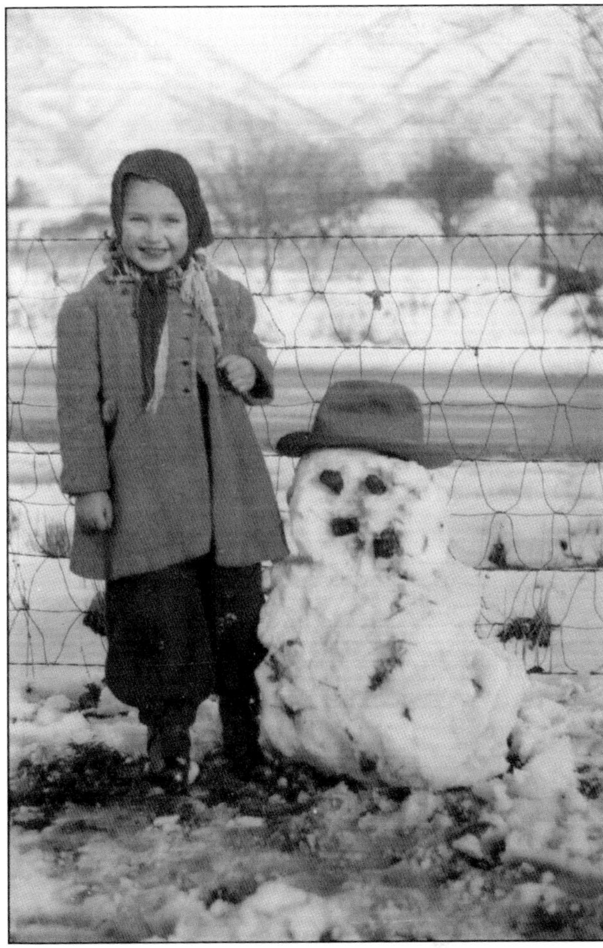

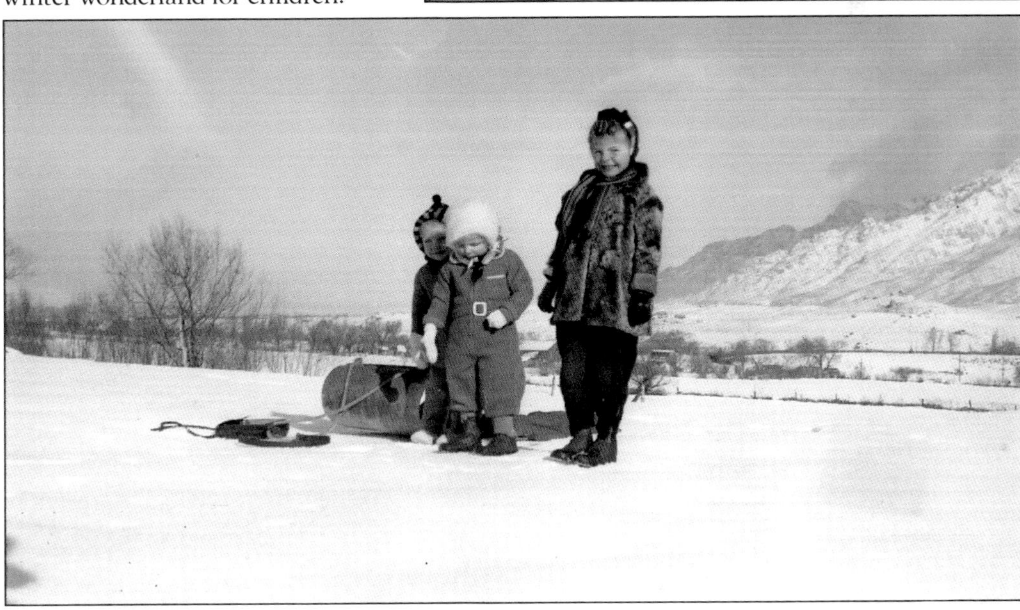

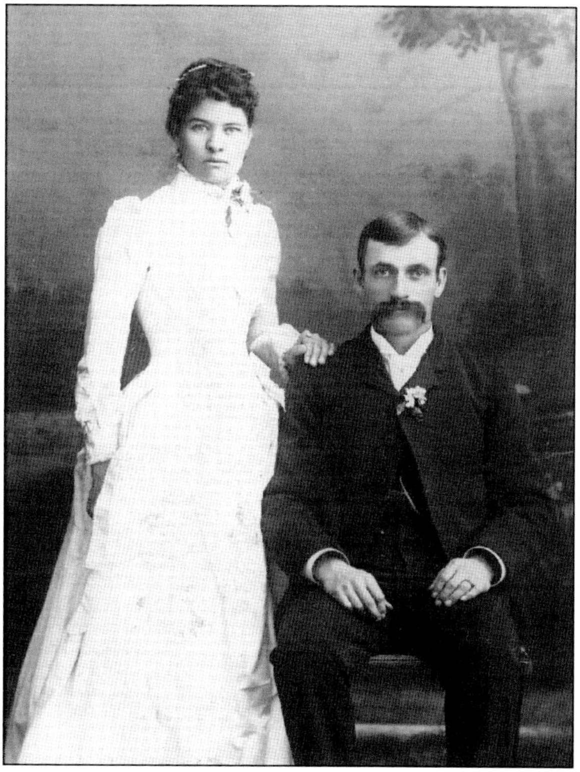

Scott Winfield and Lucinda (Strong) Campbell were married March 12, 1890. Their first home was located on the west side of 400 East between 2550 and 2600 North. Through the years, three sons were born to them, and Scott and Lucinda constructed a new home at 738 East 2600 North.

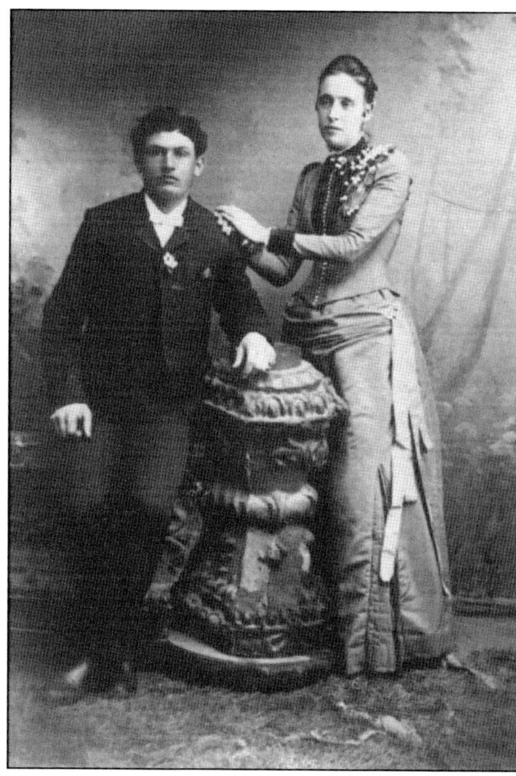

William and Celestia (Bailey) Ward were married January 7, 1891. They lived in a house constructed by William in 1890 at 2737 North 1050 East. Three children were born to this happy union. William and Celestia were among the first in the area to own a surrey with fringe on top, which was drawn by beautiful gray horses. This distinguished ensemble was loaned out for many local funerals.

The marriage of Henry Charles and Amelia (Ford) Hall took place March 8, 1893. The couple then purchased the family home and farm at 825 East 2750 North. They were the parents of five children, and together they successfully farmed many acres of orchards and crops. Henry helped develop North Ogden's water supply and assisted in the construction of the North Ogden Pass road during the Depression.

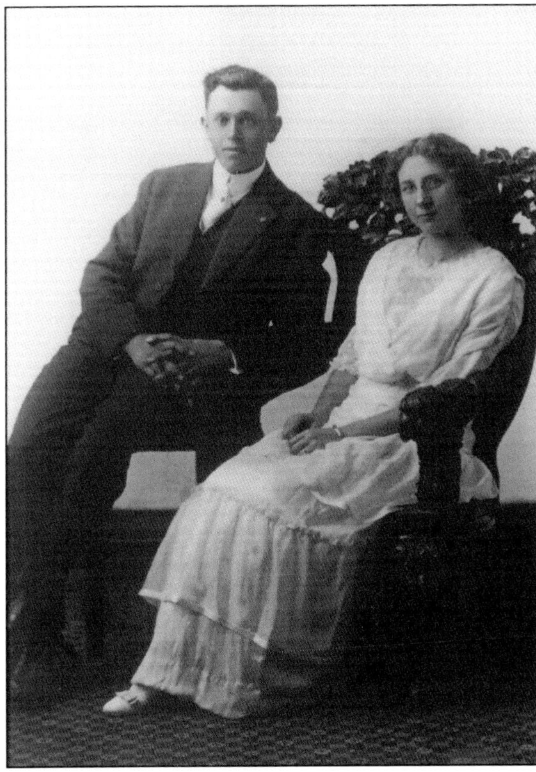

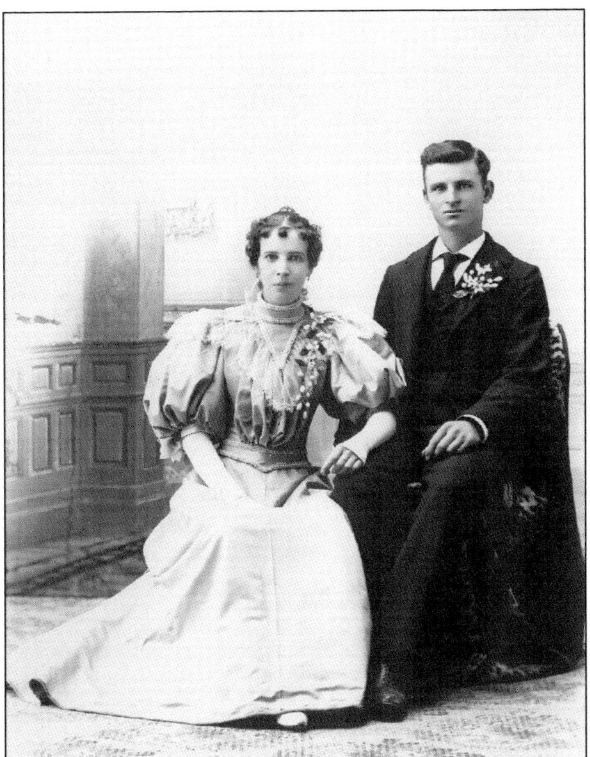

After Heber John and Lillias (Montgomery) Randall were married April 22, 1896, they lived in North Ogden's Randall District. Heber and his brothers farmed the family property and shared the harvest with their mother. Heber and Lillias were the parents of four children. They later sold their land to Percy Randall and built a new home at 426 East 2650 North.

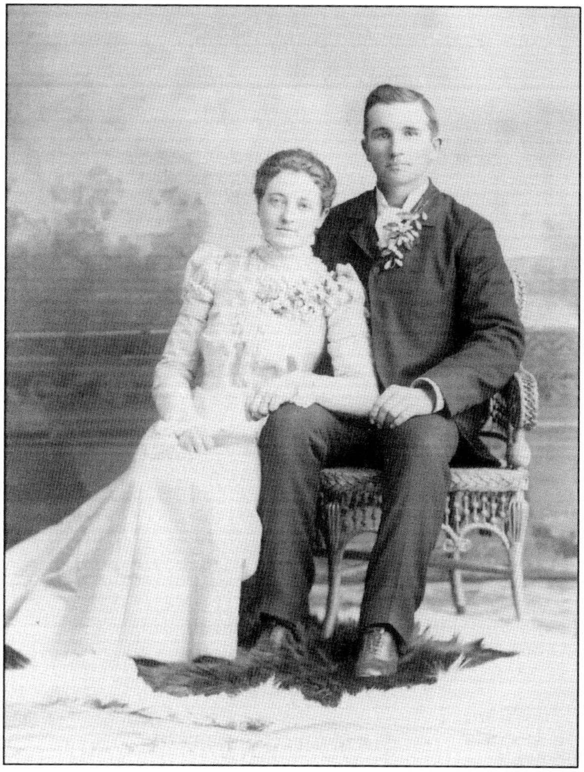

John Aaron and Margaret May (Chadwick) Woodfield were married December 13, 1899, and moved into their first home at 520 East 2100 North. They built additions to the two-room brick home gradually as their family grew to include eight children. They had a successful farm and cattle business.

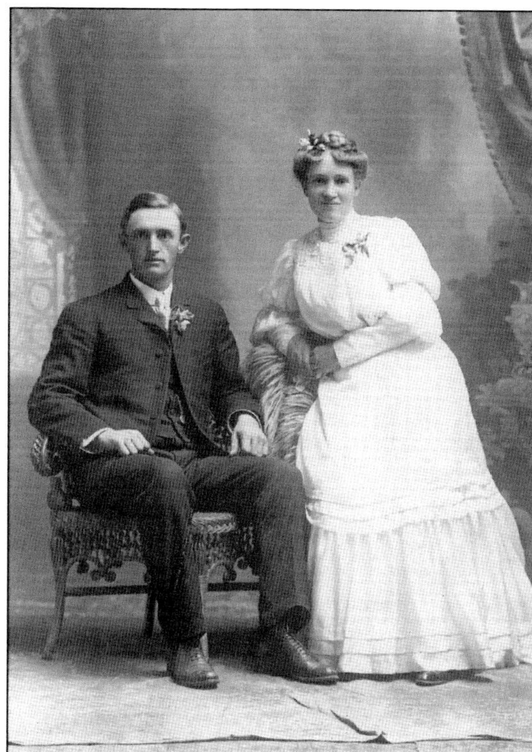

Married March 14, 1906, Thomas Francis Jr. and Margaret Louise (Storey) Brown lived in North Ogden, raising five children. Francis and "Louie" were both born in North Ogden and raised in log cabin homes. Louie grew up in Storey Town, with a Native American boy as her best friend. Francis's childhood favorites included playing the harmonica and ice-skating.

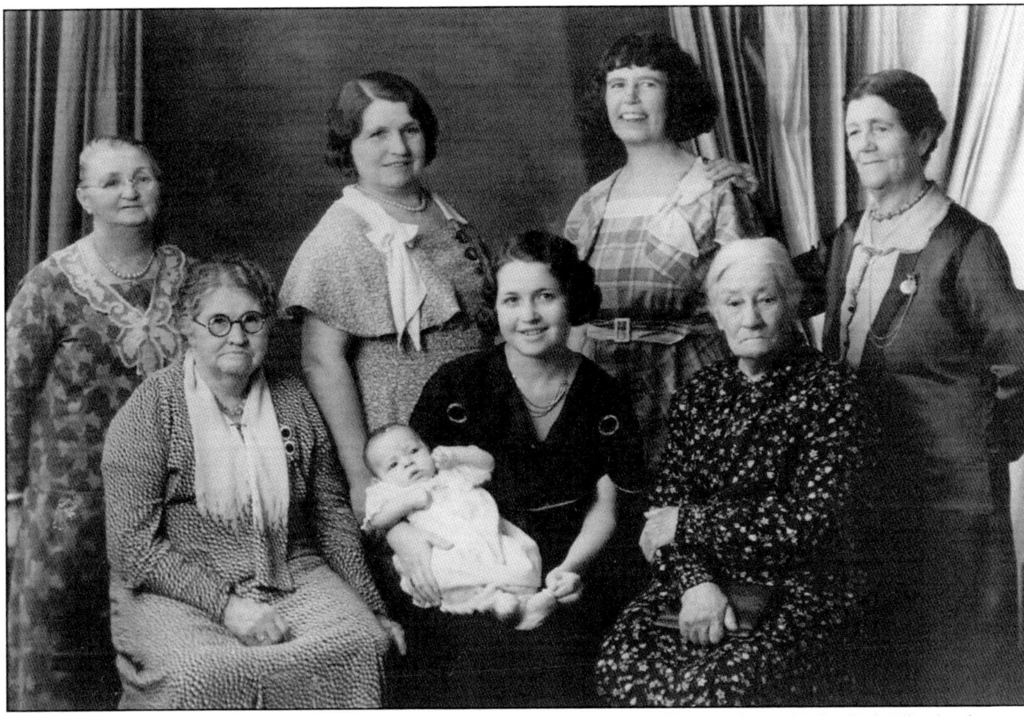

Above, four-month-old Raymond Blaylock is held by his mother, Vilate (Schultz) Blaylock, and surrounded with grandmothers and great-grandmothers. They are, from left to right, (first row) great-grandmother Artemisia (Cole) Fronk, mother and baby, and great-grandmother Annie (Land) Blaylock; (second row) great-grandmother Anna (Ninnemann) Schultz, grandmother Jane (Fronk) Schultz, grandmother Golda (Clifford) Blaylock, and great-grandmother Caroline (Clifford) Peterson. The baby also had a living great-great-grandmother at the time this picture was taken on December 10, 1933.

Marie (Stallé) Warren is shown at right celebrating her 78th birthday party in North Ogden with some of her grandchildren in 1923. Marie emigrated with her family from Italy at age 11, crossing the plains in the first handcart company in 1856. Her parents were ill on the journey, leaving the children to pull the handcart. She later married Elihu Warren in North Ogden, and they became the parents of 13 children.

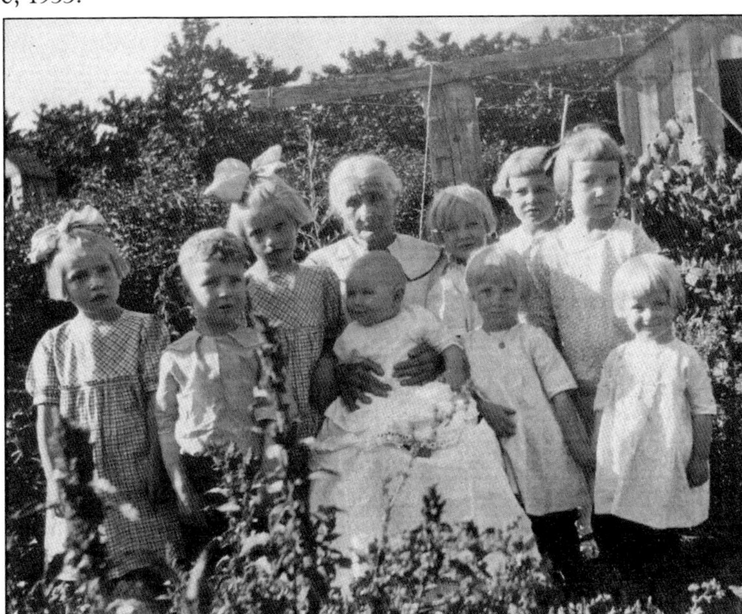

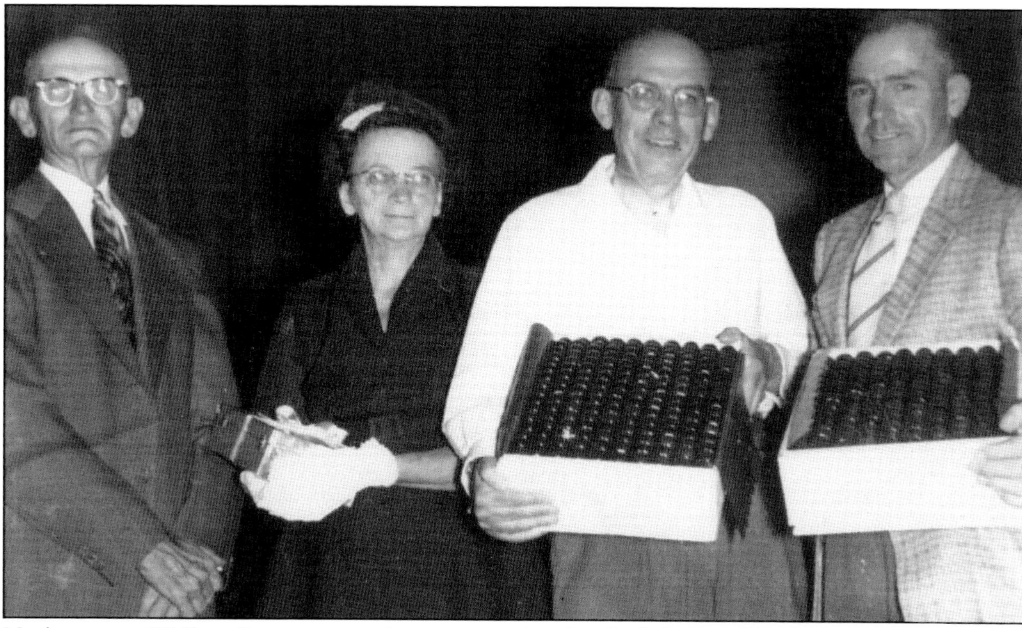

Utah senator Wallace Bennett was the guest speaker for the July 4, 1955, Cherry Day celebration, and he was presented with two boxes of hand-packed cherries. He was to keep one box as a gift, and promised to deliver the other box to President Eisenhower the next morning. Pictured are, from left to right, grand marshal LeRoy Snooks, Florence Snooks, Sen. Wallace F. Bennett, and chairman Percy Randall.

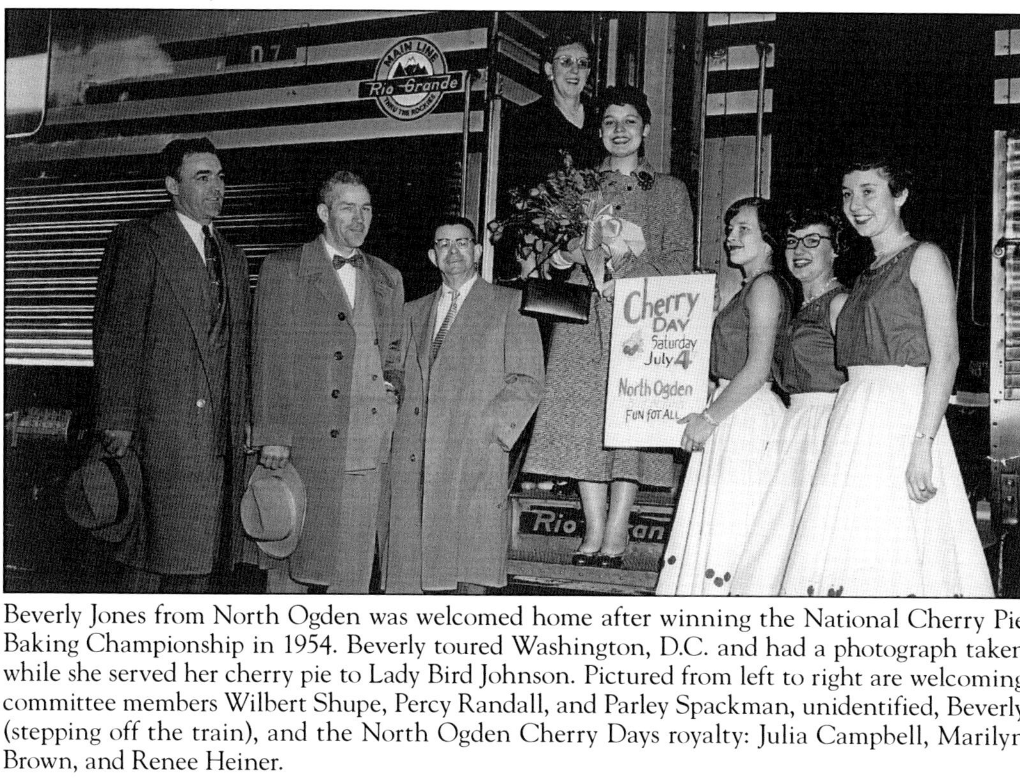

Beverly Jones from North Ogden was welcomed home after winning the National Cherry Pie Baking Championship in 1954. Beverly toured Washington, D.C. and had a photograph taken while she served her cherry pie to Lady Bird Johnson. Pictured from left to right are welcoming committee members Wilbert Shupe, Percy Randall, and Parley Spackman, unidentified, Beverly (stepping off the train), and the North Ogden Cherry Days royalty: Julia Campbell, Marilyn Brown, and Renee Heiner.

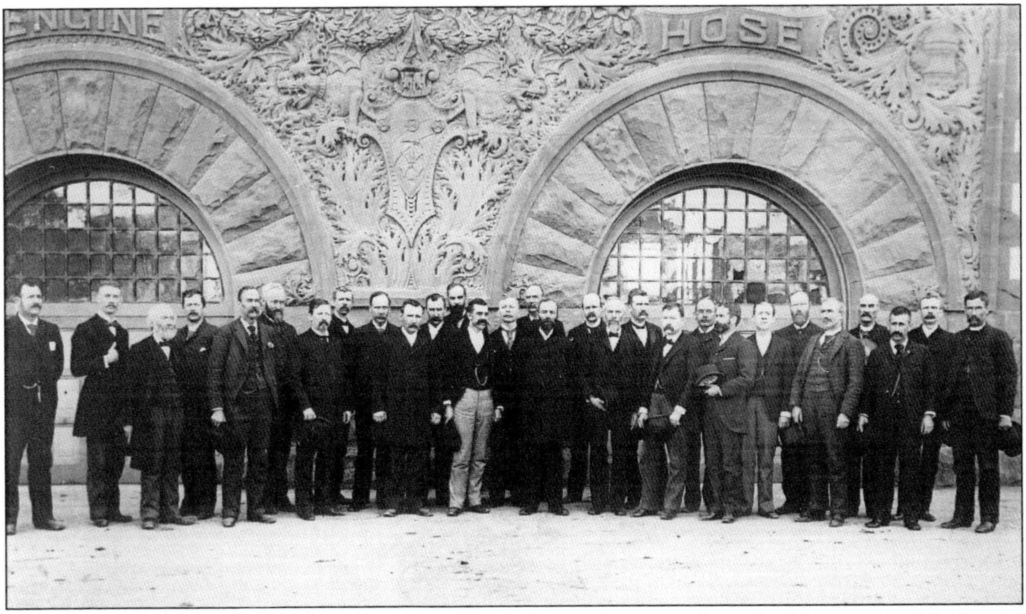

The Utah Legislative Assembly of 1892 is shown in front of an ornately crafted fire station. Nathaniel Montgomery, a prominent North Ogden citizen, was a member of the House. He is pictured in the center, 15th from the left. He served in the legislature for four years, helping to secure Utah's statehood. He later became a justice of the peace and the Weber County assessor.

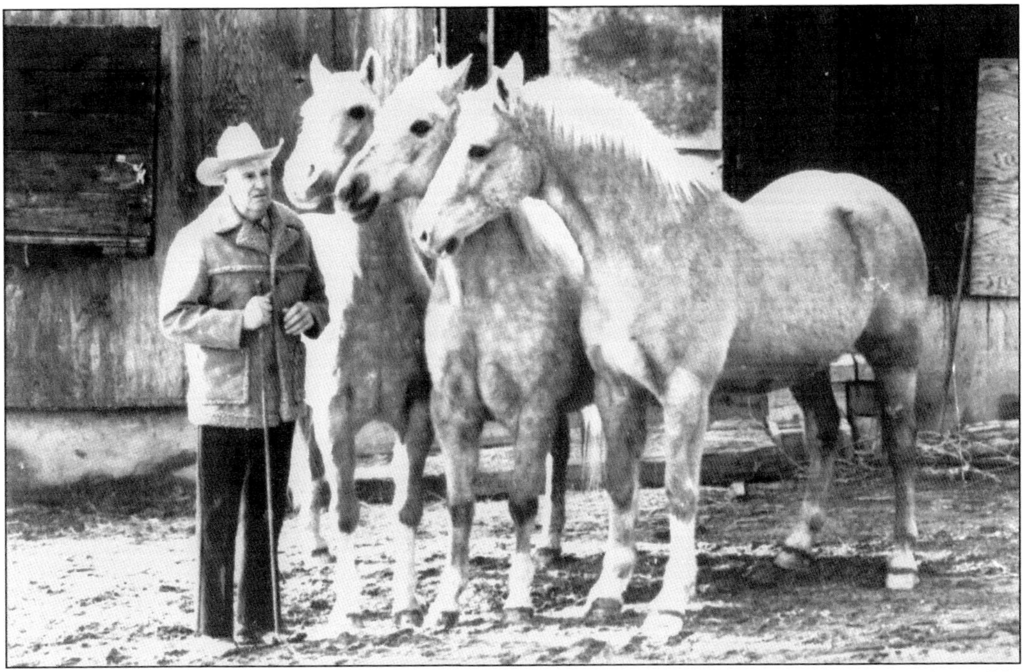

Al Warren was a world-renowned horse trainer, training three palomino horses to perform. He kept the horses in the barn during the day to keep their coats from fading. The horses were filmed in several movies and performed for many years throughout the western states. Al's granddaughter Collette rode a trained pony at the Ogden Pioneer Days rodeo. With Collette on its back, the pony walked on its hind legs, impressing the crowd by waving with a front hoof.

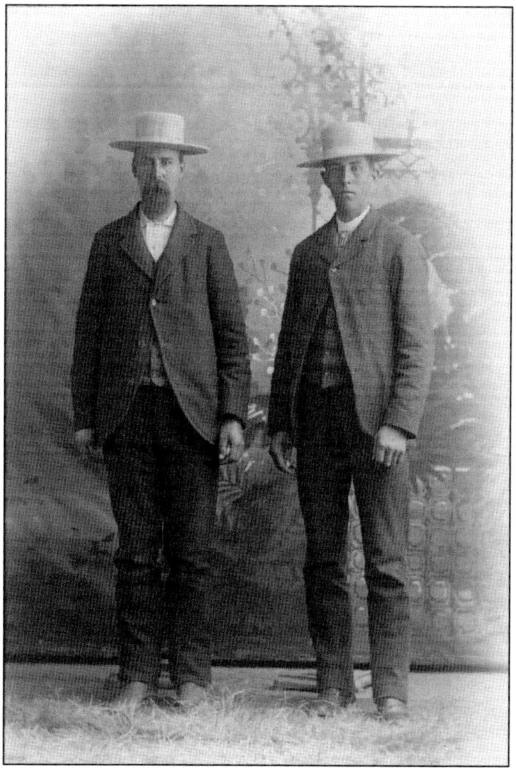

Best friends George A. Lyon and J. William Gibson posed for the photograph at left before heading off to training camp for World War I. They served in the armed forces from 1914 to 1918. Pvt. William L. Blaylock, pictured below, fought with the 168th Infantry in World War I. Blaylock was hospitalized in 1916 after being exposed to gas on the front lines of war in France. He was hospitalized again in July 1918, and was sent home after the war ended on November 11, 1918. Grand celebrations were held in North Ogden when Germany's surrender was announced.

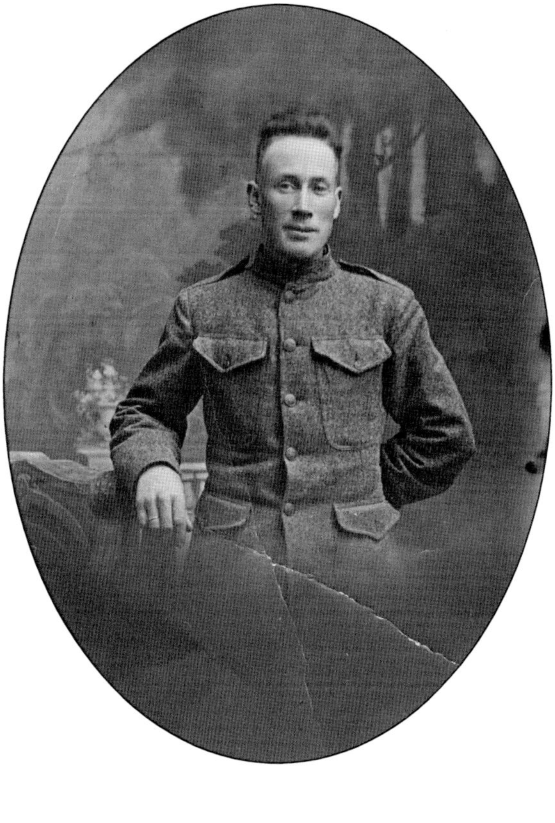

Annie Jessie Hall, born in 1885, served with the U.S. Nurse Corps during World War I. Known as the "Red Cross Girl," she is pictured here in 1910. After earning a nursing degree in Salt Lake City, she served as director of nurses at Dee Memorial and St. Mark's Hospitals. She enlisted and worked on the front lines during World War I in France from 1917 until late 1919.

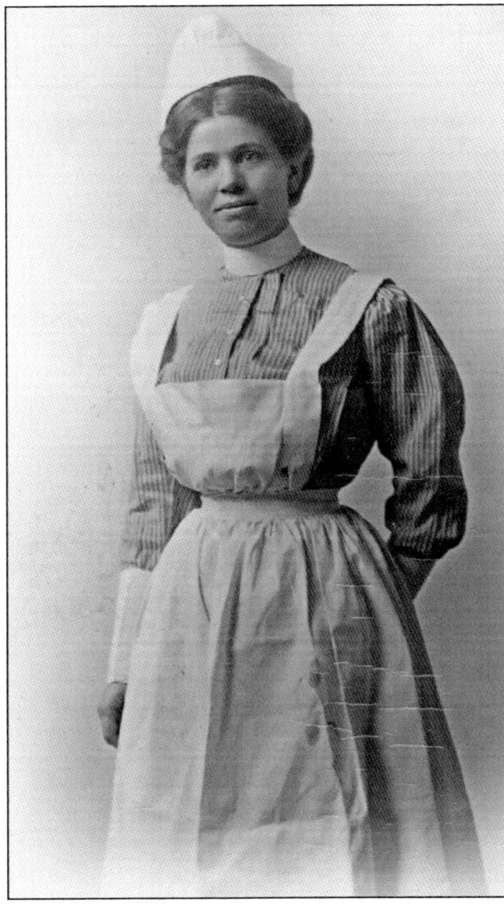

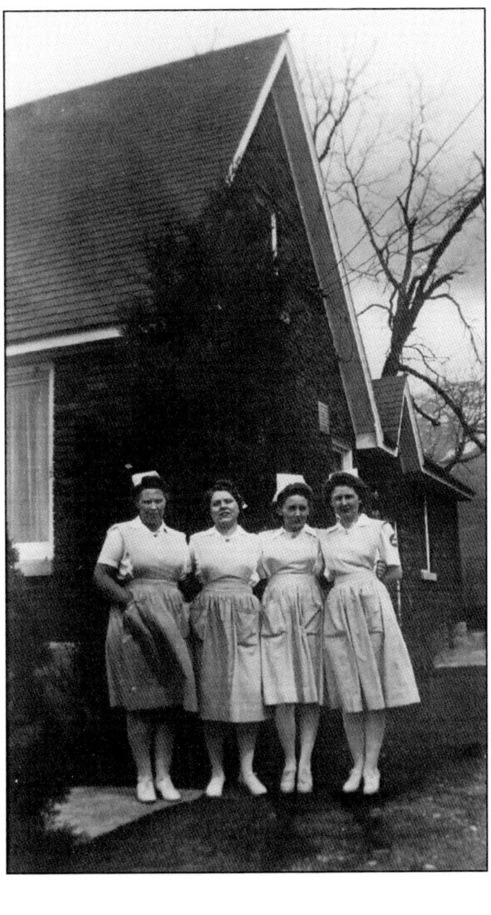

Bushnell General Military Hospital operated in Brigham City, Utah, from 1942 to 1946, treating wounded soldiers from World War II. Many citizens of northern Utah donated time, supplies, and money to support the facility. Pictured at left are Red Cross Nurses Aid volunteers, from left to right, Myrtle Layton, Norma Bailey, Agnes Berrett, and Naomi Randall in 1945. After the hospital closed, the buildings were utilized by the Intermountain Indian School until 1984.

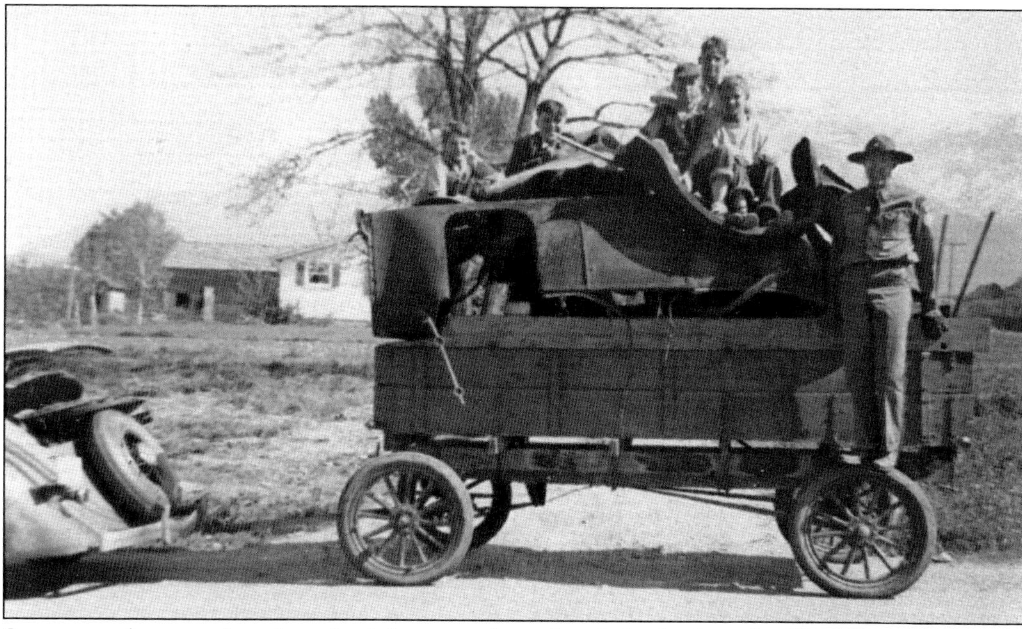

Scrap metal was gathered, melted down, and used to help further the World War II defense effort. A Boy Scout troop and their scoutmaster are pictured gathering metal. They are, from left to right, Bruce Ballif, Alton Mathie, Richard Layton, Karl Allred, Lavere "Bud" Campbell, and M. Nephi Manning, and unidentified scoutmaster. An old Ford coupe is pulling the trailer along 2600 North.

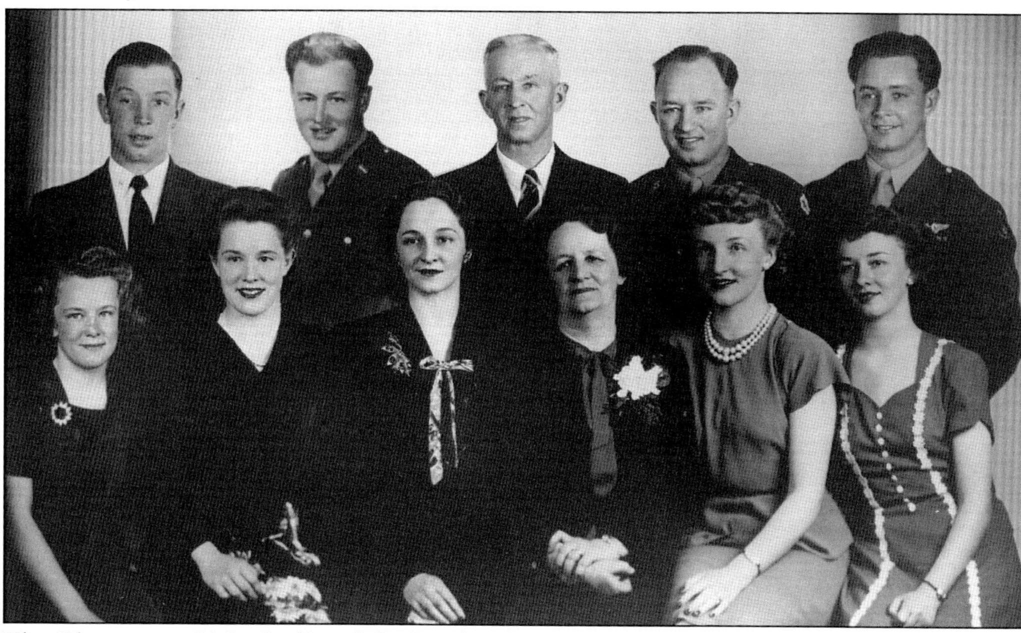

The Clarence and Myrtle (Ririe) Barker family gathered in 1945 for the memorial service of their brother and son, James, who was killed in World War II. They left a space for James's photograph to be added to their family portrait. Pictured from left to right are (first row) Elaine, Jetta, Florence, Phyllis, Myrtle (mother), Lorene, and Melba; (second row) Verle, James, Clarence (father), Wayne, and Marvin.

Eight

Business
Enterprise, Exchange, and Economy

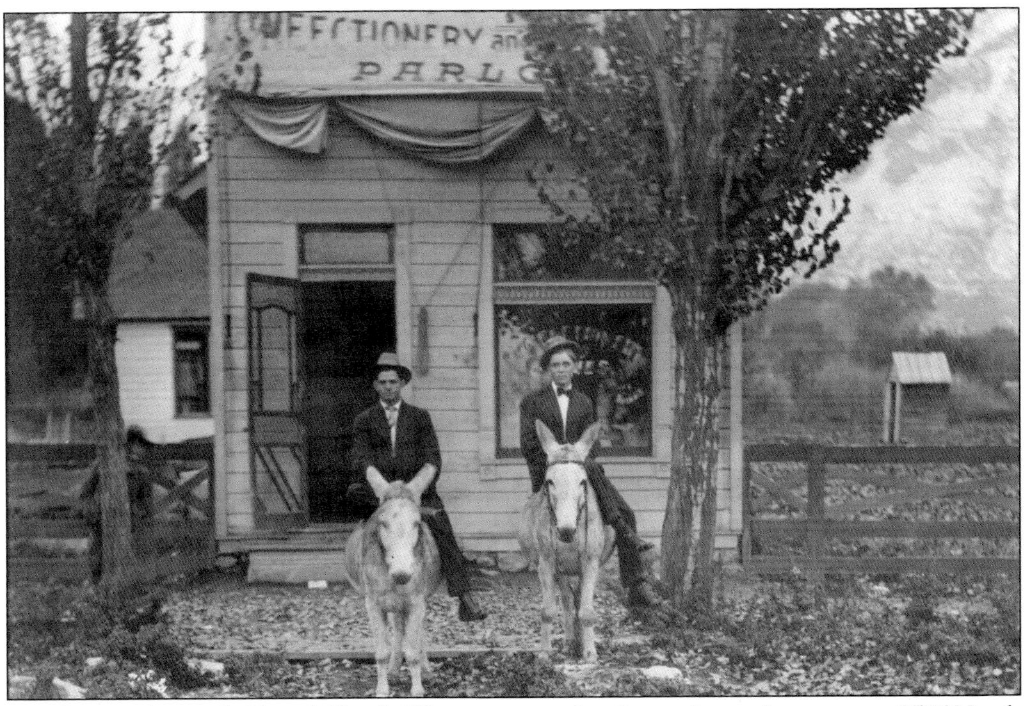

J. Parley Spackman (left) and Claude Ellis are pictured in front of a candy store near 2596 North 400 East in about 1910. They caught the donkeys and posed for a photograph. The donkeys were offspring from those used to pack ore from mines on the face of Ben Lomond Peak for Don Maguire, roaming free after mining subsided. Area youngsters with a sweet tooth affectionately called the confectionery "The Dump."

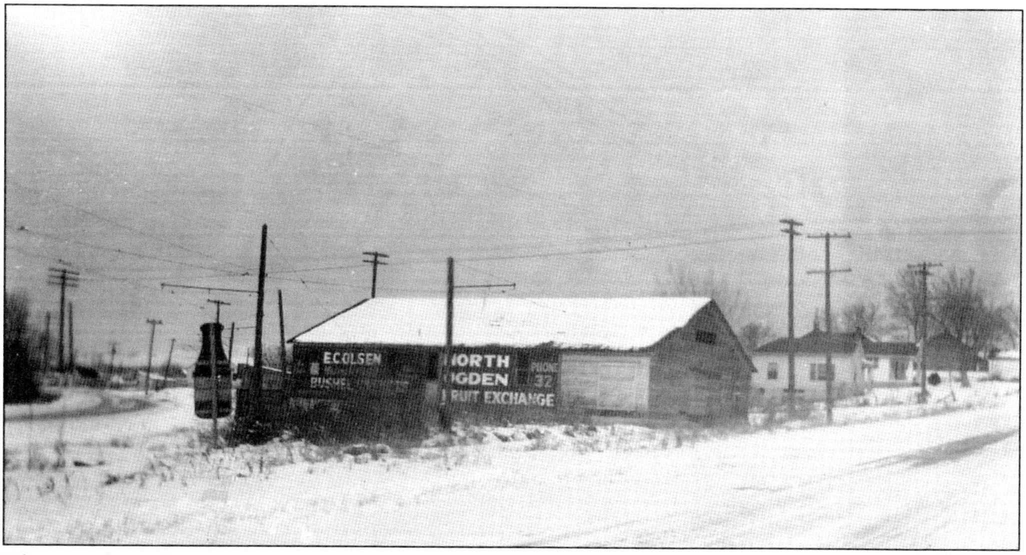

The North Ogden Fruit Exchange was formed in 1924, and continued as a profitable business for many years. The local fruit growers banded together to sell fruit to interstate markets, rather than competing with each other. In 1925, the organization shipped out 137 tons (15 railroad cars) of cherries, netting the company $20,758. In 1941, the membership divided and two organizations were formed. Shown above is the North Ogden Fruit Exchange packinghouse, which was located in the "V" of the intersection of 400 East and Pleasant View Drive. Pictured below is the organization in action. The workers are, from left to right, Harry Chandler, Claude Ellis (head showing), Lowell Shupe, Maurine Jackson, and LeRoy Snooks in 1938. After 1961, the Fruit Exchange disbanded, and many fruit growers then joined the Utah Fruit Growers Incorporated.

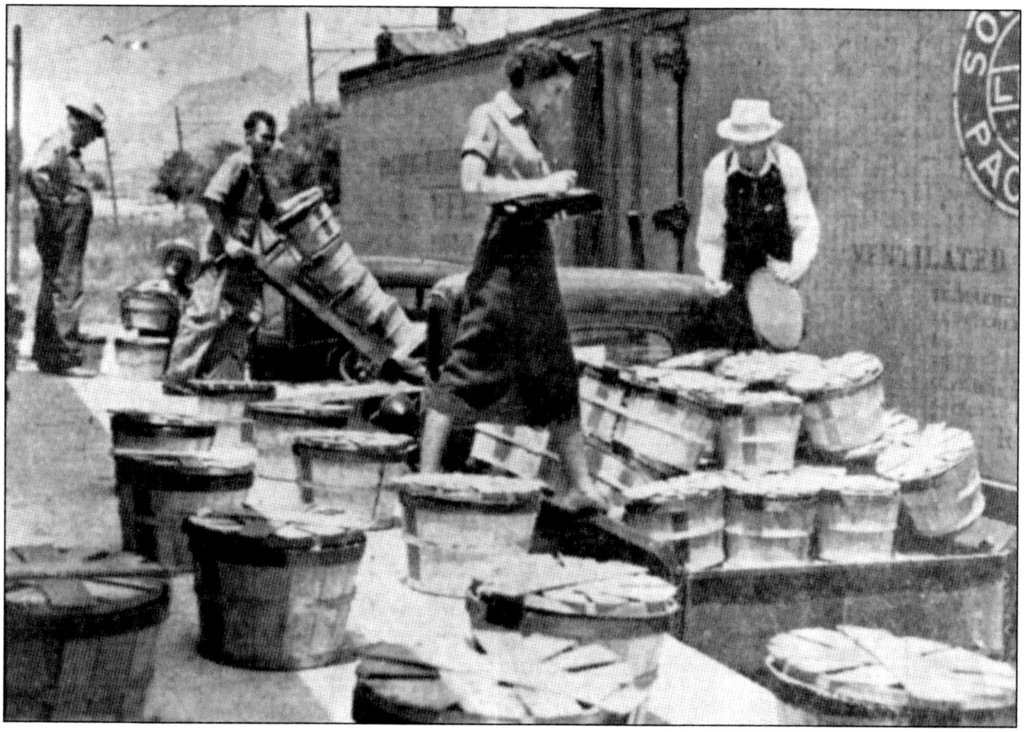

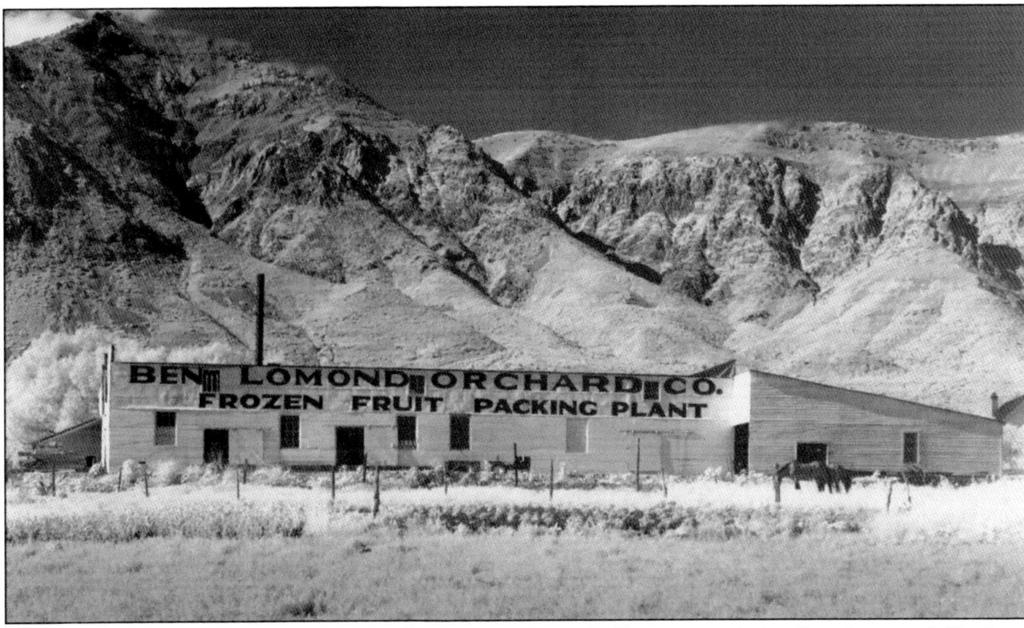

Edwin G. McGriff, James Storey, and Scott W. Campbell organized the Ben Lomond Orchard Corporation. A fruit-packing plant was constructed near 277 East Lomond View Drive. Refrigerated railroad cars were filled with boxes of peaches to be transported to the eastern states. As many as 75 carloads were shipped from North Ogden during peak season. The packinghouse was transformed into an ice-skating rink during the winter months.

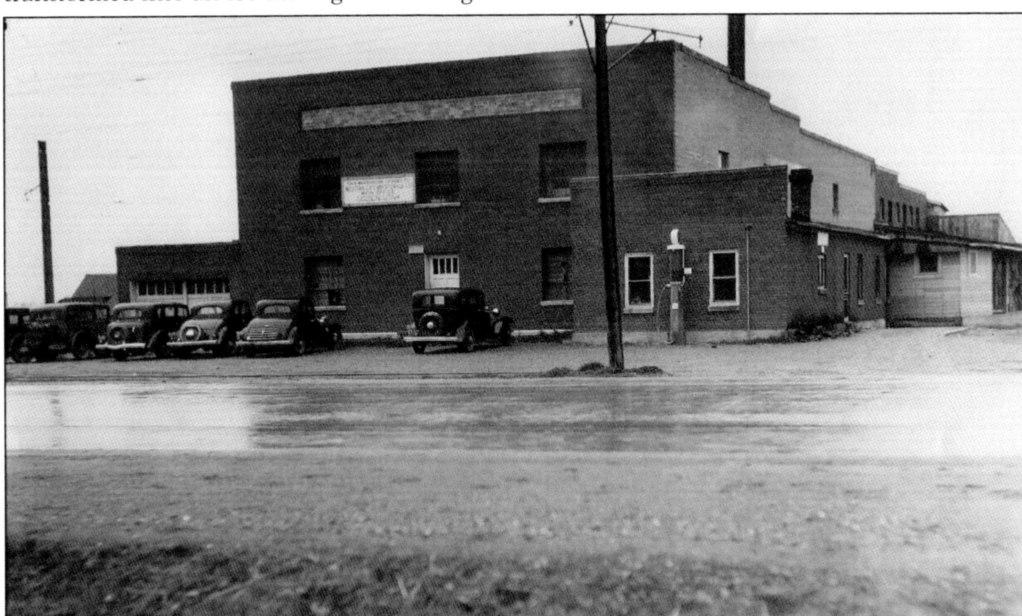

In 1900, the North Ogden Canning Factory was constructed near 2000 North 400 East. Newman Barker purchased the land for $125 from Gideon Alvord. Fruit was processed under the Utah Pride brand, and vegetables were labeled Magic Lake. The cannery employed many local people as well as selling the produce of the farmers, adding to the financial well-being of the area. The business was later owned by the Randalls.

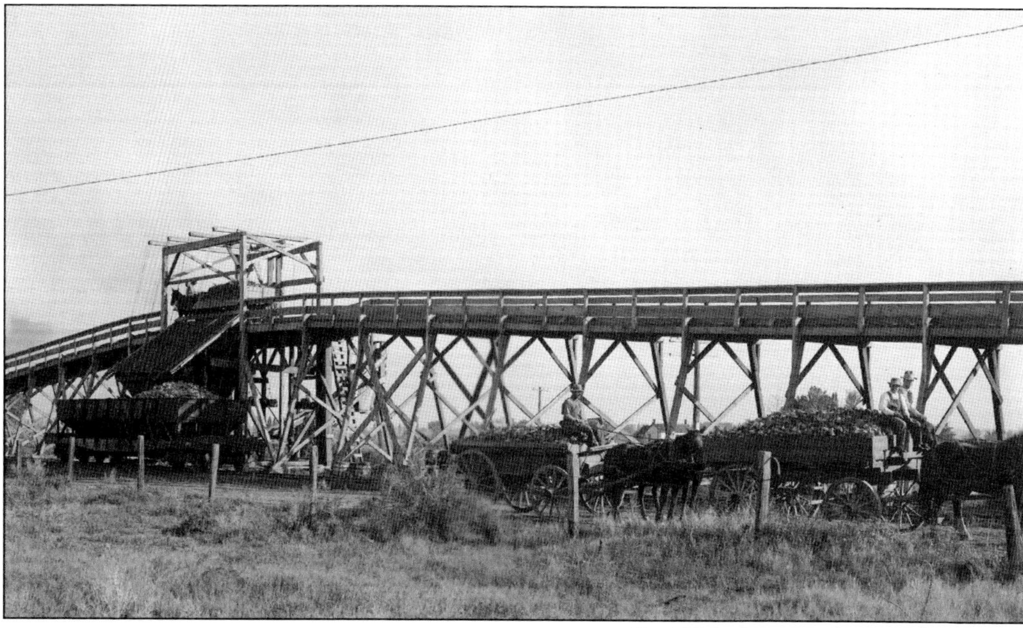

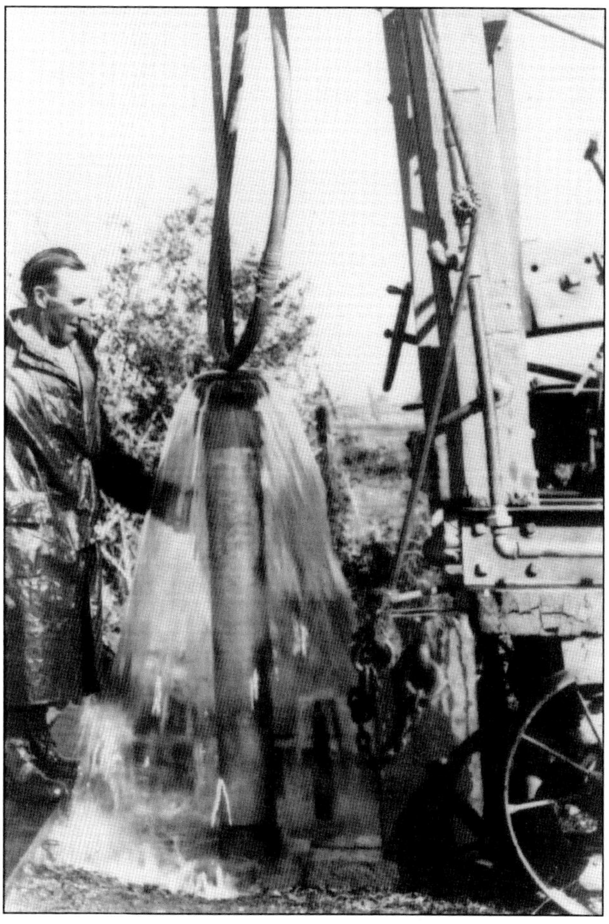

In 1900, the sugar beet industry began, and the beets were sold to the Amalgamated Sugar Company of Ogden. Entire families, including children, worked painstakingly during the growing season to thin the beets. The crops were cultivated, irrigated, and weeded until October, when they were dug and loaded on wagons to be taken to the North Ogden sugar beet dump, shown here in 1921 at 332 East Pleasant View Drive.

The first settlers of North Ogden collected their culinary water from springs and streams. In the early 1900s, well drillers tapped into underground water sources. Clyde Roylance is pictured here with a drilling rig. The earliest well drilling machines were horse-powered, and later steam and gas-powered engines were used. Early well drillers in the area included James Roylance Sr., Marlon Berrett, Scott Campbell, John Jones Jr., Henry Blaylock, and Newman Barker.

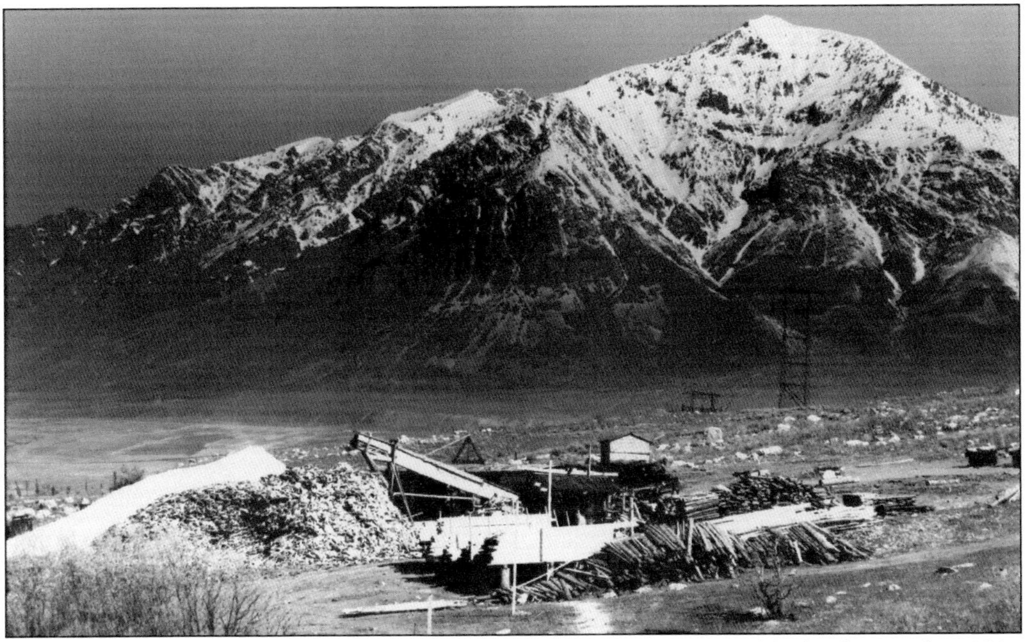

One of the first industries in North Ogden grew from the pioneers' need for lumber. In the 1850s, Samuel Ferrin and his sons constructed the first known sawmill in the area of Rice Creek Hollow. After an early spring flood washed the mill away, Robert Montgomery Jr. built another sawmill on Cold Water Creek. Daniel Hathaway and Moroni Campbell owned and operated a shingle mill near Rice Creek.

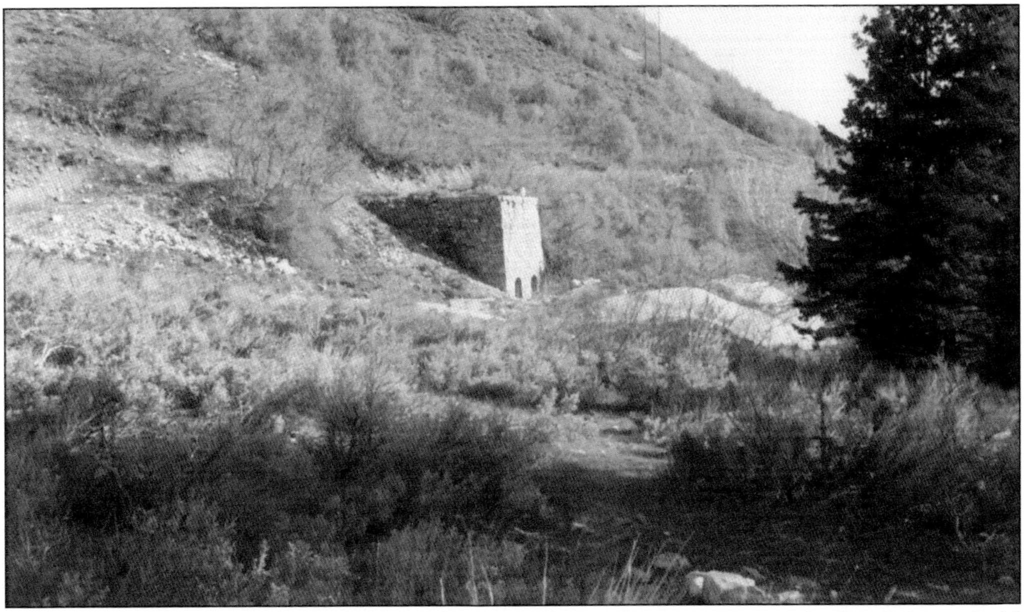

In 1890, Joseph Johnson and Charles, John and Johnnie Jones constructed a limekiln in Cold Water Canyon. Lime was used for brick mortar, plaster, as a disinfectant, and for whitewashing. The lime rock was blasted from surrounding hillsides, and then hauled to the kiln. The rock was placed in the kiln along with coal and burned to a powder. The photograph was taken in 1930, east of 2440 North Mountain Road.

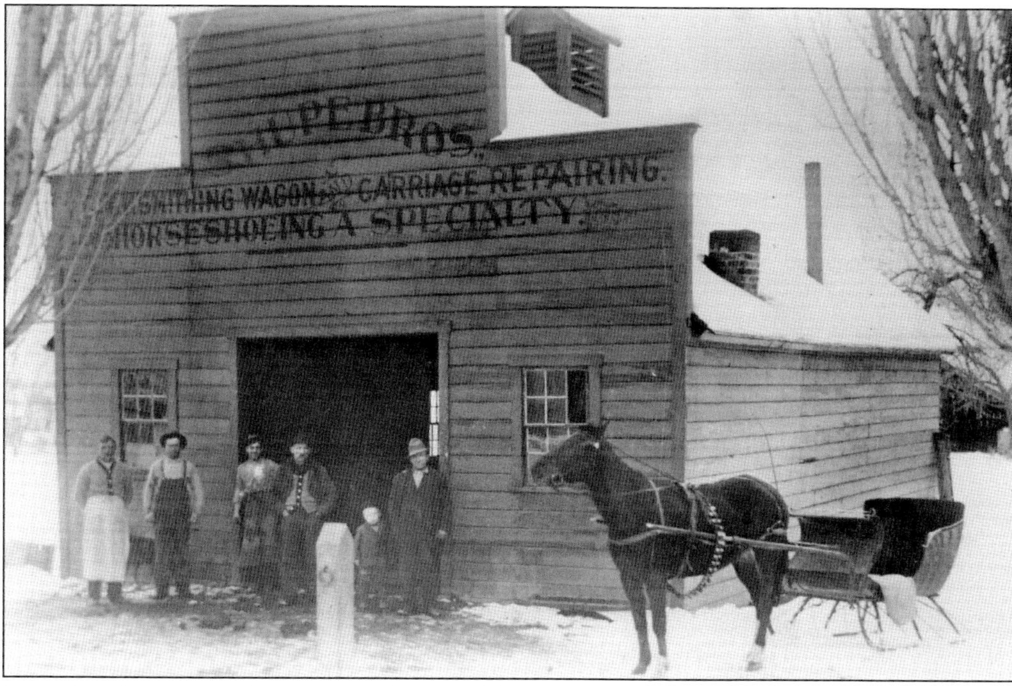

James W. Shupe started a family tradition of blacksmithing in his shop at 2565 North 400 East. He worked with his son and brothers, specializing in the repair of wagons. Pictured above is the Shupe Brothers blacksmith shop around 1910. Pictured from left to right inside the shop below are Parley G., David G., Thomas, and Isaac Shupe. Blacksmithing, one of the oldest known crafts, was necessary to repair wagons and machinery as well as making tools and horseshoes. The leather-aproned smith would use tongs to pull hot, glowing iron pieces out of the forge and hammer them into shape on an anvil, with sparks flying. A large bellows was pumped to make the fire hotter, and a tub of water was kept nearby to cool the red-hot metal, causing a loud hiss. These sights and sounds mesmerized passing schoolchildren.

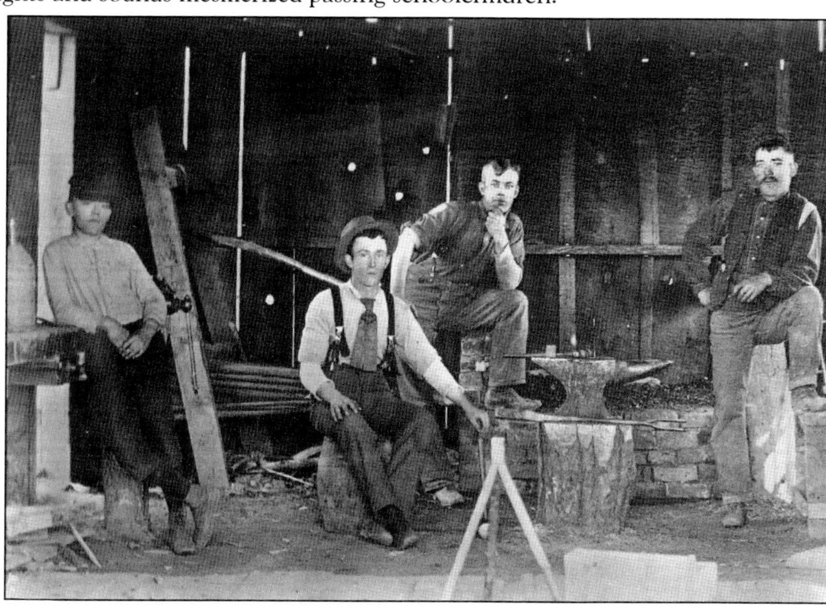

In 1881, John W. Rex, known as the "Merchant Prince," opened a general mercantile store at 2564 North 400 East, with a second floor dance hall. Shown from left to right around 1910 are Scott W. Campbell, B. E. Chatelain, John W. Rex, and an unidentified man. Signs on the store read, "Dried Apples Wanted at 6¢ per lb.," "Public Telegraph Station," and "Juvenile Instruction—$2 issued semi-monthly."

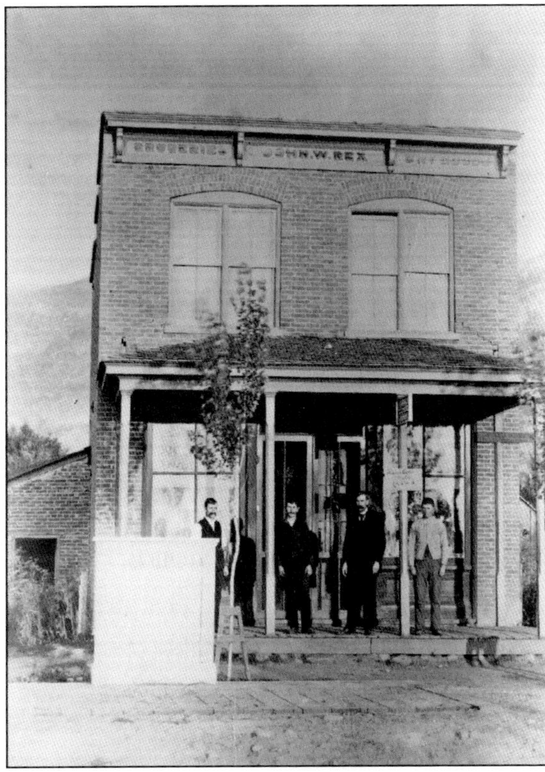

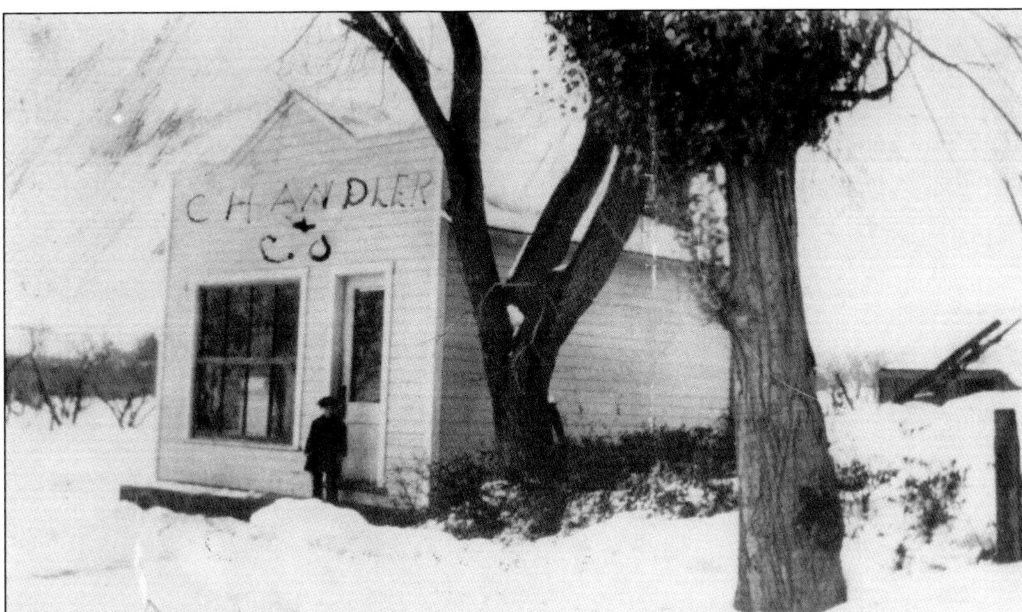

Harry Chandler opened a candy store around 1921 at 610 East 2650 North. Children from the nearby North Ogden Central School were his best customers. The store had a pot-bellied stove in the center and a display of tempting candy stretched across the west wall. Parents sometimes sent money for schoolchildren to buy sandwiches for their lunch, but the money was often spent on candy instead.

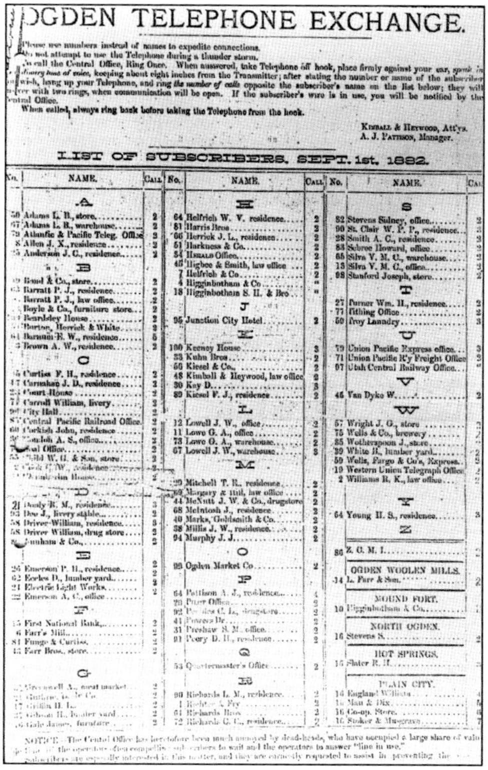

OGDEN TELEPHONE EXCHANGE.

Please use numbers instead of names to expedite connections.
Do not attempt to use the Telephone during a thunder storm.
To call the Central Office, Ring Once. When answered, take Telephone off hook, place firmly against your ear, *speak in ordinary tone of voice*, keeping about eight inches from the Transmitter; after stating the number or name of the subscriber you wish, hang up your Telephone, and ring *the number of calls* opposite the subscriber's name on the list below; they will answer with two rings, when communication will be open. If the subscriber's wire is in use, you will be notified by the Central Office.
When called, always ring back before taking the Telephone from the hook.

KIMBALL & HEYWOOD, Att'ys.
A. J. PATTISON, Manager.

LIST OF SUBSCRIBERS. SEPT. 1st. 1882.

No.	NAME.	CALL
	A	
50	Adams L. B., store	2
67	Adams L. B., warehouse	2
79	Atlantic & Pacific Teleg. Office	3
8	Allen J. X., residence	2
25	Anderson J. C., residence	2
	B	
[illegible]	Bond & Co., store	2
[illegible]	Barratt P. J., residence	2
[illegible]	Barratt P. J., law office	2
[illegible]	Boyle & Co., furniture store	2
[illegible]	Beardsley House	2
[illegible]	Burton, Herrick & White	2
61	Barnum E. W., residence	5
[illegible]	Brown A. W., residence	2
	C	
[illegible]	Curtiss F. H., residence	2
17	Carnahan J. D., residence	2
[illegible]	Court House	2
[illegible]	Carroll William, livery	2
[illegible]	City Hall	2
[illegible]	Central Pacific Railroad Office	2
60	Corkish John, residence	2
[illegible]	[illegible] A. S., office	2
[illegible]	[illegible] Office	2
55	[illegible] W. G. & Son, store	2
[illegible]	[illegible] W., residence	2
[illegible]	[illegible] House	2
	D	
21	Dooly R. M., residence	3
93	Dee J., livery stable	2
58	Driver William, residence	3
58	Driver William, drug store	3
[illegible]	Dunham & Co.	3
	E	
26	Emerson P. H., residence	2
62	Eccles D., lumber yard	2
21	Electric Light Works	2
22	Emerson A. C., office	2
	F	
15	First National Bank	2
6	Farr's Mill	2
81	Funge & Curtiss	2
13	Farr Bros., store	2
	G	
[illegible]	[illegible] A., meat market	2
[illegible]	Guthrie, [illegible] Co	2
17	Griffin H. L.	2
[illegible]	Gibson H., lumber yard	2
[illegible]	Gale James, furniture	2

No.	NAME.	CALL
	H	
64	Helfrich W. V. residence	2
81	Harris Bros	2
66	Herrick J. L., residence	2
51	Harkness & Co.	2
54	HERALD Office	2
45	Higbee & Smith, law office	2
7	Helfrich & Co	2
4	Higginbotham & Co	"
18	Higginbotham S. H. & Bro	"
	J	
95	Junction City Hotel	2
	K	
100	Keeney House	3
33	Kuhn Bros	2
56	Kiesel & Co.	2
48	Kimball & Heywood, law office	2
30	Kay D.	3
89	Kiesel F. J., residence	2
	L	
12	Lowell J. W., office	2
11	Lowe G. A., office	2
73	Lowe G. A., warehouse	2
67	Lowell J. W., warehouse	3
	M	
29	Mitchell T. R., residence	2
69	Margary & Hall, law office	2
44	McNutt J. W. & Co., drugstore	2
68	McIntosh J., residence	2
40	Marks, Goldsmith & Co.	2
38	Millis J. W., residence	2
94	Murphy J. J.	2
	O	
99	Ogden Market Co	2
	P	
64	Pattison A. J., residence	4
20	Post Office	2
92	Peebles C. L., drugstore	2
41	Powers Dr.	2
31	Preshaw S. M., office	2
91	Peery D. H., residence	2
	Q	
53	Quartermaster's Office	2
	R	
90	Richards L. M., residence	2
1	Richter & Fry	2
61	Richards Bros	3
72	Richards C. C., residence	2

No.	NAME.	CALL
	S	
82	Stevens Sidney, office	2
90	St. Clair W. P. P., residence	3
28	Smith A. C., residence	2
83	Sebree Howard, office	2
65	Silva V. M. C., warehouse	2
13	Silva V. M. C., office	3
98	Stanford Joseph, store	2
	T	
27	Turner Wm. H., residence	2
77	Tithing Office	2
50	Troy Laundry	3
	U	
79	Union Pacific Express office	3
71	Union Pacific R'y Freight Office	3
97	Utah Central Railway Office	"
	V	
46	Van Dyke W.	2
	W	
57	Wright J. G., store	2
75	Wells & Co., brewery	2
85	Wotherspoon J., store	[illegible]
39	White B., lumber yard	2
59	Wells, Fargo & Co's, Express	3
19	Western Union Telegraph Office	2
2	Williams R. K., law office	2
	Y	
64	Young H. S., residence	3
	Z	
86	Z. C. M. I.	2
	OGDEN WOOLEN MILLS.	
14	L. Farr & Son.	2
	MOUND FORT.	
10	Higginbotham & Co.	[illegible]
	NORTH OGDEN.	
16	Stevens S.	2
	HOT SPRINGS.	
16	Slater R. H.	[illegible]
	PLAIN CITY.	
16	England William	4
16	Maw & Dix	5
16	Co-op. Store	6
16	Stoker & Musgrave	7

NOTICE.—The Central Office has heretofore been much annoyed by dead-heads, who have occupied a large share of valuable time of the operators, often compelling subscribers to wait and the operators to answer "line in use." Subscribers are especially interested in this matter, and they are earnestly requested to assist in preventing the [illegible]

On September 1, 1882, the Ogden Telephone Exchange issued this list of Weber County area subscribers, as seen at left. There were only two telephones available in the area, one at the Sidney Stevens residence, and one at Hot Springs Resort, both listed as No. 16. Some hints for subscribers are listed at the top: "Do not attempt to use the Telephone during a thunderstorm; take Telephone off hook, place firmly against your ear, speak in an ordinary tone of voice, keeping about eight inches from the Transmitter." The first supervisor at the North Ogden Telephone Building Exchange was Rose Dean. Eliza (Hall) Higgins, in the photograph below, was one of the early switchboard operators. The operator connected each call manually by inserting a pair of phone plugs into the appropriate jacks on an exchange board.

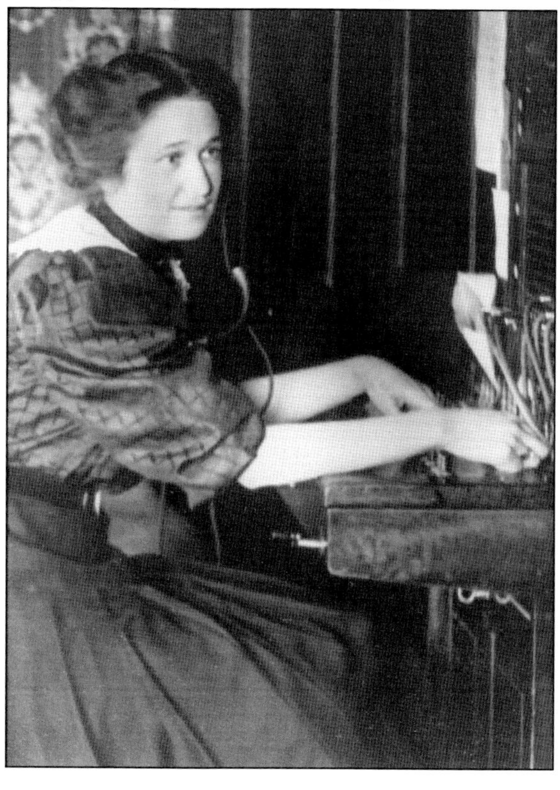

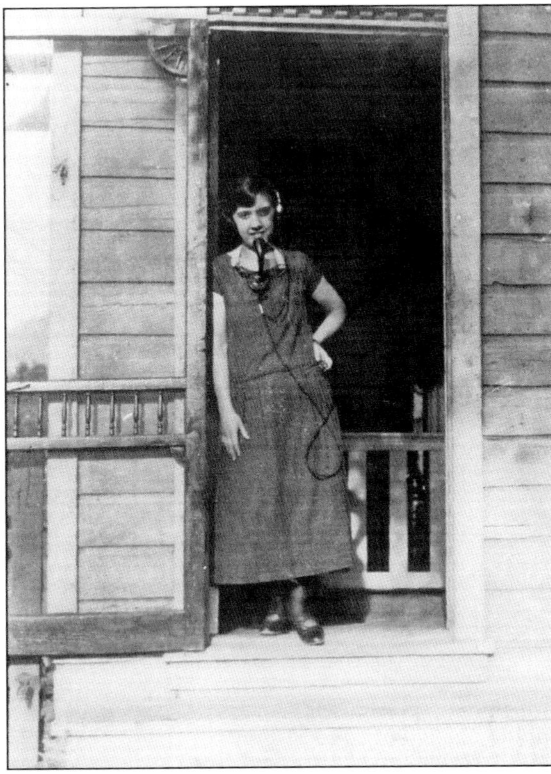

Rose (Toone) Thompson poses in the doorway of the North Ogden Telephone office in 1921 near 2596 North 400 East. The telephone operators worked three shifts per day to accommodate 24-hour telephone service to the residents. Customers came to the office to make calls from a telephone booth or pay their bill. Details of each call were recorded for billing purposes. A call to Ogden City cost 5¢.

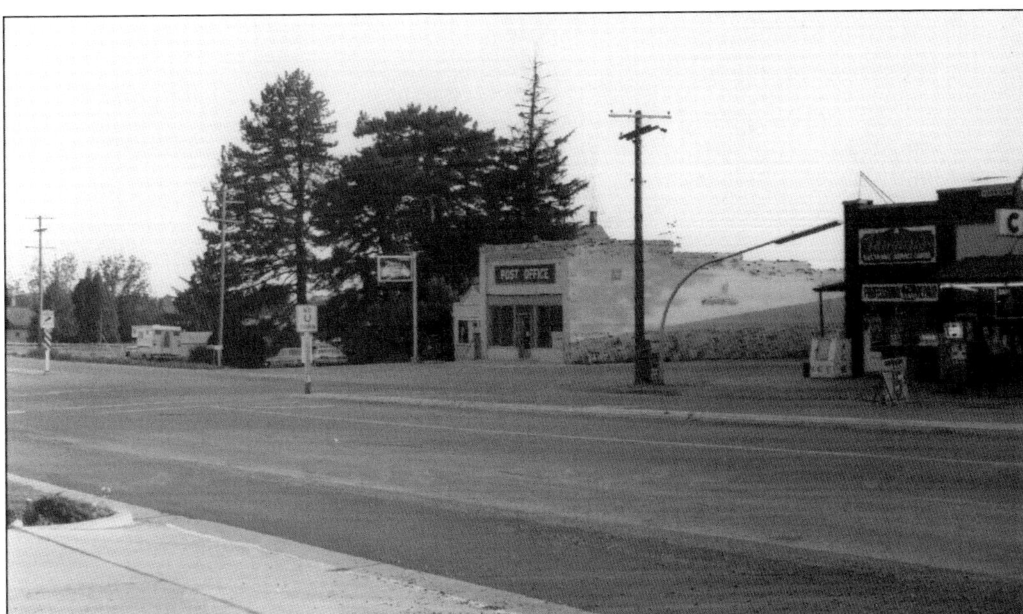

During pioneer times, North Ogden mail was collected randomly in Ogden City and distributed during public meetings. In 1864, a postal service was added to Sidney Stevens's store. Early postmasters included Henry Holmes, John W. Rex, Francis Dudman, John and George Dean, and William Ellis. The building shown at 2599 North 400 East was originally constructed in 1920, and was dedicated as a U.S. Post Office in 1961.

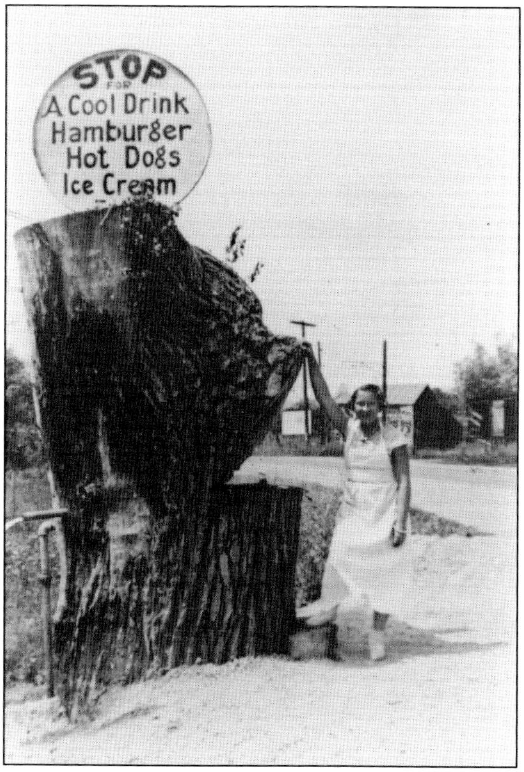

"The Stump," a North Ogden landmark, is located near Pleasant View Drive and 400 East. The stump of a cottonwood tree was moved into place by several teams of horses and chiseled into a giant drinking fountain in the early 1930s. The stump came from Frank Campbell's yard near 2580 North 400 East. A well was dug by George Roylance. Cool, refreshing artesian well water bubbled up through the stump, where many weary travelers have stopped for a drink. A sign made by Grant Huband was placed on top to advertise Joseph Ballif's hamburger stand. Joe's daughter Jennabee is pictured at left in 1936. The original stump deteriorated over time, as shown below in the early 1950s.

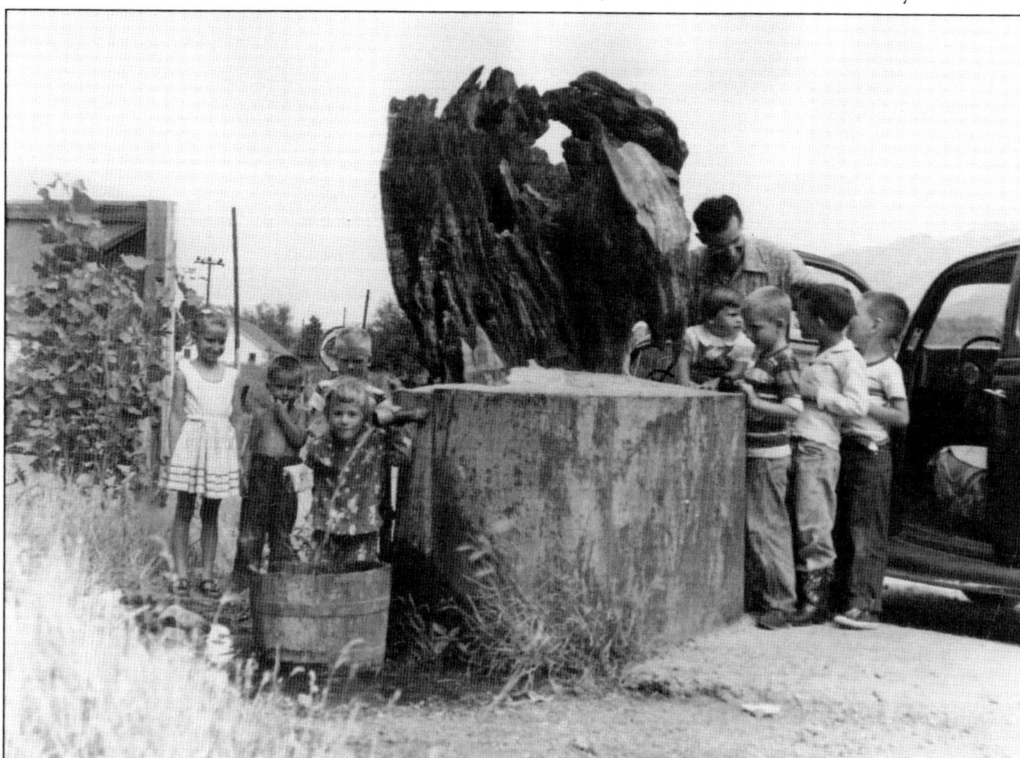

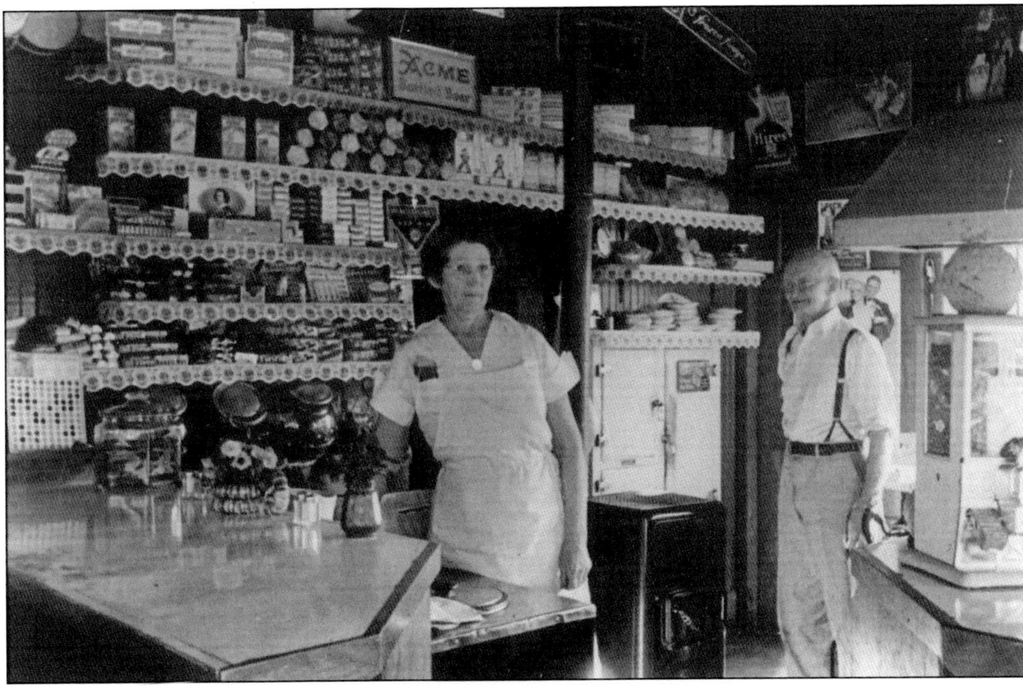

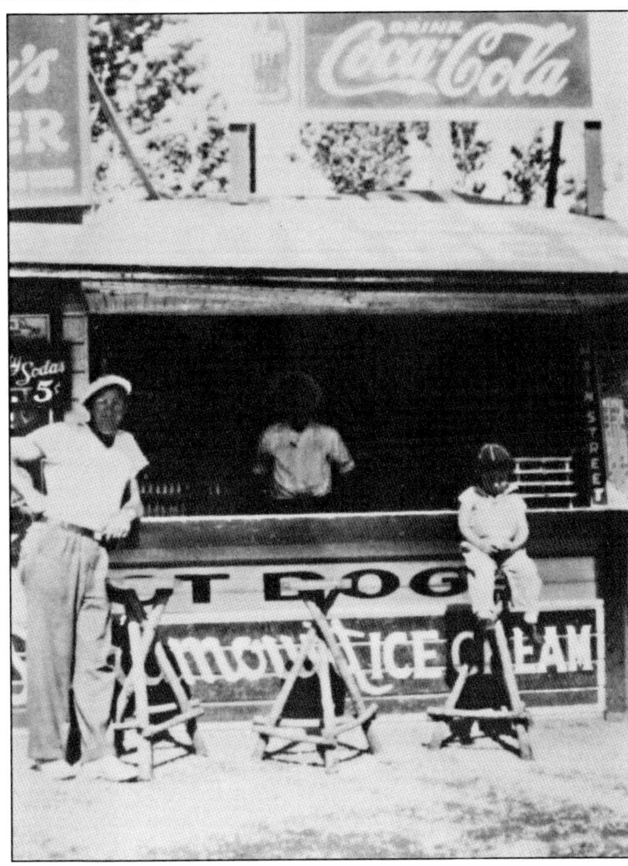

Above, Joseph F. Ballif Sr. and his wife, Florence, are working in their hamburger and hot dog stand, "The Stump," in 1935. Joe's famous burgers were fried on a pat of butter and sold for 5¢ each. A cup of coffee was also 5¢, and came with free refills. After moving his business across the street, as pictured at right, Joe and his wife lived in an apartment at the back of the store. They operated the hamburger stand at that location for eight more years.

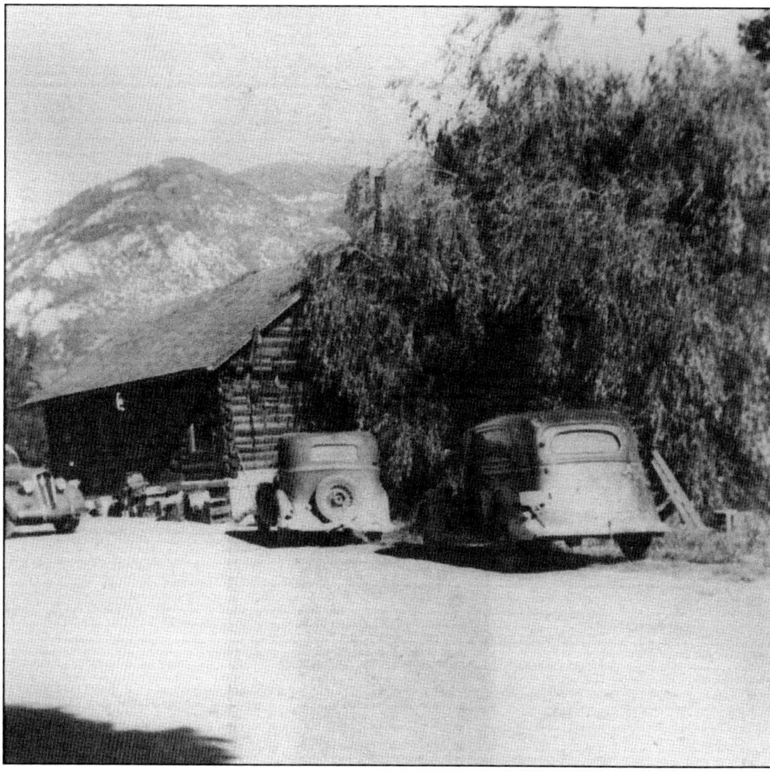

In 1932, Ira Lowder built a log cabin store at 515 East 2650 North. Ira and his wife, Theresa, operated a grocery store, a barbershop, and a beauty salon at this location. The store also had a meat-cutting room and cold storage lockers. Kenneth G. and Alice (Shaw) Burton bought the store in 1947. A newer store was constructed to the east of the cabin in 1960. A day care business now occupies the newer building.

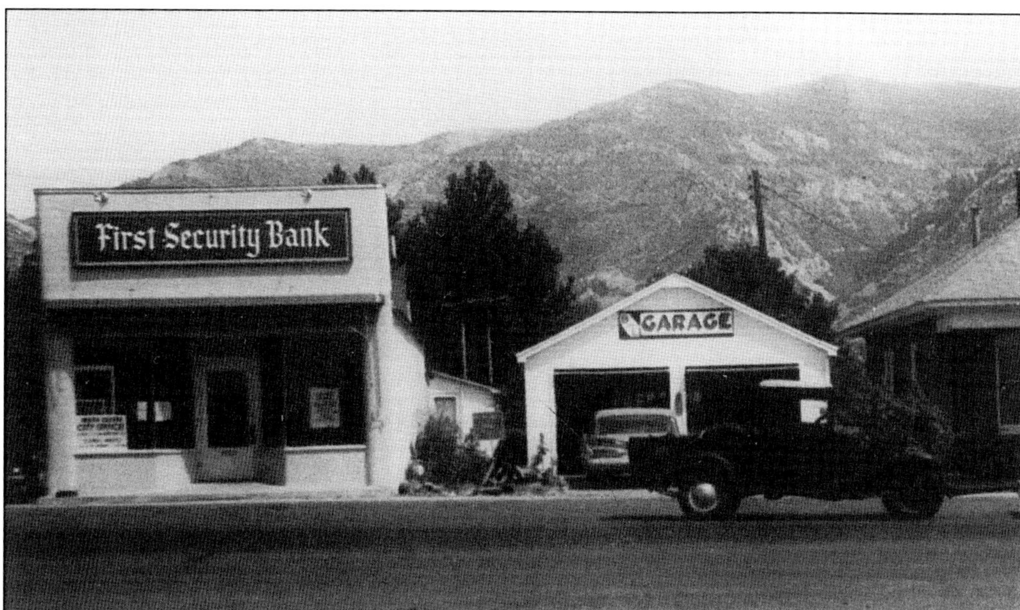

In 1926, the building at 626 East 2600 North that housed George Dean's printing business was moved to 2596 North 400 East. There Parley Spackman operated a thriving grocery store for 10 years, until Earl Randall bought the store. In the early 1940s, it was purchased by First Security Bank, with space inside utilized for North Ogden City Council meetings. Wells Fargo Bank is now located at this site.

Sidney Stevens constructed a general merchandise store in 1867, one of the first brick buildings in North Ogden. A dance hall and a public library were added on the top floor. His business block at 2599 North 400 East burned down in 1885. The fire was difficult to contain because ammunition was stocked inside. The store was rebuilt and housed businesses for over 100 years.

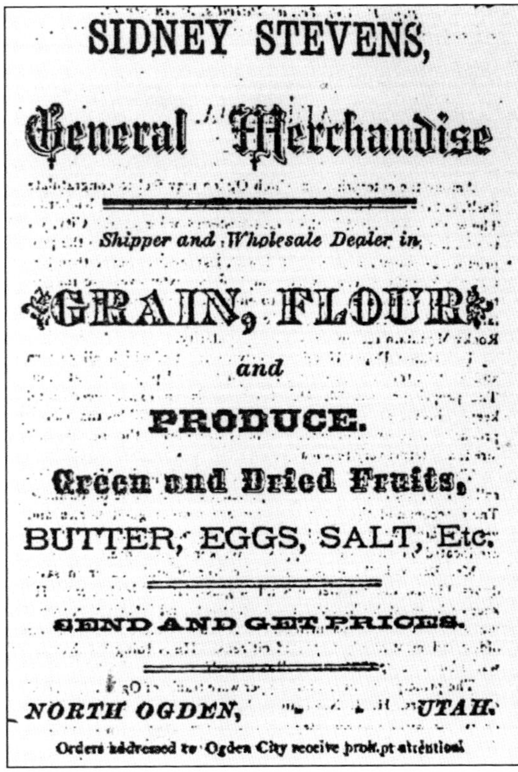

SIDNEY STEVENS,

General Merchandise

Shipper and Wholesale Dealer in

GRAIN, FLOUR

and

PRODUCE.

Green and Dried Fruits,

BUTTER, EGGS, SALT, Etc.

SEND AND GET PRICES.

NORTH OGDEN, UTAH.

Orders addressed to Ogden City receive prompt attention.

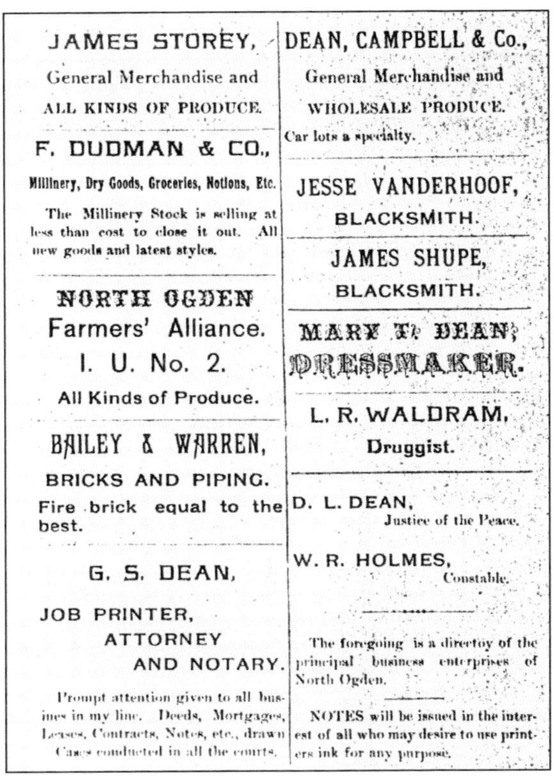

JAMES STOREY,

General Merchandise and

ALL KINDS OF PRODUCE.

F. DUDMAN & CO.,

Millinery, Dry Goods, Groceries, Notions, Etc.

The Millinery Stock is selling at less than cost to close it out. All new goods and latest styles.

NORTH OGDEN

Farmers' Alliance.

I. U. No. 2.

All Kinds of Produce.

BAILEY & WARREN,

BRICKS AND PIPING.

Fire brick equal to the best.

G. S. DEAN,

JOB PRINTER,

ATTORNEY

AND NOTARY.

Prompt attention given to all busines in my line. Deeds, Mortgages, Leases, Contracts, Notes, etc., drawn Cases conducted in all the courts.

DEAN, CAMPBELL & Co.,

General Merchandise and

WHOLESALE PRODUCE.

Car lots a specialty.

JESSE VANDERHOOF,

BLACKSMITH.

JAMES SHUPE,

BLACKSMITH.

MARY T. DEAN,

DRESSMAKER.

L. R. WALDRAM,

Druggist.

D. L. DEAN,

Justice of the Peace.

W. R. HOLMES,

Constable.

The foregoing is a directoy of the principal business enterprises of North Ogden.

NOTES will be issued in the interest of all who may desire to use printers ink for any purpose.

George S. Dean became an attorney in 1884 and formed a law practice in North Ogden, taking care of most of the legal work for area citizens. In 1887, he bought one of the first commercial printing presses in the Ogden area and published a newspaper called *Notes*. The paper published a directory of North Ogden businesses in 1894, as shown at left. George's printing press enabled him to establish a lucrative business.

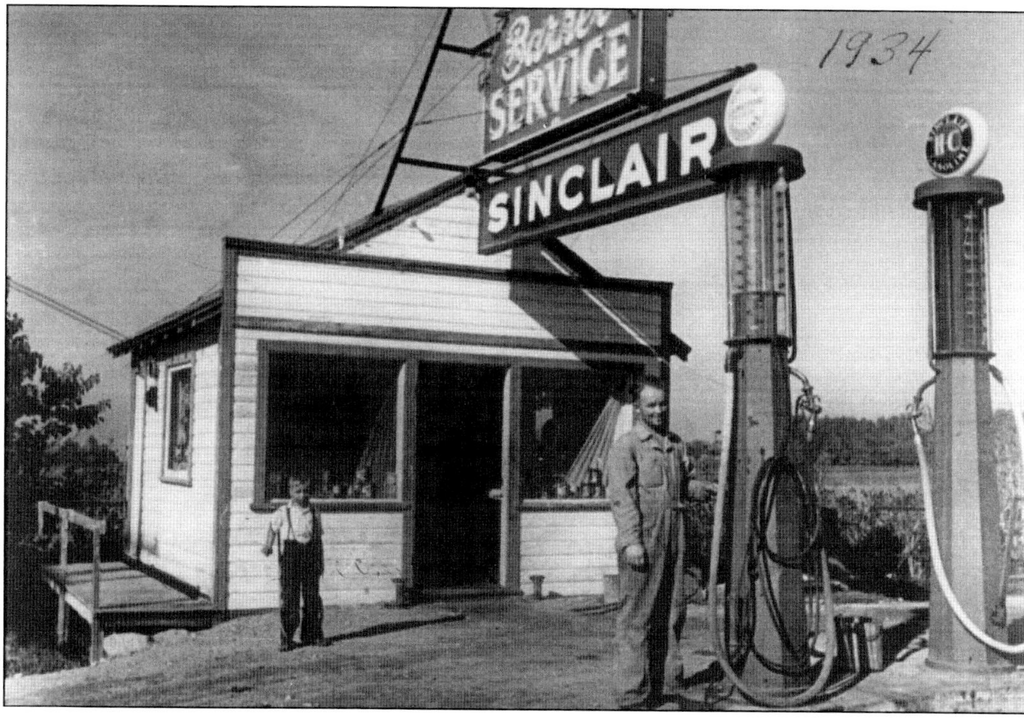

The Barker Service Station was temporarily located at 2589 North 400 East, and provided service to many loyal customers beginning in 1928. Above, a young Bob Shupe and Wayne Barker are shown at the station in 1934. The business returned to the original location at 2603 North 400 East, seen below at the left side of photograph. Wayne, his brother Verle, and Ken Wilson pumped gasoline, checked oil and tires, cleaned windows, and gave many children chewing gum for about five decades. The business performed this full-service treatment until its closure, never giving in to the trend of self-service stations.

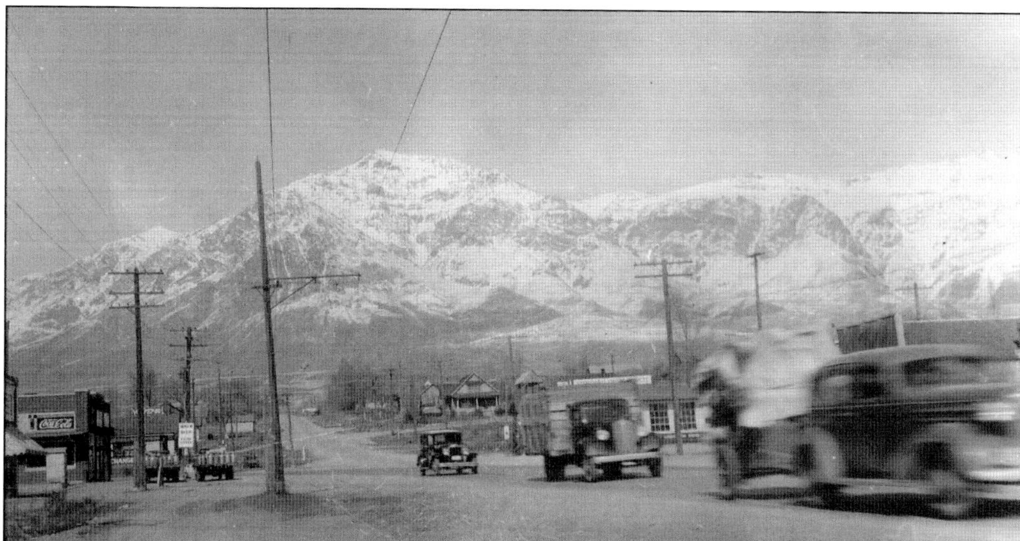

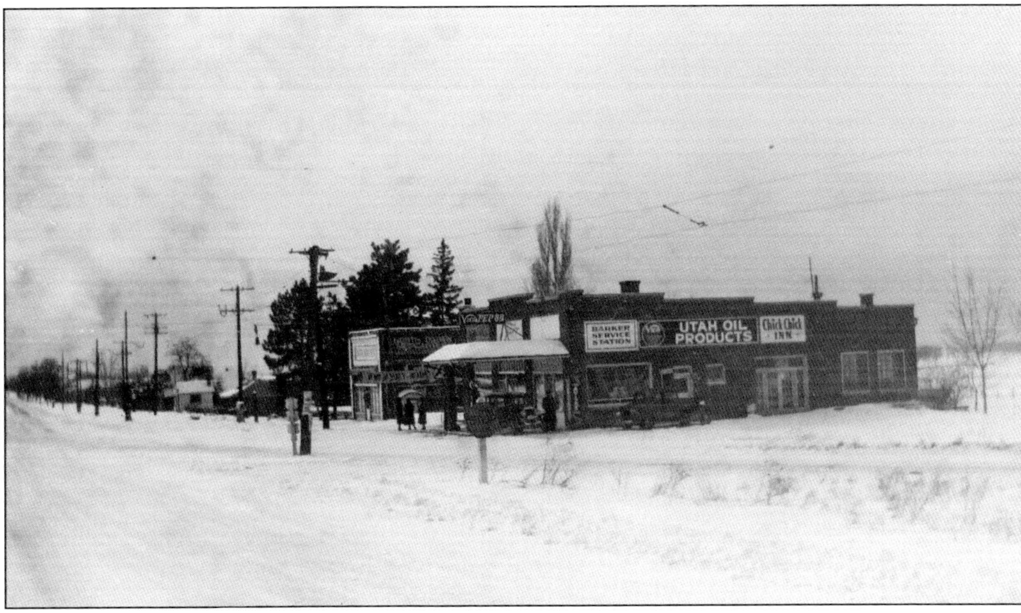

In 1936, Wayne Barker developed the Chick Chick Inn at the back of his service station. As the business thrived, he expanded the restaurant and menu, added a dance floor with a live orchestra, and served draft beer. There were also punchboards and two one-armed bandits (more commonly known as slot machines), making the hangout notoriously popular. The photograph above also shows his other service station, the small white building in the distance to the left, and the North Ogden Mercantile next door. Pictured below is a price list sign that hung in the Chick Chick Inn.

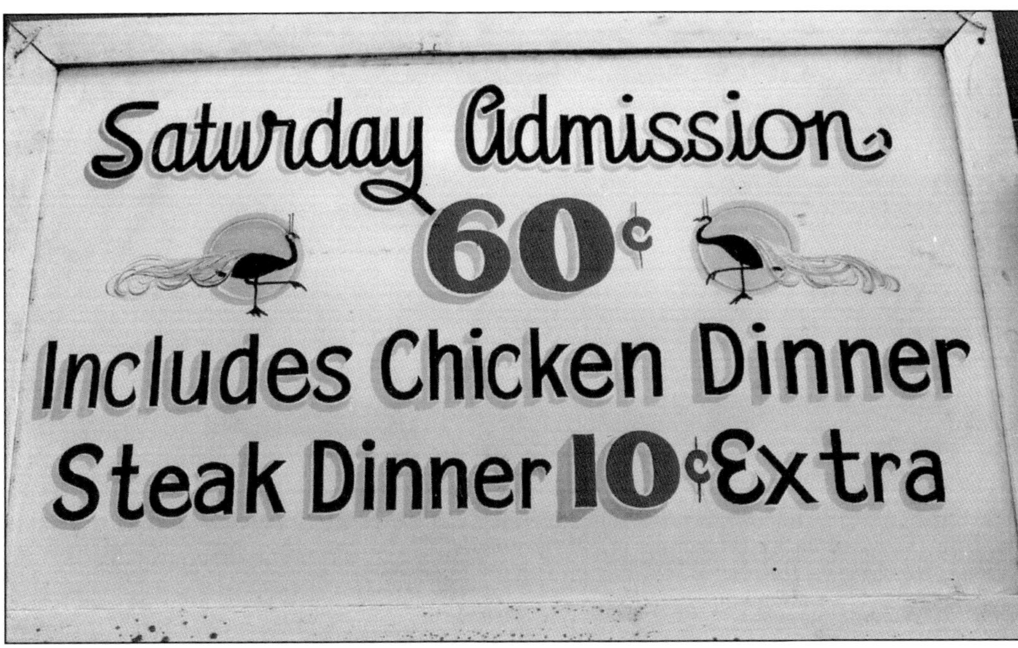

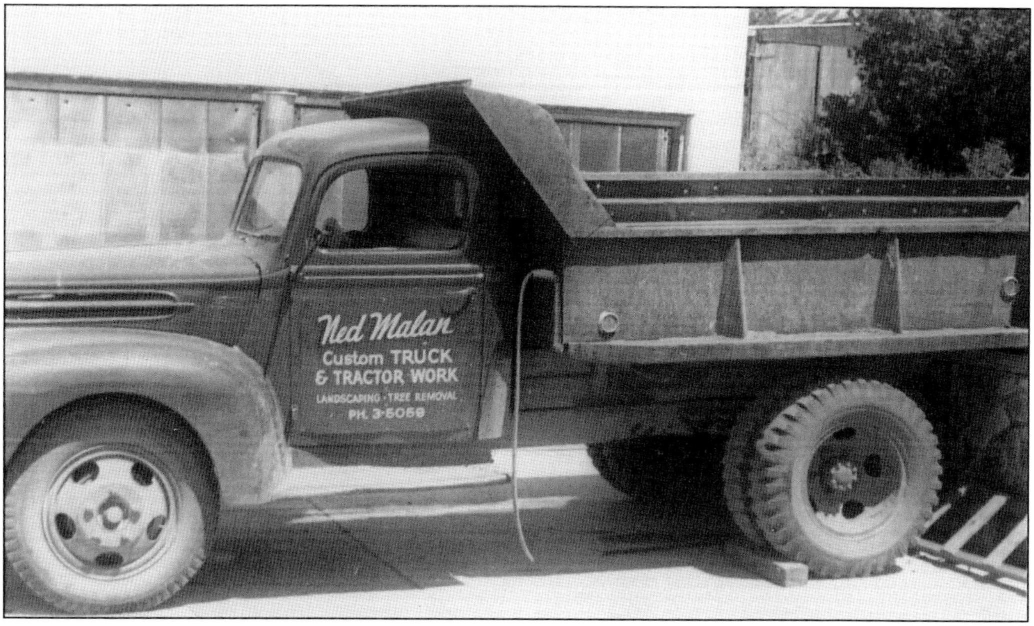

Ned Malan's "Custom Truck and Tractor Work" truck was a 1947 Ford. The business was started in 1950, hauling topsoil and working on landscape projects. When Ned was building a house and unable to find an excavator, he bought the necessary equipment to do the work himself, which gave him the experience to expand his business. He also contracted for demolition work and pipe installation.

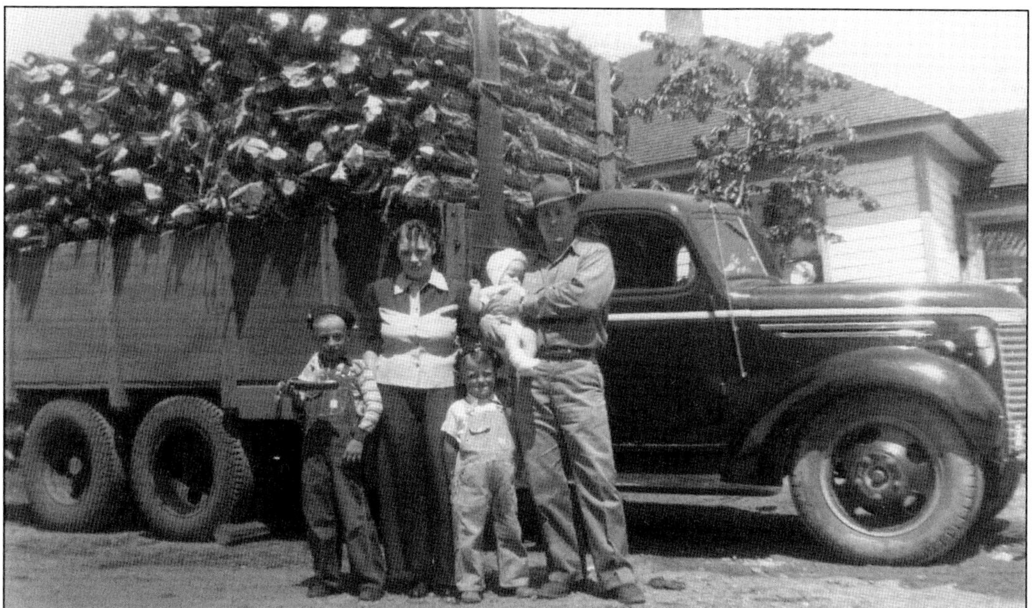

Ott L. Price and his wife Marvel brought the transportation industry to North Ogden. In 1937, they began trucking cedar posts and fence poles from Monticello and coal from Carbon County to be sold to buyers in North Ogden and surrounding communities. The family business flourished in North Ogden for many years. Pictured are Marvel and Ott with their sons, Harold, Lee, and James.

Nine

YESTERDAY AND TODAY
HERETOFORE AND HENCEFORTH

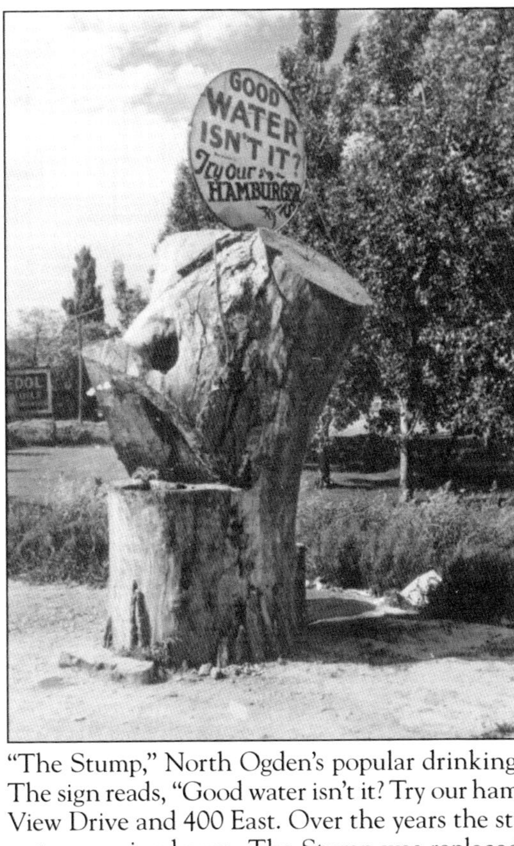

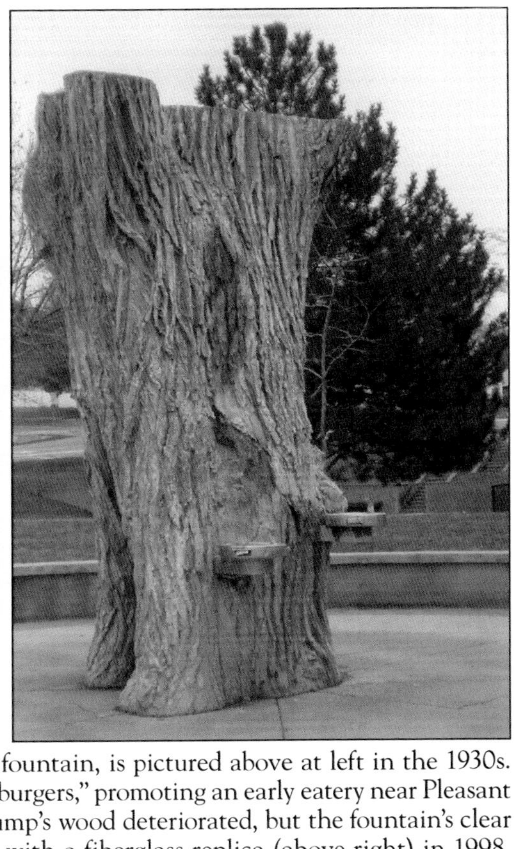

"The Stump," North Ogden's popular drinking fountain, is pictured above at left in the 1930s. The sign reads, "Good water isn't it? Try our hamburgers," promoting an early eatery near Pleasant View Drive and 400 East. Over the years the stump's wood deteriorated, but the fountain's clear water remained pure. The Stump was replaced with a fiberglass replica (above right) in 1998, surrounded by the city's beautiful Centennial Park. The park's land and water rights were donated by Verle and Rubie Barker.

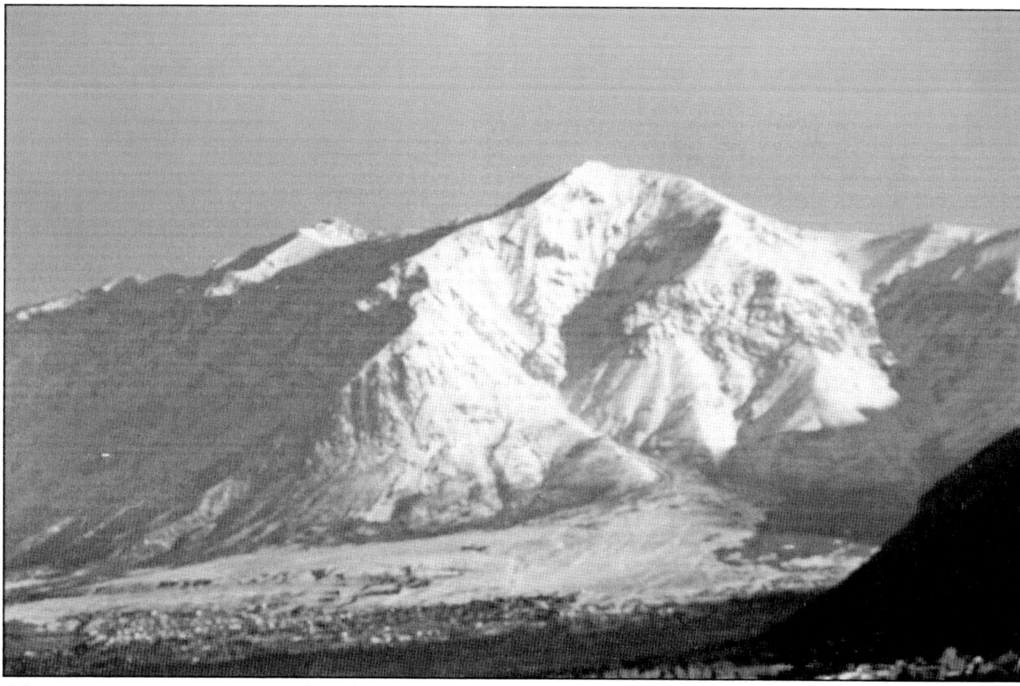

Above, a snowy Ben Lomond Peak looms in the early morning sunrise. The undated photograph, which is taken from about 600 North Harrison Boulevard, is credited to Darren Gathermen. The "face on the mountain" can be seen at the center top of the peak in both photographs. The "face" is often referred to as an "elf" or a "pixie." In the modern image below, Ben Lomond Peak remains unchanged through the years, with the exception of the ever-expanding housing areas in the foothills. The land in the foreground also shows more development.

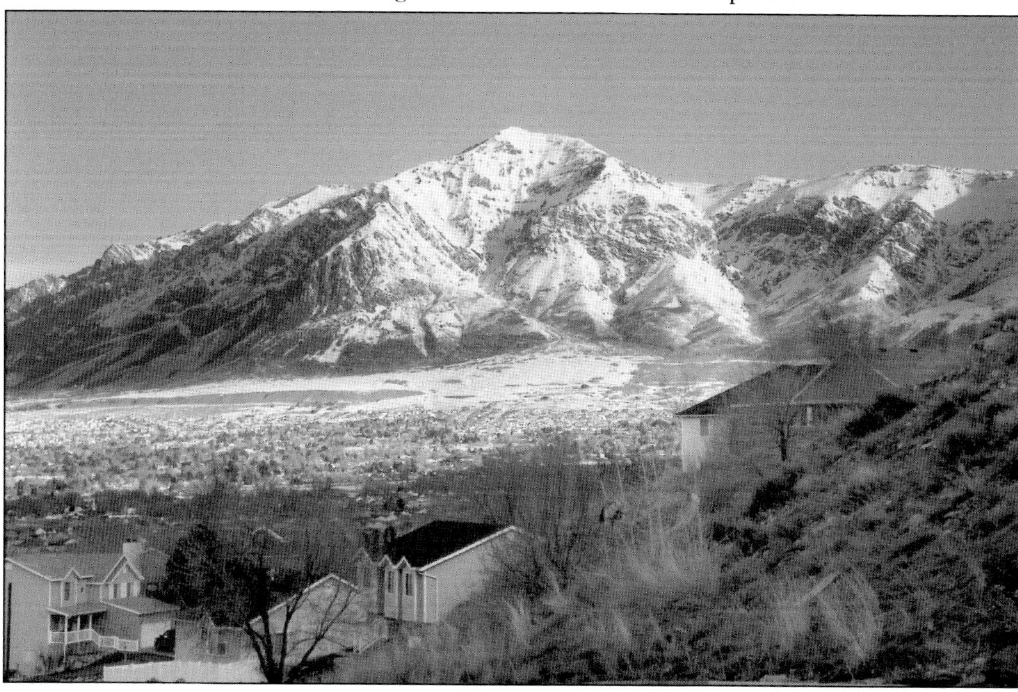

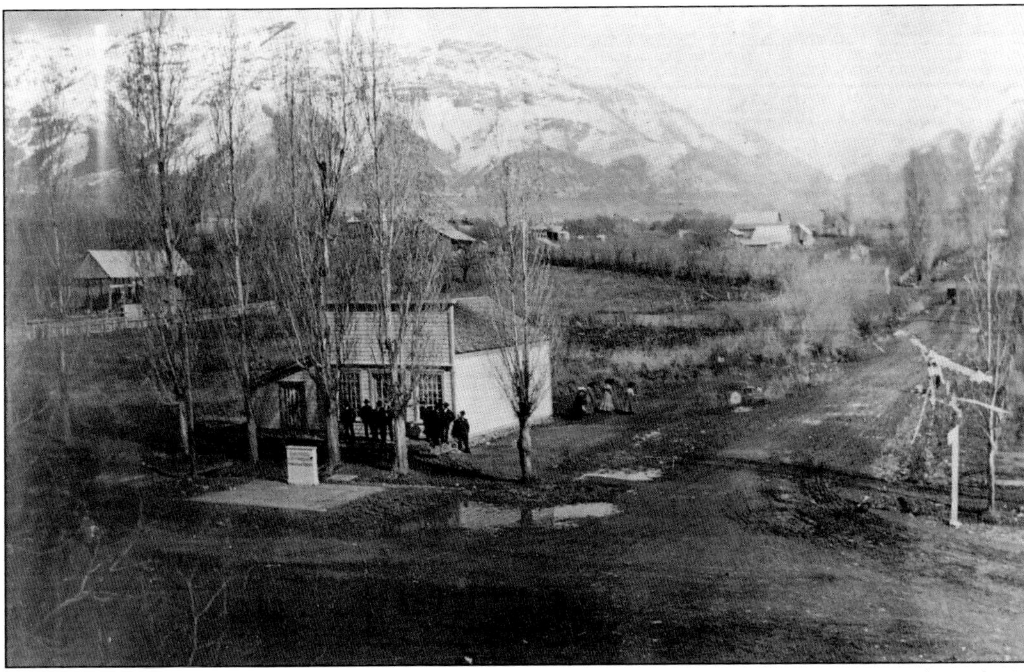

The James Storey Store is shown above in 1904 on the northeast corner of 2600 North and 400 East. The store opened in 1881 as a partnership with Benjamin Cazier Sr. and James Storey, selling merchandise, groceries, and fresh produce. The large scales in front of the store weighed grain and livestock feed. Four ladies wearing long dresses can be seen to the right of the store. The corner has become one of the busiest intersections in North Ogden. The city's first traffic light was installed at this site. Several businesses, apartment buildings, and homes have sprouted up where barns, hay sheds, and farmhouses were once located. (Below courtesy of Tim Jacobsen.)

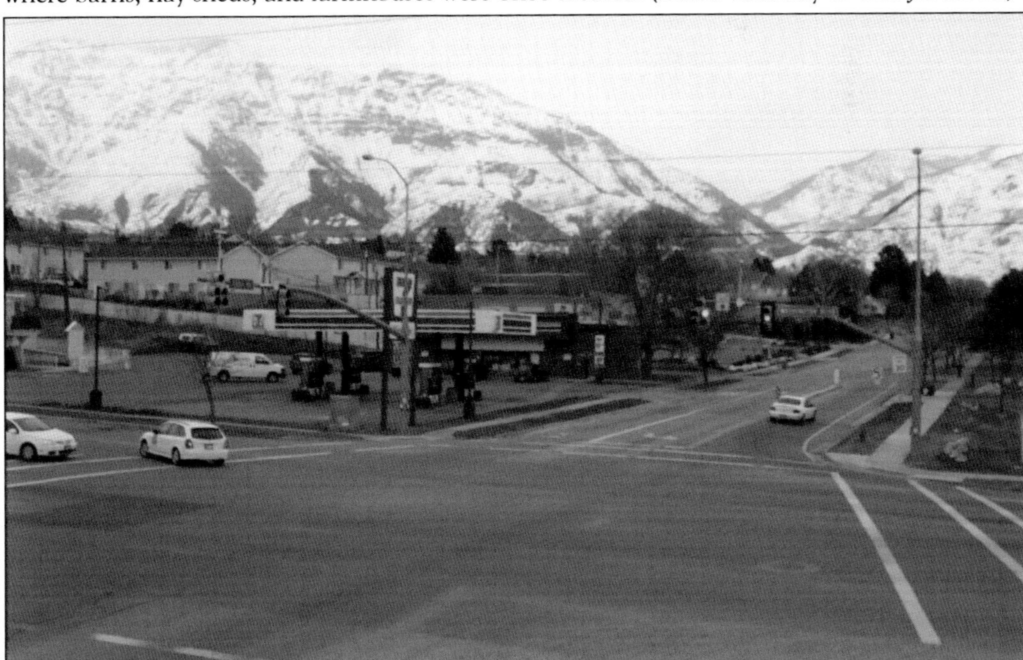

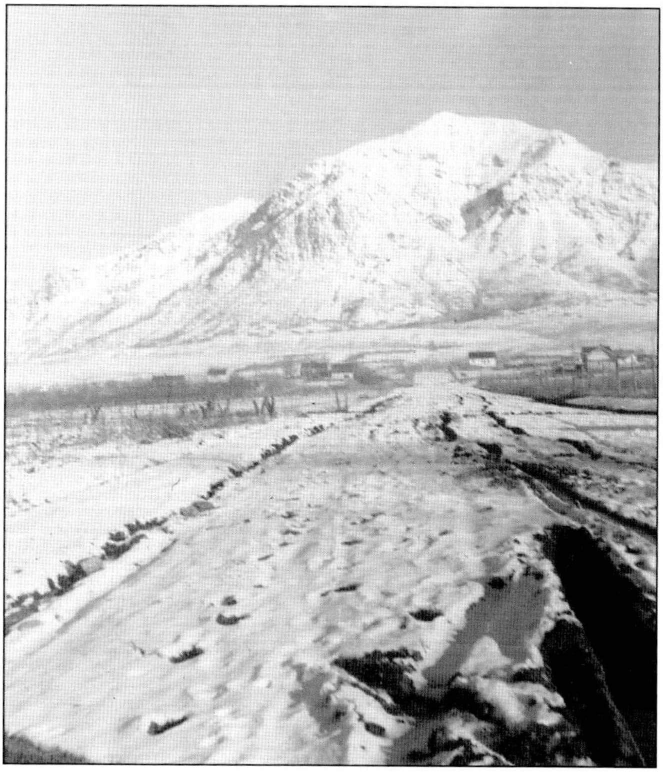

The 1910 view at left looking north up 400 East shows a much less developed city. The rutted dirt roads made travel nearly impossible after a snowstorm. Only a few farmhouses and barns dot the landscape. Today the muddy, rutted dirt road has been widened and paved. Businesses, homes, and traffic congestion are common in the area. Life has become easier in many ways, but less peaceful.

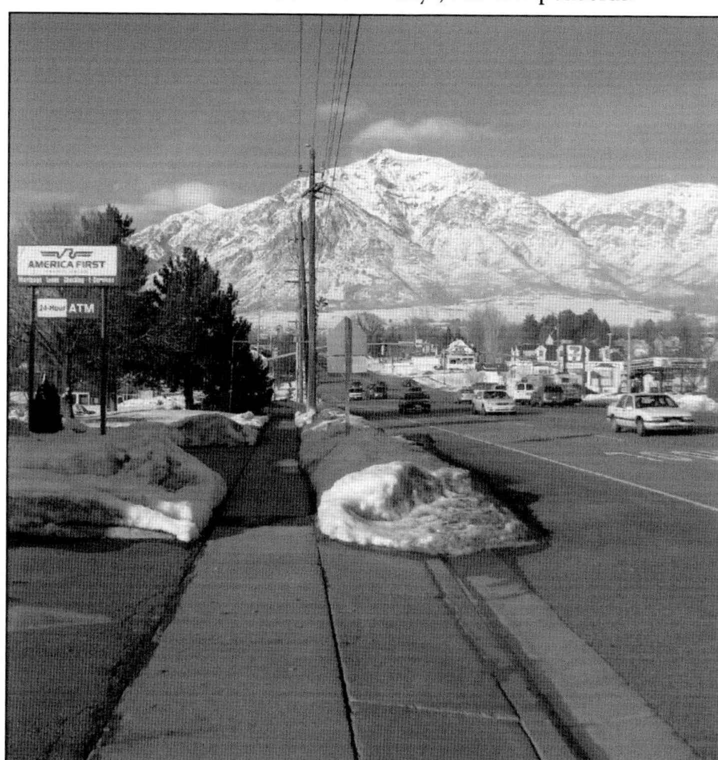

The Barker Cold Springs Trout Farm near 2284 North Fruitland Drive is pictured at right in the summer of 1960. The people are enjoying a sunny day catching fish with bamboo poles. Seen below, the present-day Barker Trout Farm is one site that has grown more beautiful over the years. The ponds have been improved, the shade trees are larger with landscaping, and picnic areas have been added. The tranquil setting provides a fun outing, and fish can still be caught with bamboo poles.

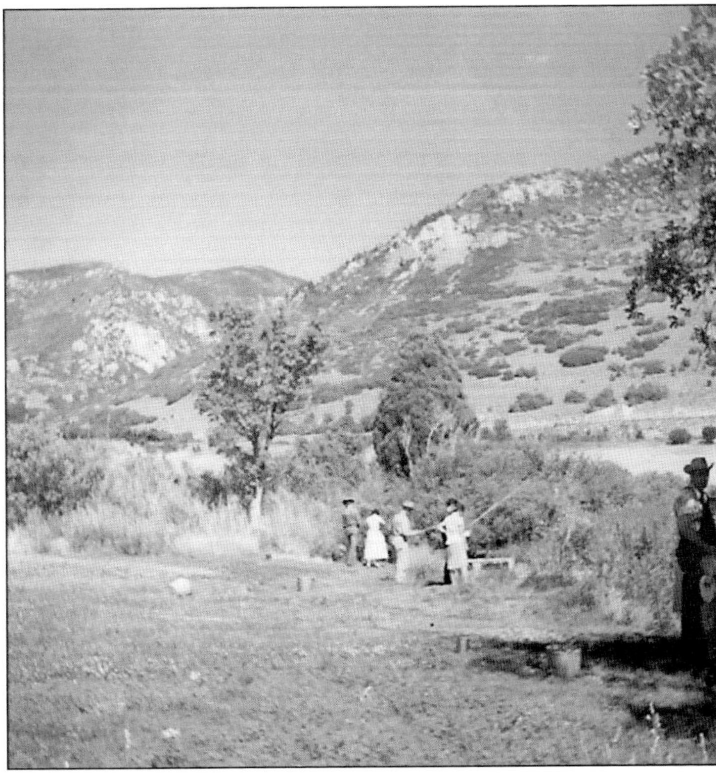

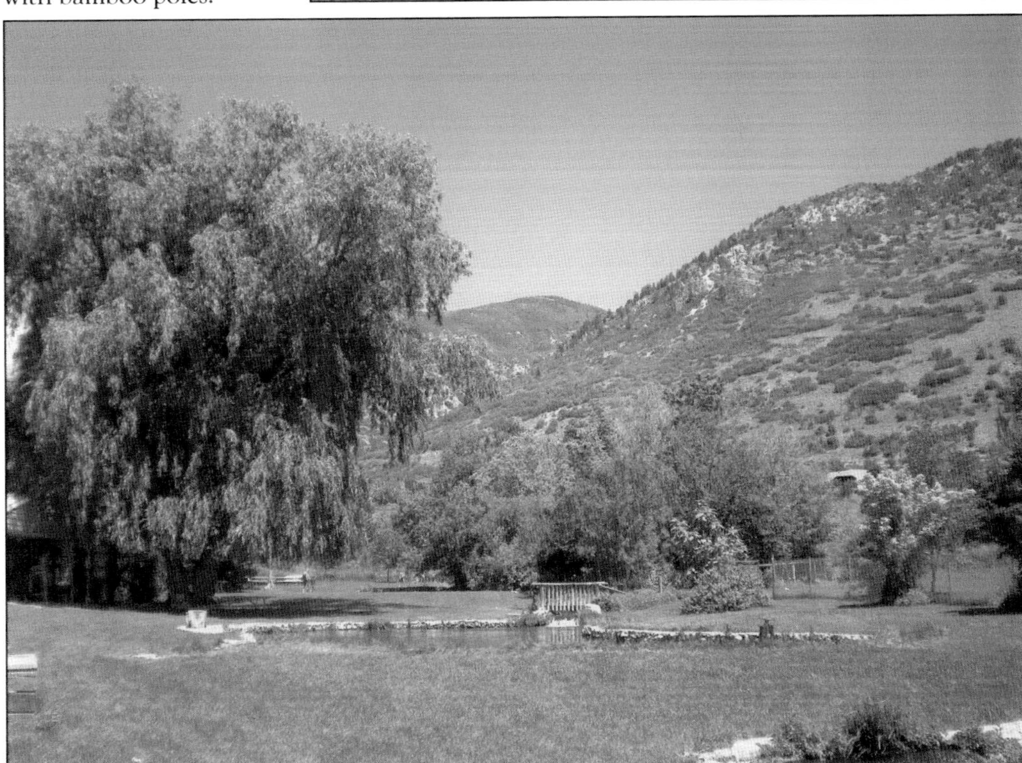

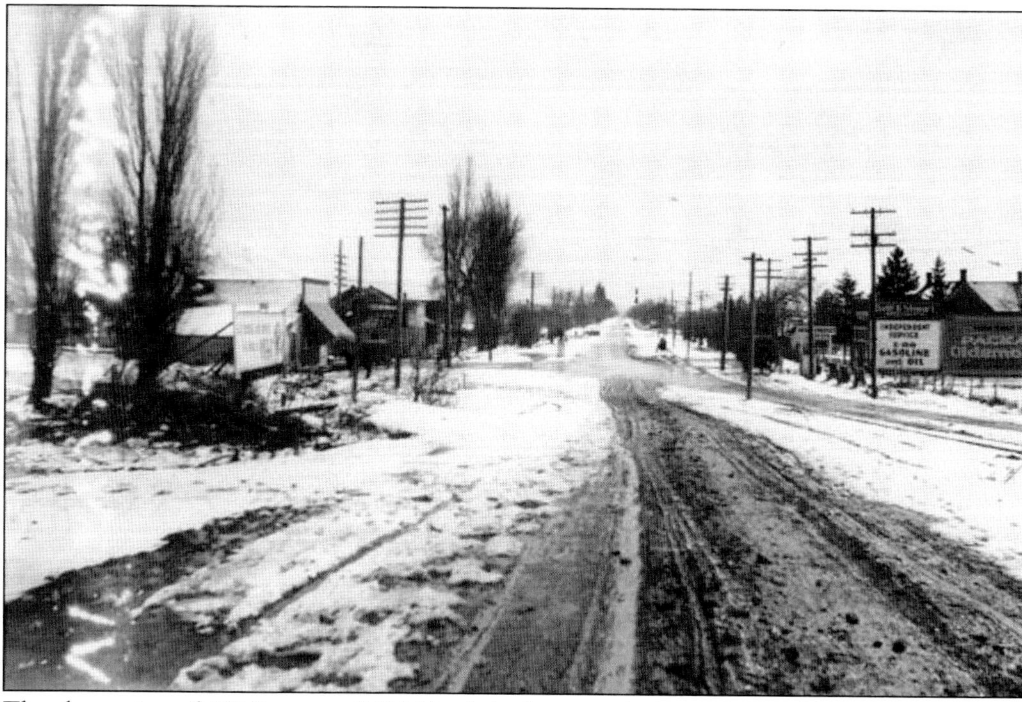

The above view of 400 East near 2600 North looking south shows the muddy roads of winter in the early 1920s. On the left, a horse is tied up in front of the Banner Ice Cream Store, which was previously the James Storey Store. On the right is the Ballif-Stewart store displaying a sign for gasoline, oil, Packards, and Oldsmobiles. There were very few automobiles in North Ogden at that time. Today this busy intersection has traffic lights, grocery supercenters, restaurants, beauty salons, banks, and other businesses. A four-lane highway was built westward to the interstate on 2600 North, and 400 East has been widened to four lanes to accommodate the increase in traffic.

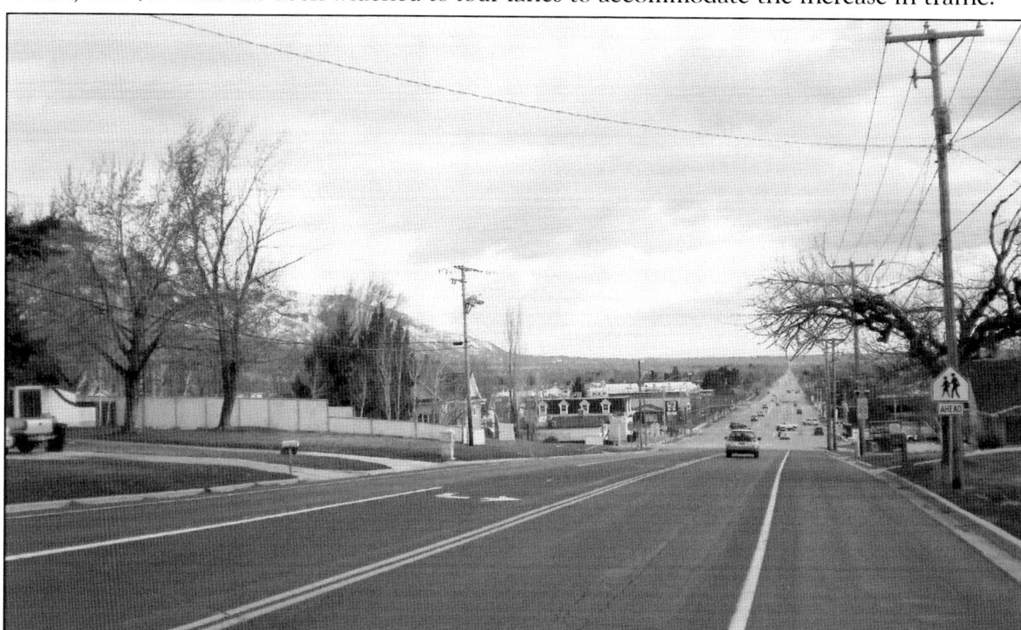

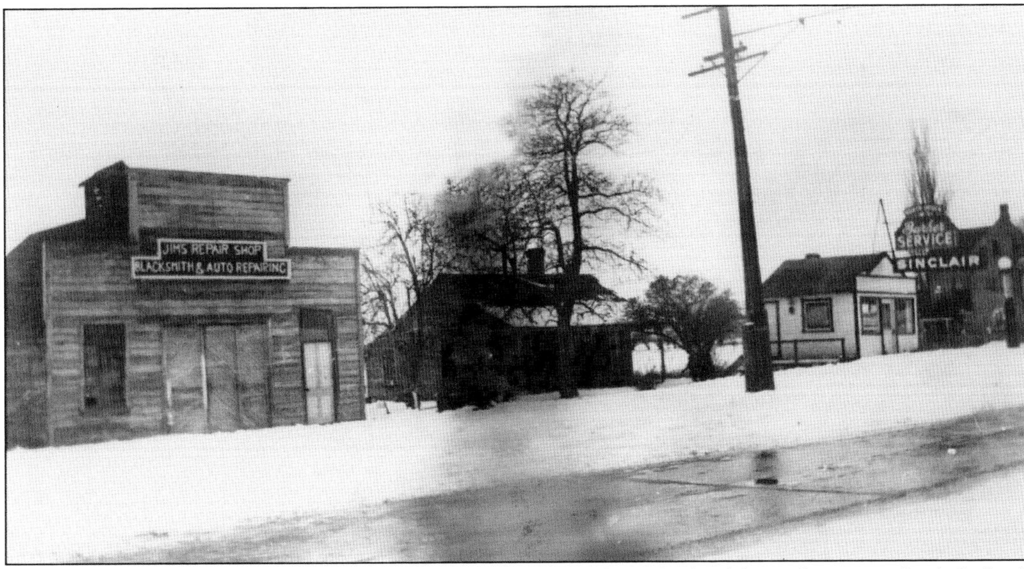

Shupe Brothers Blacksmith Shop was originally located in the building above on the left. Jim's Repair Shop occupied this building in 1936. At the far right of the photograph is the Sidney Stevens/Clarence Barker pioneer home, with Wayne Barker's Service next door. The photograph was taken of the west side of 400 East near 2600 North, around 1936. Pictured below, the area is now home to America First Credit Union on the left and a McDonald's restaurant at the far right, with a four-lane road between. The property just beyond the pine trees, zoned as commercial property, is where the Sidney Stevens/Clarence Barker home once stood (demolished in 2009).

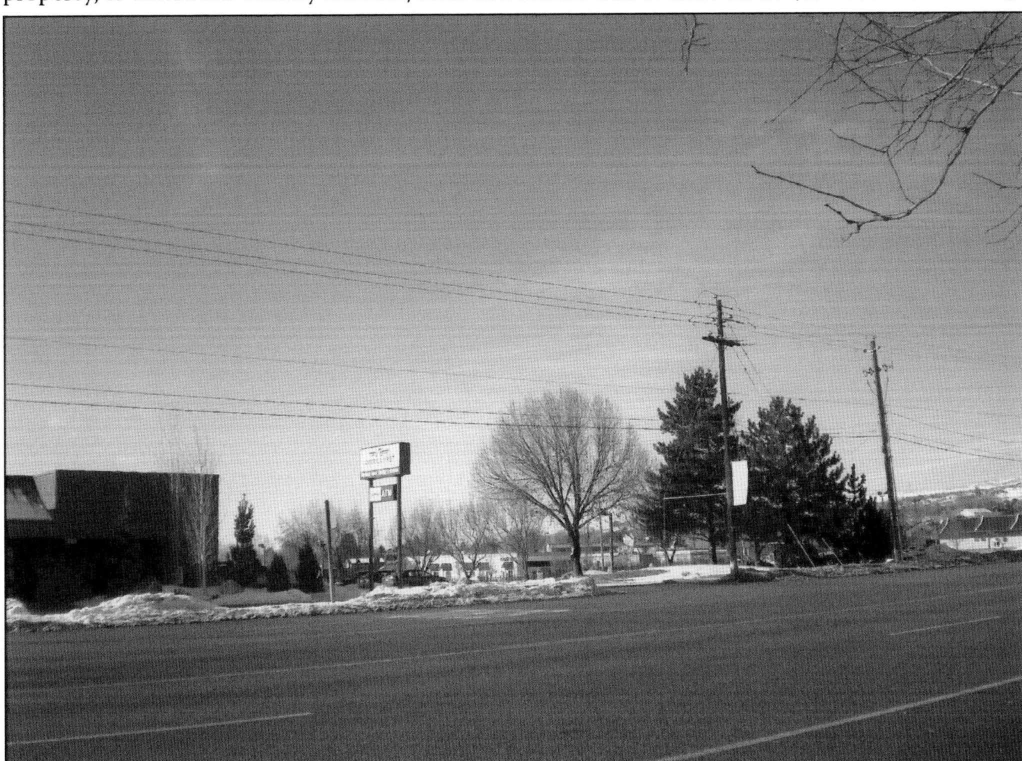

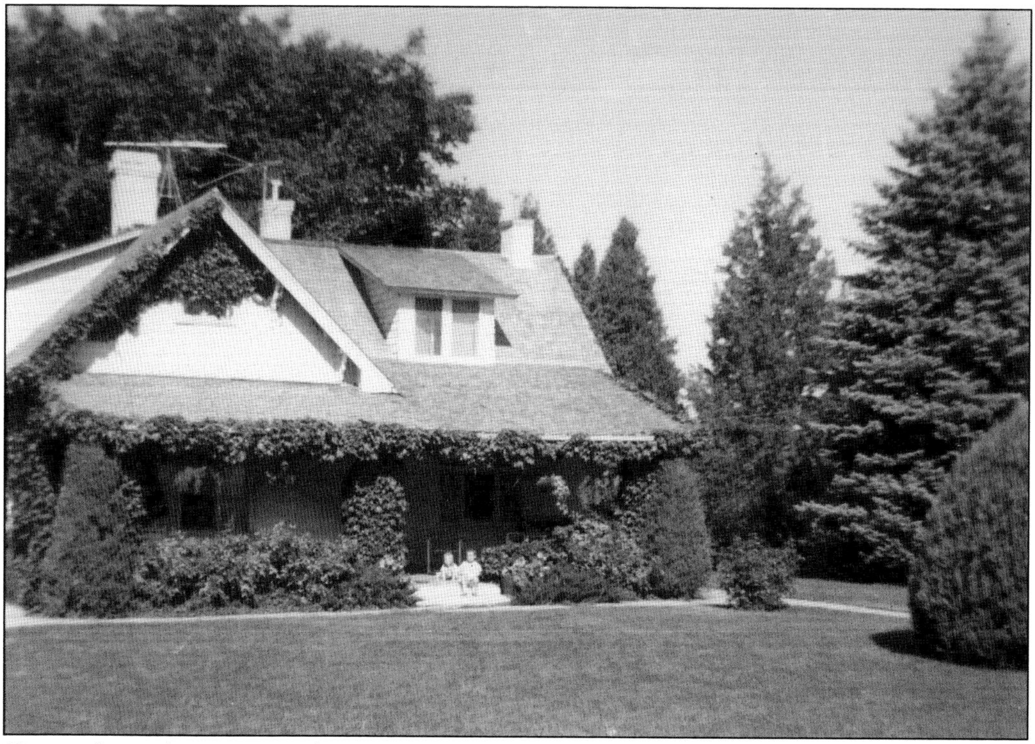

Shown above, the ivy-covered cottage-style home located on the northwest corner of 2550 North 400 East was owned by Clarence and Myrtle (Ririe) Barker. The home was the first in North Ogden to install electricity. The Barkers held a town party after dark, magically flipped a switch to light up the house, and the townspeople were amazed. Today the house and its peaceful, tree-laden yard have been replaced by a Walgreen's store. This is yet another example of how things change drastically over time, making the preservation of history even more important.

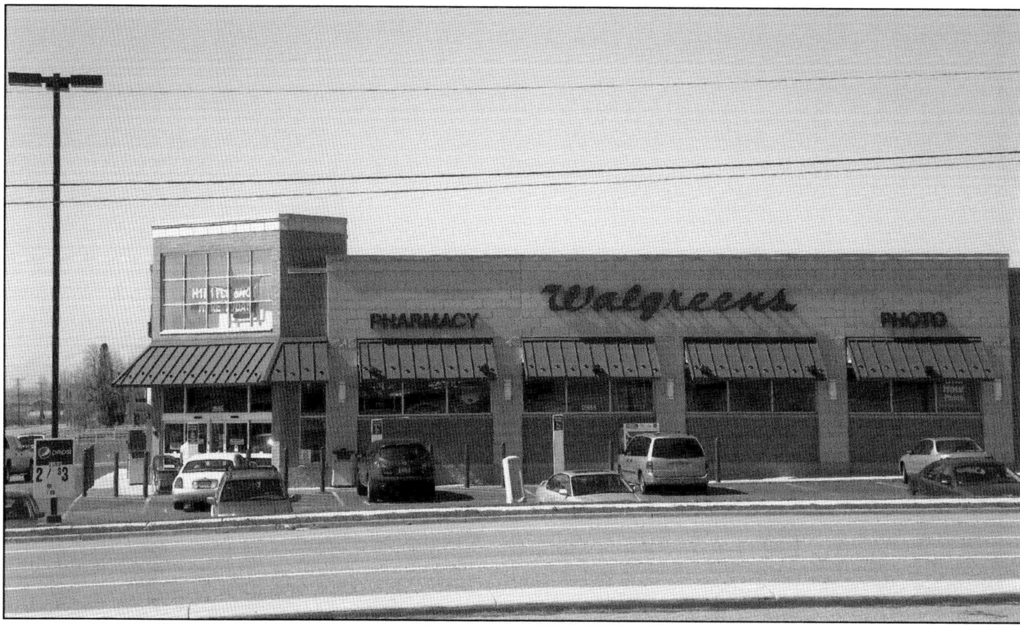

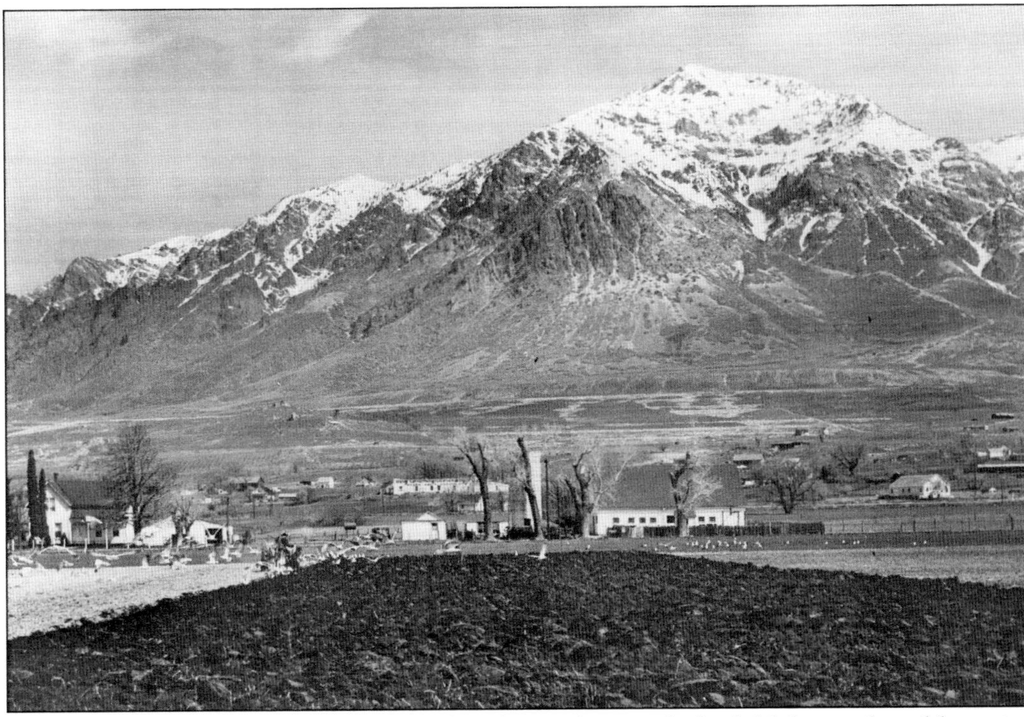

The Alvord farm near 200 East 2550 North is shown above with the fields being plowed for spring planting. The home, silo, and barn can be seen at the base of majestic Ben Lomond Peak. A few homes and barns can be seen, with the Ben Lomond Orchard's fruit packinghouse at the left of the silo. The foothills were undeveloped, and Frog Rock is clearly visible. Today the North View Fire Station is shown in the center, and the Alvord silo and barn can be seen at the left of the photograph. Blacktop and buildings have replaced the plowed fields, and homes are stretching up the foothills and around Frog Rock.

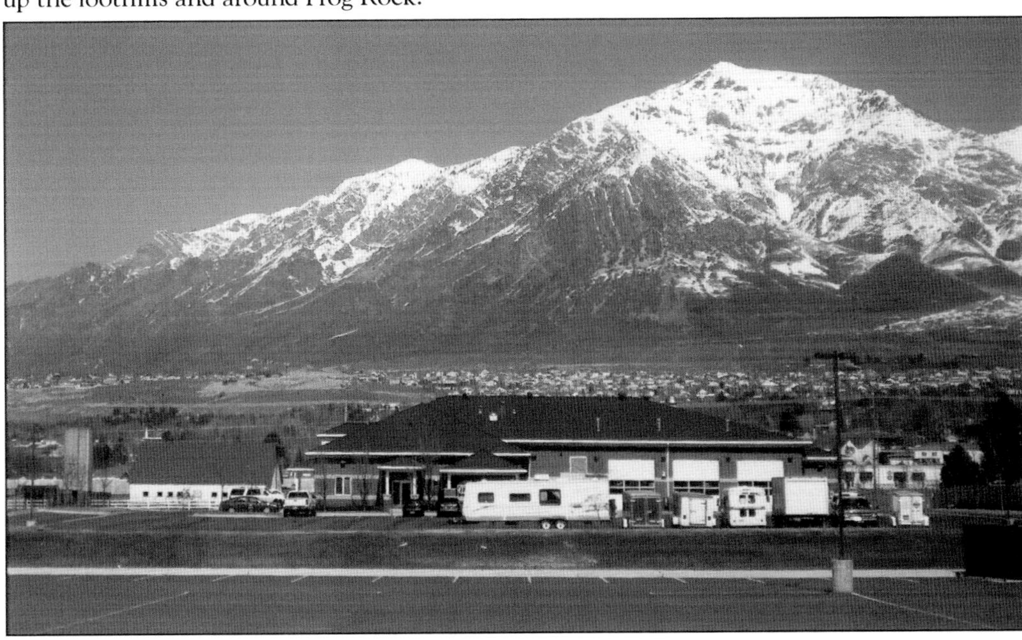

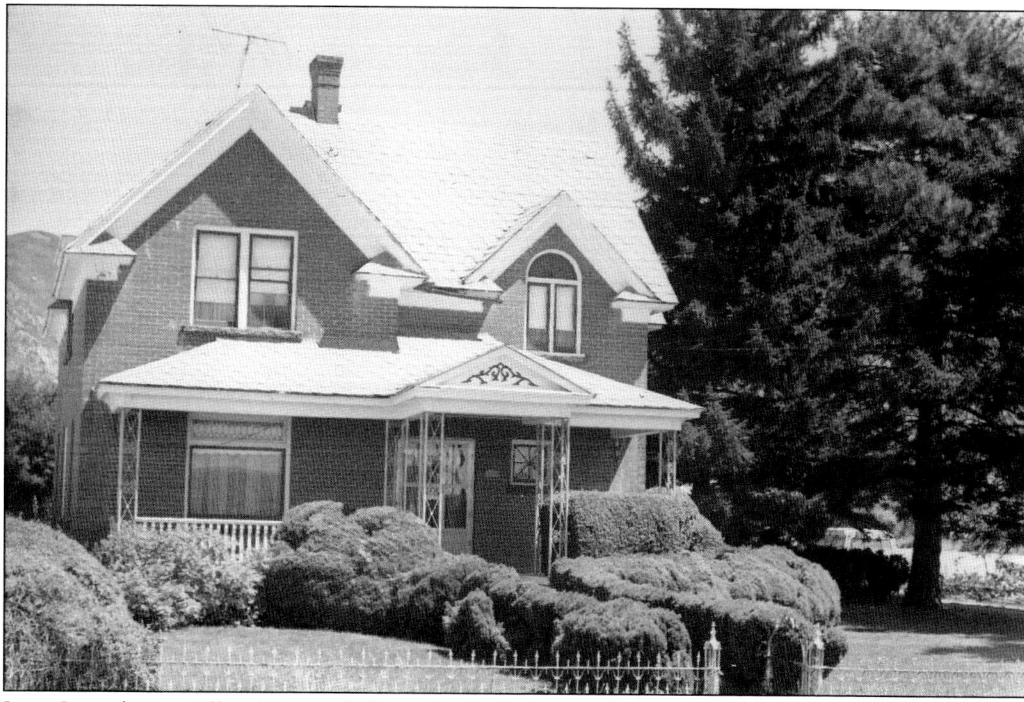

Isaac L. and Mary Ellen (Deamer) Shupe built the home above near 2480 North 400 East in 1901. The home and grounds were immaculate. In 1944, the 10-room brick home was sold to Parley and Inez Spackman, who operated a grocery store nearby. The home was well kept with its decorative iron fence and beautiful landscaping until it was demolished in 2006. Today the land is commercial property. The Smith's gas station is located to the north and Intermountain Health Care Clinic to the south. A housing project and Cold Water Canyon are visible in the distance.

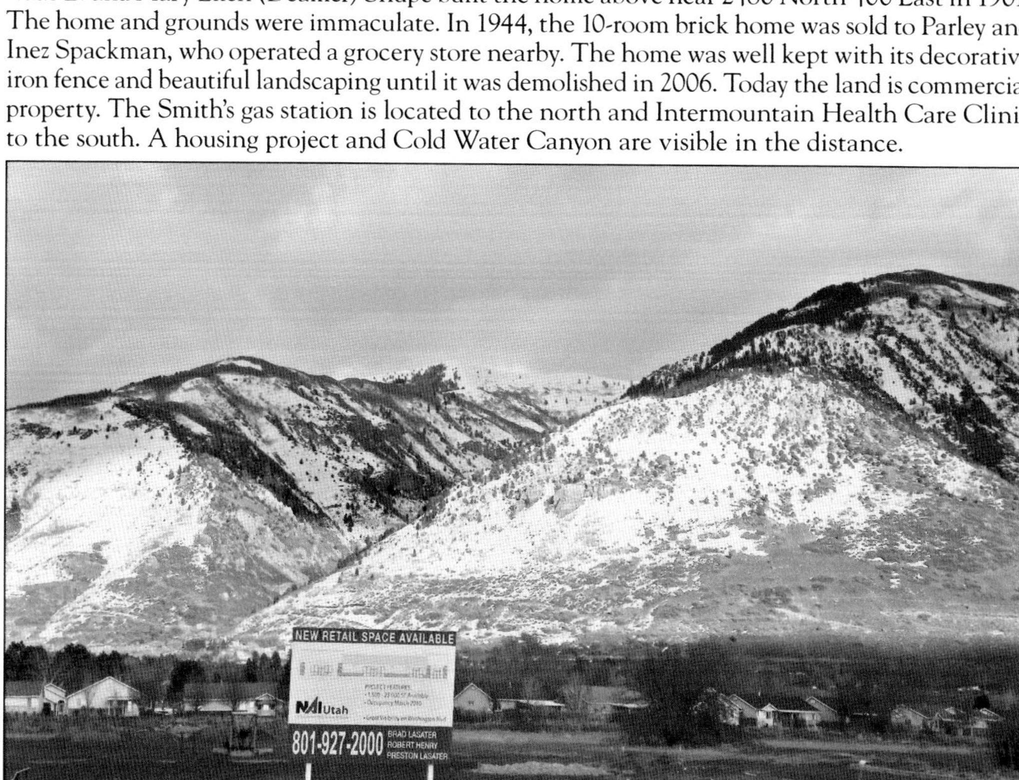

About the Organization

On behalf of the North Ogden Historical Museum, we would like to thank you for your support of Images of America: *North Ogden*. The book proudly showcases many of the photographs and histories that are preserved in the Museum's archives.

The goal of the museum is to preserve North Ogden's rich heritage and to educate the community about the legacy of its ancestors. This book encourages an enthusiastic connection to the past and an appreciative awareness of our city's natural surroundings and peacefulness.

At times I can almost feel the presence of my ancestors—
A gentle, guiding touch from those who've gone before

—Author unknown

North Ogden Historical Museum, Inc.
A 501(c)3 Nonprofit Organization
E-mail: NOHistoricalM@gmail.com
Web site: www.NOHMuseum.org